A Way Into The
Old

By

CR Biggs

and

A Grant-Henderson

ATF Press
Adelaide

ISBN 978 1 920691 81 3

ATF Press
An imprint of the Australasian Theological Forum Ltd
P O Box 504
Hindmarsh
SA 5007
ABN 90 116 359 963
www.atfpress.com

Contents

Preface v

Preface to the Third Edition vii

1. Introducing the Old Testament 1

2. The Story of God's People 10

3. God Speaks to the People of Israel 32

4. Learning from History 62

5. Building on the Past 84

6. Being Responsible to God 92

7. Recovering Faith 123

8. Singing Songs to God 152

9. Books for Special Occasions 165

10. Words to Make One Wise 171

11. Hidden Strength in Time of Trouble 180

Epilogue 189

Glossary 190

Further Reading 196

Preface

We have written this book because of the frequently expressed dissatisfaction with books that have been available for lay preachers courses in Old Testament. It has also been suggested that books ought to be produced in Australia for our lay preachers courses. This would have two advantages. First, the books could give attention to the requirements of students and teachers working in Australia, a need that has been very much in our minds as we have gone about our task. Whether we have succeeded or not will only be shown when the book has been used, both by classes and those having to study on their own.

The second point is that, with an Australian publication, we will not be dependent on books produced by overseas groups for their lay preachers and lay education courses. Supply of books should therefore be less of a problem.

We have attempted to show the importance of the traditions of Israel. We have investigated the origins of these traditions, the use to which they were put at various times, and the ways they were adapted in the different periods of Israel's history. The Old Testament is presented as the record of Israel's experience of God. It is a record which spoke to people about their past, which gave them understanding of their present and hope for their future. In all of this, the major emphasis is on the relationship between God and God's people.

We offer an introduction that covers all of the Old Testament, with some parts receiving more attention than others. For people wanting to do further study, some reading is recommended at the end of the book. Where additional material is required we suggest readers consult their minister or the lecturers at the theological college or lay education institute in their area. We hope that this book will encourage people to do further study and so be better able to discern God's word in the Old Testament scriptures.

We thank all those who have helped us in our task. The Lay Preachers' Committee of the Synod of South Australia affirmed the need for a text-book for the Old Testament course and encouraged us in the project. Several people have read the material at various stages of preparation and offered helpful criticism. We thank them all and express particular appreciation to Rosemary Mitchell, Bet McKay, Helen Boggs and David Biggs for their interest.

CR Biggs
A Grant-Henderson

Preface to the Third Edition

We offer this new edition of *A Way Into The Old Testament* in response to the many requests we have had from people beginning Old Testament study. The book has met the needs first identified and which are still being felt today. We are very grateful for the feedback we have received over the years.

However, we recognised that the material needed to be revised to give readers a more up to date approach to the Old Testament and how it is to be understood. Readers will find changes in all chapters but the basic structure of the book is unchanged. If the book encourages readers in their ongoing relationship with God through the Old and New Testaments, we will be well repaid.

1
Introducing the Old Testament

*§A review of content and purpose * Using the Old Testament*

What is the Old Testament?

The most important question for people who begin to study this subject is, 'What is the Old Testament?' Many answers may be given to the question, each of which is correct from a particular viewpoint. For example: it is a collection of ancient material written over a long period by, for, and about the people of ancient Israel; it is the record of the religious experience of a people; it is the Word of God or part of the Word of God; it is a book compiled from different sources about a central theme of the revelation of God to God's people.

The question has particular point for Christians because everything that is written in the Old Testament relates to people who lived in the period before the coming of Jesus Christ. The further question 'What has the Old Testament to contribute to our understanding of the Christian faith?' may therefore be expected. The New Testament writers showed that they believed it made a significant contribution by referring to it and quoting it frequently because the coming of Jesus Christ was a new and unique revelation of God that built on the revelation seen in the Old Testament. Paul drew on the creation stories in Genesis 1–3 (1 Cor 15:38,45) in establishing where humans stand in relation to God (1 Cor 15:38,45). He used Abraham as an example when discussing faith (Romans 4). The writer of Hebrews went to great pains to show how faith is demonstrated in characters in the Old Testament (Heb 11). Luke referred to Moses and the prophets as effective witnesses to God (Luke 16:29–31) and recorded that Jesus explained Old Testament passages which referred to himself (Luke 2.4:27).

Jesus is seen as the fulfillment of the messianic promise in the Old Testament. The gospel writers showed this as they referred to his being of the line of David (Matt 1:1; Luke 2:4–5) and as they recorded sayings in which Jesus quoted the Old Testament. For example, as he began his ministry he quoted Isaiah 9:2 (Matt 4:16) and Isaiah 61:1–2

(Luke 4:8), when in the desert he answered the tempter quoting Deuteronomy 8:3 (Luke 4:4), 6:13 (Luke 4:8) and 6:16 (Luke 4:12), and when he was dying on the cross he quoted Psalm 22:1 (Mk 15:34).

The church through the ages has accepted that the Old Testament is essential if we are to understand the revelation of God in Jesus Christ, and if we are to live a Christian life. God is revealed to us in the pages of the Old Testament.

The Old Testament brings this revelation of God through its presentation of the relationship between God and the people of Israel. Although it may appear at first glance that the Old Testament is mainly concerned to tell us about the people of Israel—their history, their worship, their relationships with other people—this is not its main concern. Rather, it is to help people to know God, God's care for people and the way they may respond to God.

The Old Testament is divided into a number of parts, each of which is intended to serve this purpose. In the process it also tells us about the people so that we may learn about the history of Israel from the Old Testament. What it tells about them has not been made up. It can be shown to have a basic historical accuracy. But it is not told as history. It is rather told as theology; i.e. so that we may learn of God, of humanity, and the relationship between God and people.

Basic to understanding the Old Testament is the recognition that everything takes place within the context of God's chosen relationship with Israel. This act of choice on God's part is expressed in a number of places; for example, the call of Abraham (Gen 12:1–3) and the exodus from Egypt (Exod 12 to 15).

Each of these choices is followed by an agreement (covenant) between God and the people in which it is acknowledged that God is their God and the people belong to God (Gen 15,17; Exod 19:5, 24:3–8).

Accounts of Israel's experience of God within the relationship were used to help later generations to understand God and to seek God's help as they faced their problems. People were reminded how God had cared for them in the past, and so helped to see that God would continue to care for them and aid them if they remained faithful to God. An example of this is the Pentateuch (Genesis to Deuteronomy), which shows God among the people from the time of creation. It tells of God leading Abraham, Isaac and Jacob to the land God chose for them, of God's promises that the land would be for them and their descendants, and that their children would become a great nation (Gen 12 to 50). The Pentateuch also contains the laws that provided the framework for the people's response to God within the covenant relationship (for example, Exod 20:1–17).

Another example is the collection of 'historical' material in the books from Joshua to Second Kings. The major purpose of this body of material was to help Israel understand why its life had developed in the way it had and why the relationship ended with many of the people exiled in a foreign country. The writers of this 'history' intended the people should learn from this reflection on the nation's life and so avoid the same mistakes in their present and future.

The prophetic books serve a similar purpose. The prophets were significant people in the life of Israel. They attempted to bring their people back to God and away from those things (gods and practices) that threatened the relationship between God and the people. The prophets' method was to remind the people of what God had done for them in the past by recalling the traditions of their religion and then showing how God was active in the present situation. This usually resulted in a message of judgment on the people and a reminder that if the people were to remain in relationship with God, they were to respond to God with obedient.

In one sense the prophets were failures. Their message did not bring the desired change in the lives of the people. But in another sense they were a success. Their words and actions were remembered and preserved by those who came after them. Some of the words of the earlier prophets were used as part of their message by later prophets; for example, material from Hosea was used by Jeremiah, and Ezekiel used material from both Hosea and Jeremiah. The prophetic books are now presented to us as further reflections on the relationship with God so that people may recognise the warnings contained in the prophets' messages and apply them to current situations.

The relationship between God and Israel may be characterised as one of gift and response. God is the giver who expected Israel to respond to God. One part of that response is obedience to God, which is shown in the requirements of the covenant. Another is the worship life of the people. The book of Psalms contains material that enabled the people to make their response. Whether this was made by individuals in private or by congregations, whether it was to praise God, or to make confession, or to lament their position and seek God's help, it was all done to celebrate the God who gives and to bring people nearer to God.

The wisdom material (Proverbs, Ecclesiastes and Job) is a contrast to the Psalms. The wisdom writers had little interest in the formal structure of the religion. Rather, they were taken up with the everyday things of life. In particular, they discussed the right way to live so that a person's life may be a credit to the individual and the community. They were also concerned with the great questions of life that come to people in all ages. Both of these aspects of the wisdom writers' work were set within the relationship between God and Israel. The writers do not often refer to this relationship explicitly, but it is there in the background to inform the instruction given and the discussion of the great questions. Indeed, there is recognition that humans may plan and devise, but this is within the limitations imposed by God (Prov 16:1, 2, 9; 19:1, 21). The thought behind all the wisdom material is, 'The fear of the Lord is the beginning of wisdom' (Prov 9:10. See also Prov 15:33; 14:26–27; Job 28:28; Ps 111:10).

As with all books, the Old Testament comes to us as written material and is, to that extent, static. This is emphasised for us because the book comes from the ancient world. The last incidents that may be dated with any accuracy occurred over 150 years before the birth of Jesus. However, the process by which the material was preserved and passed on is not in any way static. It was rather a dynamic or living process and the intention of those who were involved in it was that its living quality should continue.

The process involved the continued use of the traditions that were contained in the material used for worship, the teaching of the priests and the message of the prophets. These traditions were not simply recited to give an answer to a particular problem the people faced. Rather, they were adopted so that they spoke directly to the problem. As this new application conveyed to the people the word of God for their situation it, in turn, became part of the deposit of tradition and was available to be applied to later situations.

Two examples of this process will demonstrate the vitality of the Biblical tradition. In a number of places in the Old Testament, Israel or its land is compared to a vine and/or its produce. In Genesis 49:8–12, the comparison is used to show the power and fruitfulness of the land (see also Num 13:21–24 and Deut 8:7–10). Psalm 80:8–13 traces the history of Israel as a vine that grew well in the beginning but had become spoiled (see also Hos 10:1–2; Isa 5:1–7 and Jer 2:21).

Ezekiel uses the comparison to emphasise the failure of Israel and desolation that will befall Jerusalem by dealing with the wood of the vine rather than its produce (Ezek 15). Israel is no longer a vine that may produce fruit and be restored by God; it is a useless piece of wood that has been charred and can only be used as fuel for the fire.

Second, Hosea, Jeremiah and Ezekiel use the marriage motif to deal with the relationship between God and Israel. As the bride, Israel is expected to faithful to her husband (God) and not go after other lovers (gods). Hosea is the first to use this illustration. Addressing Israel, he charges her with being unfaithful and behaving as a harlot in her association with other gods (Hos 2 to 3; 4:7–19). The result of this activity will be divorce, that is, total rejection by God. Jeremiah takes up this thought from Hosea and applies it to the people of Judah as they neared the end of their existence as a kingdom (Jer 2 to 6). The words used, as well as the use of the concept, show that Jeremiah was deliberately using the material left by his northern Israelite predecessor.

Ezekiel, especially in chapters 16 and 23, takes up this message against apostasy as it is presented in Hosea and Jeremiah. Again the words used, along with the concept, show that Ezekiel was drawing on his predecessors. He applied their words to a new situation and supplied more elaborate details so that the word of God made its impact on the people of his time.

This process of applying the traditions to the needs of the people continued within the material, both in its oral and written forms, until the written material was accepted as standard and no longer able to be added to. In this sense the Old Testament is the deposit of living traditions and should be read as such by us. The process has, of course, continued in the traditions of those who are the inheritors of the Old Testament—Jews, Christians and Muslims.

Using the Old Testament

The purpose of this book is to help Christians to bring the teaching of the Old Testament to the needs of people today. The main thing required to do this is to become involved in and familiar with the Old Testament itself. To that extent this book is intended to point beyond itself to the Old Testament and to exegesis and theological study. It is therefore a beginning to a process of understanding for you. It provides introductory and background material that will help you to study and understand the Old Testament. It is not a substitute for the Old Testament. To gain the most out of it you should read the parts of the Old Testament as they are discussed, to become familiar with them and to see what they say for themselves.

Before we go on to look at some of the details of our approach to the Old Testament, we need to be reminded that if we seek to hear God's word to us, we must acknowledge our need of the guidance and inspiration of God. Preparation of ourselves by way of prayer before we approach the scriptures, while we are reading them, and for the outcome of our enquiry, is essential. In our prayer we ask God that the Holy Spirit, who guided and inspired those who wrote the scriptures and the many people who have interpreted them through the ages, may be with us. We ask not only for heightened understanding and deepened appreciation, we ask also for resolve and courage to do what is revealed as the will of God for us. When the aim of our study is that we may proclaim the word of God in preaching, our prayer is also that God's word which came to people in the preaching of God's servants long ago may come to people today, that they may know God who offers us life in Jesus Christ, and that they may choose that life.

When we are considering a passage from the Old Testament there are three things we need to remember, or three steps we need to take.

1. We look at the passage as an address to people of long ago. To understand it we need to find out as much as possible about the people addressed, and what was happening to them at the time. What was happening in the nation? Were the people happy and prosperous? Were they suffering oppression from a foreign power? Were they being addressed in their own land, or when they were in exile in a far country? We also need to know about the person who presented the passage. Who was he/she—a priest, prophet, wise man, or king? Where did he/she fit into the religious life of the people, and what emphasis did he/she bring to that life? We need to know these things because the meaning of what is said is conditioned by the situation of the people and the messenger. For example, compare the words of Amos the prophet to the self-satisfied people of Israel in the eighth century (Amos 8:4–8a) with those of the prophet of Second Isaiah to the exiles in Babylon (Isa 40.1).

> Hear this, you who trample upon the needy,
> and bring the poor of the land to an end,

saying, 'When will the new moon be over,
that we may sell grain?
and the sabbath,
that we may offer wheat for sale,
that we may make the ephah small and the shekel great,
and deal deceitfully with false balances,
that we may buy the poor for silver
and the needy for a pair of sandals,
and sell the refuse of the wheat?'
The Lord has sworn by the pride of Jacob:
'Surely I will never forget any of their deeds.
Shall not the land tremble on this account,
and everyone mourn who dwells in it . . .'
(Amos 8:4–8a)

Comfort, comfort my people,
says your God.
Speak tenderly to Jerusalem,
and cry to her
that her warfare is ended,
that her iniquity is pardoned,
that she has received from the Lord's hand
double for all her sins
(Isaiah 40:1).

2. The things we discovered in the first step (above) help us to know about the passage we are studying. The second step is to discover what the passage had to say to the people who first heard it. Here we consider what was said and the way it was said to discover what the writer wanted his people to understand about God, themselves, and their relationship with God.

In this step we seek to discover the theological concerns of the passage. We ask such questions as: What does the author mean here? What would the people to learn from this? These questions need to be asked of the statements by prophets, lists of laws, psalms used in worship, and accounts of Israel's history. All parts of the Old Testament were intended to help people to know God, God's action on their behalf, God's requirements of them, and to help them make their response to God. We are looking to discover, not just what the law said, but the theology expressed by the law; not just the abuses Amos attacked, but the theological concerns that made him attack them.

For example, in Amos 8:4–6 we learn of the way the poor were treated by the wealthy in the time of Amos, the attitude of the wealthy to the Sabbath, and the general dishonesty of the traders. These things are interesting as they tell us about the social problems of the time, and about God's requirements of the people. God required the wealthy to care for, rather than exploit the poor, to be honest in their dealings with people, to respect opportunities to worship God and not see them as duties to be observed and to be got out of the way so that business may be carried on, and to see worship and dealings with others as part of the whole act of response to God. When we read verses 7–8 we see that Amos made it plain that these are the things required of God's people. Because they were not offered to God, the people were called to account and to face punishment. Within the relationship with God there are requirements and there are consequences for disobedience. That is what Amos told the people of Israel.

Isaiah 40:1, in addressing the people in exile, is concerned with another side of the relationship; God's continued care for the people through their disobedience and subsequent judgment and punishment. It shows that judgment and punishment are not in conflict with God's care, but are part of the process by which God deals with the disobedient people to bring them to obedience and renewal. Punishment was not avoided—it was suffered in the exile in Babylon. Now the pardon of God is extended to the people and the relationship, which they broke by their disobedience, is renewed by God's forgiveness and acceptance of them.

3. The third (and final) step is to consider what we have discovered in step two in the light of the New Testament and its revelation of God in Jesus Christ. The New Testament writers have taken into the structure of their presentation of Jesus Christ and the beginning of the church all the major themes of the Old Testament. In doing this they have given the themes a new significance. We now see them in the light of what Jesus has done. When we, as Christians, study the Old Testament we are to do the same thing. When we have completed step two we ask: What does the knowledge of God brought to us in Jesus Christ do to this understanding of God and our relationship with God? Does it extend it, modify it, or confirm it as it is?

How we answer these questions may be best shown by looking again at our earlier examples. The New Testament confirms the underlying message which we saw in Amos 8:4–6. Jesus' teaching and example is clear—an attitude of care and concern for our fellows is an essential part of our response to God. He sent his disciples out to *'Heal the sick, raise the dead, cleanse lepers, cast out demons'* (Matt 10:8). Jesus' action in healing, raising, and cleansing, as well as preaching the good news to the poor (Matthew 11:2–6) was the sign to John the Baptist that Jesus was 'he who is to come'. The parable of the Good Samaritan, given in answer to the question of response to God, shows that such care has no limits (Luke 10:25–37). All of our actions toward one another are to reflect the recognition that God cares for us with forgiving love. In the parable of the debtor servant this is brought out with great force. (Read Matt 18:23–25)

In the opening address to the exiles (Isa 40:I), forgiveness comes to the exiles after they have been punished. We know from other places that willingness of the people to return to God is a requirement of forgiveness (for example, 'let the wicked forsake their way . . . let them return to the Lord, that he may have mercy on them . . .' Isa 55:7), but the burden of punishment as the way to forgiveness remains the strong emphasis in much of the Old Testament. The New Testament does not make this condition. Rather, it shows that God is ready to forgive those who return to God (repent). The prodigal son decided to return to his father and was forgiven and restored to the family (Luke 15:11–32). The king forgave his servant a massive debt because the servant returned and threw himself on the king's mercy (Matt 18: 23–35). Of course, returning to God means accepting God's love and being willing to align ourselves with God's purpose as it is shown in Jesus Christ. Rebellion against God brings its own punishment, but punishment is no longer a precondition for forgiveness.

When we deal with the text in this way we see not only the meaning of the words to the people of the time, we also find truths which apply to the relationship with God at all times.

Question

What steps need to be taken in our study of the Old Testament?

2
The Story of God's People

*§The origins * Early history * The monarchy * The divisions * Exile * Restoration * Time chart * Maps*

(The maps and time chart should be consulted during the reading of this chapter.)

Israel's religion was never separate from its historical and political setting. To help the reader identify the situation of the various writers as we progress through the book, a brief summary of Israel's major historical events is given in this chapter.

While we are looking at historical events we must realise that in fact the Old Testament is not an historical document, but a theological story. It describes the relationship of the people, Israel, to their God, and it is against this understanding that all the history is viewed. No historical document is ever objective, and any account of events in the life of Israel in the Old Testament is interpreted in the in terms of the writers' understanding of God. For example, the writer does not give a full account of every king's reign. He only writes of each king in terms whether of he was true to God and walked in the way of David, or of Jeroboam 1.

The journeys of the Israelites can never be fully described because we do not have enough factual geographical information. The writers were concerned with major events in relation God, not a strict record of their treks. The Old Testament is a faith statement, not a chronological account of events. The writer of Chronicles was not interested in the kings of the northern kingdom and left them out of his 'so called history'. He had a message to proclaim, and the northern kings were not part of that message.

The reason for this chapter at the beginning of the book is to present the major events as we can discern them from the sources given. Readers then can understand that when the authors wrote they were addressing a specific situation in the life of the people. They were interpreting God's word for the people of that time. Readers, we hope, will be able to place the writings in the context of Israel's life through the centuries, and see the message in a more vital and clear way.

Israel played only a very small part in the overall history of the ancient Near East. It was its geographical situation that forced it to be a part of a larger complex of events. Israel was situated in a vulnerable position between Egypt to the southwest, and the great centre of civilisation known as Mesopotamia to the east beyond the desert. To the north of Palestine lay Syria, Lebanon and Asia Minor.

Much of the political and religious history of Palestine was determined by conditions in these three regions. If all three powers were weak at one time, it meant that the kings of Israel could assert themselves to gain power over or overcome any smaller nation that dominated them at that time. The most significant period of Israel's military and political power was during the reigns of David and Solomon and came at such a time. The power vacuum at that time allowed the empire to reach its greatest geographic extent and influence. This power was diminished after the division of the kingdom into (Northern) Israel and Judah. For most of her history, Israel was the buffer between the bigger powers, of Egypt, Syria, Assyria and Babylon. As the countries impinge on the life of Israel or Judah they are recorded in the pages of the Old Testament. The nation's response to the situation was seen often as a reflection of their relationship with God.

The origins

Bible reading: Genesis

Where did Israel come from? What were its beginnings? To try to answer these questions it is necessary to go back a long way into the movements of peoples of the Near East. Between the years 3000 BCE and 2000 BCE there were constant uprisings of peoples in Mesopotamia with first one group and then another gaining ascendancy. However, during the early part of the second millennium BCE, various areas in Mesopotamia, Syria and Palestine came under the domination of Semitic invaders, who are generally known as Amorites. It is in this period that we place Abraham, who moved out from Ur with his family flocks and herds, migrating first to Haran and then into Canaan (Gen 11:31 to 12:5).

The reason for suggesting that Abraham is part of the turbulence and movement of this time, is that many of the names of Abraham's relatives correspond to those found in archaeological discoveries of the Far East. Tablets from the period 1900 BCE to 1800 BCE give valuable information of events in that era and describe the customs and conditions of the Hurrian people who had infiltrated into Mesopotamia, Syria and Palestine during the second millennium BCE. They speak of such customs as the provision of a concubine by a barren wife for her husband, and the law against expelling such a concubine and her children. There are close parallels to such customs in the story of Abraham and Sarah (Gen 16).

It is against this background that Genesis 12–50 tells of groups of semi-nomads moving through Canaan, settling for short periods, and then moving on to new feeding grounds for their livestock. Abraham, Isaac and Jacob are the ancestors who moved around Canaan in the years 1900 to 1700 BCE. The story of Joseph, Jacob's son, who was sold into slavery by his brothers, precedes the tribe's need to go to Egypt to buy food for their flocks when a drought was in the land of Canaan. Joseph's father, brothers and all their families moved to Egypt where they lived for a long time. At first they were well accepted and given preferential treatment but eventually they became slaves of the Pharaohs. The time of release was in the reign of Rameses 2 around 1300 BCE.

Exodus–Judges: entry into the Promised Land and the period of the Judges (1250 BCE–1020 BCE)

Bible readings: Exodus; Joshua and Judges

Against this background of slavery, Moses was called to lead his people out of bondage. The name 'Moses' is Egyptian in origin giving credence to the belief that he was born in Egypt. The story says he killed an Egyptian and had to flee, finding sanctuary with a tribe of Kenites on the Sinai Peninsula. He married a girl from that tribe and whilst shepherding was called by God to go back into Egypt and lead the Hebrews out of their misery (Exod 2 to 6).

The call of Moses, recorded in Exodus, states that it was on that occasion God's name was revealed to Moses (Exod 3:13–15). God said, 'I am who I am', or 'I will be who I will be'. Both interpretations are possible and are represented by the letters YHWH. It suggests a God who is revealed by actions rather than as an impersonal, remote deity. God was one who cared enough to hear the cry of the people and raise up a leader to bring them from bondage to freedom—a God who acted in the events of history. In the same way, Christians worship the God who acted within history in God's Son, sent to save us.

The story of Pharaoh's reluctance to let the people go is told in the early chapters of Exodus (6 to 12) and includes the account of the plagues God sent on the Egyptians to persuade Pharaoh to release the Israelites. Finally, the last plague convinced Pharaoh of the power of Israel's God, and the people were allowed to leave Egypt. Later, Pharaoh changed his mind and the Egyptians chased the slaves in an effort to return them to Egypt. When they came to the Red Sea the people were trapped but there was a miraculous crossing of the Red Sea. The Israelites were safe on dry land and then the water returned and the Egyptian chariots were swept away in a rush of water.

Once the Hebrews were free and in the wilderness, it was not long before there was murmuring against the leaders and against God because of the trials the people were facing. They had been rescued from a situation that was bad, but one that was familiar to them. Now they lived in the desert, uncertain of their final destination and facing starvation. They are pictured as an ungrateful people with little trust in God who provided for their needs.

The Israelites are thought to have spent around forty years traveling in the wilderness, but Old Testament records do not provide clear evidence for us to trace the route with any degree of certainty. The major event that occurred in the wilderness was the revelation of God to Israel at Sinai. This experience of God was vital to their understanding of themselves as a people chosen by God for God's purposes. At Sinai God made a covenant with them and gave them the Ten Commandments which would enable them to live in relationship with God and all of humanity. The commandments were written on tablets of stone that were placed in a special box and carried by the Israelites wherever they went. It became known as the Ark of Covenant and a symbol of God's presence in the midst the people Israel.

Moses had a very important role in the making of this covenant with God. He acted as mediator between God and the people and spoke to God on their behalf when they accepted the conditions and promised to be obedient to God (Exodus 19:8). The Ten Commandments were the core from which other law codes developed. For example, see the Book of the Covenant (Exod 20:22 to 23:33), the

Deuteronomic Code (Deut 12 to 26) and the Holiness Code (Lev 17 to 26). These later laws were specific in the way they dealt with all areas of community life, whether it is in relation to one's neighbours, slaves, worship life, criminal offence or animals. In their history the Jews have always perceived and understood the law as a helpful tool to enable them to stay in relationship with God. It is not the negative view we have of law today but a positive view, seeing the law as a help in enabling the people of Israel to enjoy the fullness of life.

Moses led the people through the wilderness, but he died prior to occupation of the Promised Land. He saw the land from the bank of the Jordan but it was Joshua who took over leadership at the time of entry into the land of Canaan. The entry took place around1250 BCE and is portrayed in different ways. One version is a concerted attack by all Israel, with a quick victory and assimilation (Josh 1 to 12), while another is of a slow process of infiltration and a gradual assimilation and acquisition of Canaanite land (Jud 1 and the later parts of Joshua).

The Biblical accounts of the conquest cover four main areas: Trans Jordania, the central high country, the southern region and the north. There was some infiltration from the south into the central Negev with which the tribe of Judah had earlier connections. This was a gradual penetration into cultivated land accompanied by resistance and fighting. There is very little information about these southern tribes, the Kenites, Othnielites, Simeon and Levi.

Another group of tribes left Kadesh, journeyed south and east of the Dead Sea and skirted the territories of Edom, Moab and Ammon. These latter kingdoms were established and Israel left them alone, attacking further north into the territories of Og and Sihon. This territory became the tribal of land of Reuben, Gad and Eastern Manasseh. So, part of the community adopted a settled agricultural life prior to crossing the Jordan because it was impossible to occupy the land west of the river at that time. The reason for this was that the heavily populated areas of Canaan were able to defend themselves very well against any invasion by Israel at that time.

Other tribes came in from the central land west of the Jordan, especially the hill country of Ephraim and Samaria. This settlement took place over long period of time. The tribes found it easier to gain control in the rough terrain of the sparsely populated hill country. It was harder to gain access and control on the coastal plains and on the trade routes because they we more densely populated and not easily overcome. The total process of settlement was complex and varied.

The different tribes settled and consolidated themselves in their positions throughout Canaan, but were still separate groups of people with their own leaders and traditions. They were not under a central governing body at that time. However, it is in the period of the Judges, 1250 to 1020 BCE, that men and women were raised up by God to call the tribes together when they were threatened an enemy force. These men and women who were military commanders were called Judges and were given gifts of leadership by God to meet needs of the current situation. The areas that came under most threat were strategic points west of the Jordan were many of the inhabitants of coastal plains lived. When the threat was removed, the tribes returned their own land until another crisis arose.

While the process of settling into the land of Canaan was proceeding there was a group of people called Philistines who were entering into Canaan to settle in the coastal areas. They were the descendants of people who had been forced by events in their Aegean lands to search for new homes. They were capable military organisers and made full use of the Iron-age implements available to them. They gradually expanded eastward to take more and more of the central land of Canaan. As they expanded east and Israel expanded west, each intent on gaining more and more land and consolidating their positions, the inevitable happened and they came into conflict. For Israel it became a battle for survival and one of the precipitating factors in the emergence of the monarchy in Israel.

The beginning of the monarchy (1020–922 BCE): Saul, David, Solomon

Bible readings: 1 and 2 Samuel; 1 Kings 1–11

While the struggle for survival showed the need for a king, there was strong opposition to this idea, as we see in the books of Samuel. Kingship was seen as evil and not what God intended for Israel. This tension, between those for and against kingship, continued for as long as there were kings in Israel, and beyond.

The persistent call by the Israelites for a king began when the Philistines seemed to be at the point of completely crushing them. They had been defeated at a significant battle at Shiloh in 1050 BCE, when the Ark, an important religious symbol, was captured by the enemy. To the people of Israel it seemed as if the very presence of God had gone from their midst and was now with the Philistine army. The ark in past history had been the symbol of God leading them to victory, and eventually into the Promised Land. To be defeated and to lose this sacred symbol was a double disaster.

During this disastrous time in Israel's history Samuel came to the fore. He is represented as the first and greatest kingmaker in Israel. He was also a prophet, a priest, and the last of the judges. It was through him that the monarchy was introduced into Israel and he anointed both Saul and David. He had been brought up at the sanctuary at Shiloh, under guidance of Eli, the priest. After the destruction of Shiloh, Samuel took over the priestly duties. He kept alive the traditions of the past by traveling around proclaiming the covenant and reminding the people of their relationship with God. There were frequent battles with the Philistines and these forced the Israelites to take refuge and consolidate their position in central highlands of Canaan. This continuous pressure resulted in the people begging Samuel to let them have a king as his successor. He was very unhappy with their lack of faith in God and their continuing insistence that they should have a king, but finally he nominated and anointed Saul. This story is told in 1 Samuel 8 to 12, where two traditions are interwoven. One tradition (1 Sam 9:1 to 10:16) sees Saul as God's instrument for deliverance of his people. His name had been divinely revealed to Samuel and he had gifts of leadership given by God (1 Sam 8, 10:17–27). The other tradition presents the request for a king as a rejection of the authority of God and is critical of the monarchy, which was seen as a dangerous innovation, however important the benefits it would bring.

It can be seen in later history how these two traditions were represented in the kingdoms of Judah and Israel. In Judah, the bloodline of David was carried down through the centuries and blessed by the promise of God to David; that is, the line of David would last forever and his throne be established forever (2 Sam 7:8–17). In Israel, there were frequent uprisings and new kings were raised up. There was no unbroken bloodline of kings. In the end, leaders in both countries were condemned; Israel was annihilated and Judah exiled in Babylon (1 and 2 Kgs).

Saul manifested the gifts of prophecy and leadership in the initial stages of his rule. Whilst we speak of him as a king, in fact he was still very much like a charismatic judge, as there was no formal apparatus of state at this time. The Philistines saw the election of a king as a threat to their supremacy. This was heightened by Jonathan's (Saul's son) exploits at Geba, where he and his armour-bearer killed a small group of Philistines. Saul followed up this attack and gained further victories, but was soon under great pressure from the Philistines.

Saul began to suffer in his personal life and relationships. He encroached on Samuel's priestly duties (1 Sam 13:8–14) and a growing alienation occurred between Saul and Samuel. It was at this time that young David joined the court, so that by his skill as a musician he could bring relief to the king in times of mental stress. Despite David's close friendship with Saul's son Jonathan and his marriage to Michal, Saul's daughter, his presence caused Saul severe fits of jealousy. This may have been caused by David's success as a warrior and his popularity with the people, with the consequence that David became the victim of Saul's persecution mania and nearly lost his lift on some occasions. Finally, David had to flee, gathering around him a band of fugitives and mercenaries whom he formed into an effective guerrilla group.

Much of the record of Saul's reign is concerned with the worsening relations between the two men. David was first outlawed in the hill country of Judah where Saul tried hard to eliminate the guerrillas. David then went into exile in Philistia. Soon after, Saul's last struggle with the Philistines took place. Saul, Jonathan and two other sons were killed in battle and the Philistines then had a tight grip on the land of Israel.

David, who had been in the doubtful position of a mercenary serving Achish, king of Gath, then moved to Hebron, where he was anointed king of Judah (2 Sam 2:1–4). He inherited a country in disarray and disunited with the Philistines in a very strong position for final victory.

Saul's son Eshbaal became king in Trans-Jordan. This did not last as he was a weak king and defection and dissention occurred among his followers. Eshbaal was murdered and the tribes that had supported him then sent delegates to David to ask him to be their king. This resulted in David and the elders of Israel making a covenant with God at Hebron (2 Sam 5:3) and he was anointed king of Israel. David thus became King of Judah and Israel and so posed a serious threat to the Philistines.

The Philistines, seeing the danger of the tribes unified under one leader, brought an army against David. David defeated them in two decisive battles in the vicinity of the valley of Rephaim. It seems likely that these victories preceded the capture of Jerusalem, although they follow it in the narrative (2 Sam 5:4–10). David needed a place from which he could rule his kingdom. Jerusalem was an old Canaanite citadel situated between the two parts of David's kingdom. The city was considered to be impregnable until David led an assault into the city through a water shaft and captured it (2 Sam 5:6–10). Due to its position, Jerusalem was an ideal city to serve as the political and religious centre for Israel.

Jerusalem, the City of David, became the focus of worship and administration for the united kingdom, and later, after the division of the kingdom, for Judah. David brought the Ark from Kiriath-jearim and installed it in a sacred tent in Jerusalem (2 Sam 6). This was a shrewd move because it signified that God's presence was now in the place where central rule was established. The Ark had been the symbol of success and now, established in the city, it gave authority to David's rule, and served to overcome any religious influence from Canaanite practices. Jerusalem became known as an invincible city because it was the place where God rested. This tradition of Jerusalem being under God's protection was prominent in the prophet Isaiah's proclamation. Because the people believed that Jerusalem was always safe from destruction it caused great anguish and shock when it was destroyed by the Babylonians in 597 BCE.

It is from this period (950 BCE) that the traditions about David and Jerusalem developed. Both David and Jerusalem were chosen of God, and David received the promise that his dynasty would last forever (2 Sam 7:13–16). Both David and Jerusalem are presented as favoured by God and chosen for God's purposes. These traditions can be seen in more developed patterns in later writings of Israel.

After establishing the city of Jerusalem and consolidating his leadership, David went on to further military victories. He conquered Edom, Moab and Ammon and went as far south as the head of the Gulf of Aqaba. The whole of the Trans-Jordan came under David's rule; to the north he won Zobah, Damascus and a Hittite kingdom became a subordinate state, and so David ruled from the Egyptian frontier to the Euphrates. It was the only time in the history of Israel that the Israelites ruled such a large area and had such glory and power. It must be recognised that this was due not only to David's charisma and military prowess, but also to the weakness of countries such as Assyria and Egypt, who exerted no influence in the region during David's reign.

David consolidated his territories and set up structures for governing effectively. In some ways his court resembled those of surrounding cultures. He had many wives and their offspring caused him trouble later in his reign (2 Sam 9 to 20). He set up a trading link with Phoenicia and the whole of Israel enjoyed a peace and prosperity that was unique in its long history. In this period, the cultural life of Israel began to flourish, poetry (psalms) and music developed along-side, and as part of, worship. The quality of life changed from a survival existence disturbed by tribal fighting to a settled urban and agricultural lifestyle.

Towards the end of David's reign he had to contend with rivalry between his sons. Absalom, his eldest son, led a revolt, which David succeeded in putting down. Another son, Adonijah also made a claim for the throne. He secured the support of Joab, a general, and Abiathar, a priest; two men who had been with David in his early years of struggle. This group was opposed by another headed by Nathan, the prophet, and Zadok, the priest, who supported the claim of Solomon to be the future king. Solomon was the son of David from his wife Bathsheba (2 Sam 11 and 12) and, with the aged king's agreement, Solomon was anointed and publicly proclaimed king (1 Kgs 1). This rivalry and fighting between the sons was a sad ending to a reign that had begun so gloriously.

Solomon (961 to 922 B.C.) was not a warrior like his father, but was a very able statesman. He made political and commercial agreements with the surrounding countries and Israel grew exceedingly prosperous. He instituted magnificent building programs in Jerusalem and was responsible for the construction of the temple. There was continued peace and prosperity and the arts flourished. The wise became part of the court scene and court annals were written. Using past oral traditions as a source, the Israelites created their first written theology, telling of their experience of God from its beginning.

Solomon's revenue did not keep pace with his extravagant spending so he began to tax his people heavily and implemented a system of forced labour which initially was imposed on non-Judeans, but later they too were conscripted. Gradually people became disillusioned and murmuring against Solomon grew towards the end of his reign.

The ten tribes in the north of Israel were particularly unhappy. The prophet Ahijah enacted a prophecy to Jeroboam, an officer in the labour force, in which the prophet tore his cloak in twelve pieces, gave ten to Jeroboam and two he threw away, symbolising that Jeroboam would become leader of the ten tribes. Jeroboam after this incident fled to Egypt, where the Pharaoh Shishak offered him sanctuary (1 Kgs 1:26–40).

After Solomon's death, (922 BC) his successor needed to be very sensitive to tribal feelings of oppression and injustice. They wanted Rehoboam (Solomon's son) to return to the covenant that they felt Solomon's oppressive measures had violated. Rehohoam was badly advised and refused, causing immediate reaction from the ten northern tribes who threw off their allegiance to Rehoboam, recalled Jerohoam from Egypt and proclaimed him their king at Shechem. All that Rehoboam had left under his command was the large tribe of Judah and the small tribe of Benjamin on his northern boundary.

The immediate cause of the division was Solomon's extravagant building programs and the ensuing oppressive measures. However, a smouldering jealousy between the tribes of the north and south was always present just below the surface of their relationship. David had been able to keep this in check with his charisma and so maintain a unified kingdom. Neither Solomon nor Rehoboam were able to match David's example. It must be noted that the prophets played a significant role in the politics of the state. Religion and politics were never separate in Israel's history. The kings were to be God's agents on earth and all of life, political and religious, came under God's rule and jurisdiction. In these early years, the prophets chose and anointed future kings, spoke in times of crisis, witnessed rulers' wrong behaviour and even suggested revolt. Ahijah had been party to the secession of the ten tribes of Israel and he was one of the prophets who played a major role in Israel's political affairs.

In the following brief history of the divided kingdoms, there will be mentioned only some of the disturbances, revolts, battles and alliances that abound in Israelite and Judean history. Full details are available in other books. The purpose here is to show something of the turbulent history of kingdoms caught between the rise and fall of the empires that surrounded them.

Israel: 922 BCE–721 BCE

Bible readings: 1 and 2 Kings

We will refer to the ten tribes, which seceded in 922 BCE as Israel and the remaining tribes of Judah and Benjamin as Judah.

When Jeroboam 1 was king, he realised that he would need to set up other places of worship because he did not want his people traveling to the Temple at Jerusalem. He established Dan and Bethel as the worship sanctuaries for Israel, and they were served by a priesthood which could trace its beginning to the time of Moses. In these sanctuaries, golden images of bull-calves were installed to serve as a visible focus for worship of God. This violated the second commandment and was similar to Canaanite practice. It was condemned vigorously in the later writings of the Deuteronomist (*circa* 600 BCE—1 Kgs 11:26–40; 2 Kgs 13:11).

In addition to these internal difficulties Israel, along with Judah, suffered from the invading army of the Egyptian Pharaoh Shishak who came north through Palestine, looting cities in both countries. Judah was weakened by these attacks and could not concentrate on subduing the rebel tribes in the north, or regaining the land. To preserve her own position, Judah made an alliance with the king of Damascus, which meant that Israel could not risk an attack on Judah for fear of reprisals on her northern border by Damascus.

This situation is often repeated in the history of Israel, where either Judah or Israel negotiated treaties, sometimes together, against a foreign power, or sometimes against each other in co-operation with a foreign state. Prophets like Isaiah and Hosea condemned Judah and Israel for their manner of arranging treaties instead of relying on the power of God to resolve their difficulties.

In the 200 years of Israel's history, leaders were often raised up in quick succession and there were relatively few long stable periods of peace and prosperity in the kingdom. There were some brief periods of succession in the bloodline of kings, but it was mainly rule by revolt and conspiracy rather than a continuous line as in the southern kingdom of Judah.

Jeroboam ruled for twenty years (922 to 901 BCE) and his son succeeded him for a brief time before being killed (as was the rest of Jeroboam's line) in a conspiracy in 900 BCE The northern kingdom had five rulers within the period of King Asa's rule in Judah (913 to 873 BCE). This indicates some of the turbulence that beset Israel. In the reign of Omri (876 to 869 BCE) the country had a period of consolidation and peace with growth in prosperity and expansion of territory. Omri gave Israel a new permanent capital city named Samaria and, through a policy of alliance and co-operation with Phoenicia, brought stability to the region.

When Israel first settled in the land of Canaan they had come into contact with the local worship of the Canaanite baals. There was a constant temptation to follow local customs and worship local gods. The first and second commandments spoke directly against this practice, and the kings and leaders of Judah and Israel were meant to enforce these laws of God. Worship of God alone was the only acceptable way for the people. When they were tempted to worship other deities and encouraged their people to do likewise, the prophets pronounced judgment on them.

Ahab (869 to 850 BCE), the son of Omri, was a person whom the prophets condemned for his apostasy. His wife Jezebel came from Tyre and brought with her the worship of Asherah and Baal Shamen. This worship was condoned by the king and the court prophets did not speak out because of fear of persecution. The queen's enthusiastic promotion of the Tyrian cult was a direct challenge to God's claim on the total allegiance of the people of Israel. This was a greater threat than the constant presence of Canaanite baals because it had such active support from the king and queen.

Elijah emerged on this scene and spoke out against such practices, condemning both Ahab and Jezebel for their treachery against God. Elijah had some connections with a band of prophets (2 Kgs 2:1–18), but we read of him pre-eminently as a prophet who acted by himself. He challenged the prophets of the court to show their power on Mount Carmel (I Kgs 18) and called on the people to choose between Baal and Yahweh. Elijah pronounced judgment on Ahab and on his house (1 Kgs 21:17–24), and this was seen to come true when Ahab was killed in battle in 850 BCE. Ahab's sons, Ahaziah and Joram, reigned only briefly before Jehu, a military commander, fulfilled the prophecy of Elijah by killing all the remaining descendants of Ahab (842 BCE). Jehu (842 to 815 BCE.) had a long reign and we read that he banished Baal worship from the sanctuaries, but we have little knowledge his domestic po1icies. He must have maintained some stability to reign for twenty-seven years, though paying tribute to Assyria for a time.

The next great king of Israel was Jeroboam 2 (786 to 746 BCE). He was king when the prophets Amos and Hosea made their appearances. His reign is depicted as a happy and prosperous period prior to the final crises caused by recurring Assyrian invasions and the later annihilation of Israel by that nation. It was a peaceful time because Damascus was busy keeping an enemy at bay on its northern border and so was not able to harass Israel. In the preceding years there had been continual losses of cavalry and infantry to the kings of Damascus and Israel had also lost territory in the northeast to the Aramaeans. Due to these losses Israel was not able to expand to the north and east to recapture some of its lost land. While enjoying the respite from the tyranny of the bigger powers, Israel was in fact enjoying the lull before the storm. Assyria was gathering force and momentum and the prophets in this period gave warning about possible punishment for Israel's perverse behaviour in the areas of politics, religion and justice (Amos, Hosea). The fortunes of Israel and Judah can never be viewed in isolation from events in the surrounding countries. They often only had peace when countries like Assyria and Egypt were busy in other areas, or were too weak internally to worry about outside conquests.

After the reign of Jeroboam 2 there were further brief reigns punctuated by bloody revolts to overthrow the kings of Israel. In 745 BCE Tiglath-pileser 3 ascended the throne in Assyria and began a very active program of expansion. He did not necessarily conquer all countries, but made some pay tribute and declare an oath of loyalty. Israel became one of these subordinate states on the outer edge of Assyria's power.

Syria tried to gain independence from Assyria in 733 BCE and Pekah, king of Israel, joined in an alliance with Rezin, king of Syria. Both powers then tried to induce Judah to join them in a coalition but when Judah refused, Syria and Israel exerted further pressure and Judah called on Assyria for help. Isaiah the prophet urged King Ahaz of Judah to trust in God and not run to Assyria for aid, but he was ignored (Isa 7:3–4). Tiglath-pileser, with remarkable effectiveness, swooped on Syria and Israel; he divided Syria into three provinces and Israel again became a tributary vassal of Assyria. Pekah was assassinated by Hoshea (732 to 724 BC). Hoshea paid tribute to Assyria for a while, but then entered into negotiations with Egypt. Later he withheld tribute from Assyria with the result that Shalmaneser 5 and then Sargon 2 waged war against Israel. In 72I BCE Samaria fell to the Assyrians and severe punishment was meted out by the conquerors.

Thousands were deported and mixed with other races and nationalities, so they were prevented from retaining any identity of their own. Only a few of the poor and illiterate were left in Israel. So the ten tribes of Israel ended in ignominy and defeat.

Judah: 921 BCE–721 BCE

Bible readings 1 and 2 Kings; 1 and 2 Chronicles

After the secession of the ten tribes, Judah was considerably weakened as a military power by the constant invasions into her territory by Shishak, the Egyptian Pharaoh. Rehoboam was unable to win back the northern tribes and lost some of the states won by David but neglected by Solomon. These states now took the opportunity to grasp their independence.

Asa (913 to 873 BCE), grandson of Rehoboam, continued the fight against Israel by weaning the king of Damascus from his alliance with Israel. Asa's successor, Jehoshaphat (873 to 849 BCE) extended some degree of control over Edom, and into Philistia and northern Arabia. He was loyal to Yahweh, a faithful worshipper and an advocate of true worship.

His son Jehoram (849 to 842 BC) was influenced by his wife Athaliah and established the Baal cult in Judah (2 Kings 8:18). Athaliah was the daughter of Jezebel who introduced pagan worship into Israel and drew the anger of the prophets against her husband Ahab and herself for their active promotion of baal worship. When a king, who is supposed to be the agent of God on earth, strongly supports the pagan gods, his behaviour always brings a very strong condemnation from the writers of the books of Kings (2 Kgs 8:18).

When Jehoram's son Ahaziah was killed only one year after ascending the throne, Athaliah seized power and murdered nearly all the royal house. Only an infant son of Ahaziah, Joash, was rescued and hidden from the murderous actions of his grandmother. Six years later he and his followers retook the throne from Athaliah and he reigned for thirty-seven years (837 to 800 BCE)

Uzziah came to the throne in 783 BCE and officially reigned until 742 BCE but he contracted leprosy and his son Jotham acted as regent from about 750 BCE. This was a period of stability and prosperity, reasonably free from serious external interference, so Judah was able to recover lost territories and develop trade with neighbouring states.

On the world scene, Syria was having severe struggles among its own city-states. Assyria tried to expand its empire during the first half of the ninth century BCE and failed, but by the middle of the eighth century had gained control of land to the west of Mesopotamia including Syria, Palestine, Israel and Judah.

Jotham (742 to 735 BCE) refused to be coerced into joining with Syria and Israel against Assyria but after his death, Ahaz turned to Assyria for help. Assyria not only conquered Israel but subdued Judah and made it a vassal state. As consequence, Ahaz had to pay very heavy tribute. In addition, Ahaz remodeled the Temple altar to a design similar to one he had seen in Damascus for worshipping Assyrian idols. He actively encouraged pagan practices and even offered his own son as a sacrifice (2 Kgs 16:2–4). His reign was a gloomy time of territorial and financial losses, political subservience and apostasy. Whilst Judah was in this position however, it did at least stay intact and did not meet the fate of the northern part of the former united state of Israel.

Apostasy and reform: Hezekiah, Manasseh and Josiah

Hezekiah 715 BC–687 BCE

For Judah, it was both humiliating and financially crippling to be a vassal state to Assyria, but under the submission policy of Ahaz (735 to 715 BCE) it had been the only way to survive. During the reign of Hezekiah, important changes took place both internally and externally. Assyria had to cope with a number of its vassal states rebelling and throwing off the yoke of their master. Hezekiah took advantage of this situation and began a program of cultic reform whereby the temple was cleansed of all foreign idols and people were strongly encouraged to worship Yahweh alone (2 Kgs 18:1–4). He also attempted to suppress ancient Canaanite baal worship and encouraged Israelites to make Jerusalem the centre of worship. This reform was very similar to that of Josiah many years later.

In the Old Testament, Hezekiah is portrayed as a good king because of his actions in purifying the religious practices of Judah.

Hezekiah's bid for political freedom from Assyria did not last very long. Egypt had sought Hezekiah's assistance in trying to break Assyria's power. This failed when Sennacherib came west, subdued Phoenicia, defeated Egypt, and then ravaged Judah. Jerusalem was surrounded by the Assyrian army but was spared by the intervention of God. The story is told in Isaiah 37:36–8 and 2 Kings 18:35–7 of how a plague was sent among the Assyrians who fled in fear. There is another record of this event giving a different reason for the survival of Jerusalem. Herodotus records an Egyptian tradition that Sennacherib's army had to retreat because during the night mice gnawed their quivers, bow strings and shield handles, and so they had no weapons with which to fight. Whatever the true story, the fact remains that it was a remarkable deliverance for Hezekiah, at God's hand.

After Sennacherib's withdrawal he was killed and his successor soon led another campaign west, not only regaining Judah as a vassal state, but successfully invading Egypt in 671 BCE.

Manasseh: 687 BCE–642 BCE

Manasseh was the opposite of Hezekiah. He was a king who was willing to compromise his religious principles to those of Assyria and to pay exorbitant tribute into the coffers of the overlord. Manasseh did not just tolerate Assyrian cult worship he encouraged it. For this he is condemned in the writings of the Old Testament (2 Kgs 21)

Assyria reached the peak of its power when it invaded Egypt and sacked the ancient city of Thebes in 663 BCE. Within a decade Assyrian influence began to wane and Egypt was successful in reasserting its independence. Assyria not only had Egypt resisting on its southern border but Babylon and Media were asserting their power in the east. Both of these countries made damaging attacks into Assyrian lands and, by 612 BCE, Nineveh was captured by a combined assault of Babylon and its allies.

Josiah: 640 BCE–609 BCE

These acts of international drama all helped Judah adopt an independent policy. It was possible for Josiah, who had ascended the throne when he was eight years old, to pursue an active policy of both internal and external reform. The reform was a thorough program of cultic purification and centralisation. Josiah abolished all pagan practices, including human sacrifice, and made every effort to make the Jerusalem temple the sole place of sacrifice. This meant that proper practice of sacrifice could be maintained, and removed from the local shrines any possibility of wrong forms of the worship of God. Josiah is highly acclaimed in the Old Testament writings for his movement to purify worship. This reform resulted in the local Levites being out of work and laws were made to ensure they did not suffer from the loss of employment (Deut 14:28–29). Levites were heredity successors to the priestly function bestowed on Levi, son of Jacob. Their role seems to have varied through the history of Israel but at one stage they were priests who functioned at the local shrines, leading worship and offering the sacrifices to God.

As the temple in Jerusalem was being restored to its former holiness with the removal of foreign gods and the Assyrian altar, the workmen found 'the book of the law' (2 Kgs 22 to 23; 2 Chron 34). On reading the book, Josiah discovered that many of the themes and sermons dominant in the writings supported his own reform. The book of the law—Deuteronomy 5 to 26, 28, was then read to the people as part of a ceremony renewing the covenant with God. Some scholars believe that the book of the law was found prior to any reforms initiated by Josiah and it was the discovery of the book that gave the impetus for reform. However, Judah's brief period of political freedom ended in 609 BCE when Josiah was killed in battle by the Egyptian Pharaoh Necho 2. This was a disaster for the people of Judah who were in desperate need of wise and determined leadership. The successors to Josiah were not able to provide this and Judah teetered ever more closely on the brink of disaster over the next ten years.

Fall of Jerusalem, exile and restoration (587 BCE–538 BCE) and the period of exile

Bible readings: Jeremiah; Ezekiel; Haggai; Zechariah; I and 2 Chronicles; Ezra; Nehemiah

Judah came under the rule of Egypt in the years following Josiah's death, 609 to 604 BCE. In the meantime the Medes and the Babylonians had divided the remainder of the Assyrian territory, and Babylon, in 609 BCE, turned its attention to Egypt and the lands of Syria and Palestine. The Egyptians were defeated in 605 BCE by Nebuchadnezzar and yielded Syria, Palestine and Judah to Babylon.

Egypt was still able to contest Babylon's bid for power and defeated the Babylonians in 600 BCE. Jeoiakim of Judah decided to exploit this and assert his country's independence. Babylon re-organised its troops and sought to keep control of Syria and Palestine. Jerusalem was surrounded by the Babylonian army in January 597 and over-run two months later. Jehoiachin, son of Johoiakim, had only reigned three months and was removed to Babylon with all his family and a great many other leaders and officials.

The manner of deportation was different from that exercised by the Assyrians for the people of Israel. The Babylonians allowed the people to remain together in a group and did not scatter them through the nations. It was still the practice though to remove the elite of the defeated country's society and leave behind the ordinary population. The temple was heavily plundered, but was neither destroyed nor completely stripped of its sacred vessels.

Nebuchadnezzar appointed Zedekiah, an uncle of Jehoiachin, as king in Jerusalem. However, he did not have the strength of character to lead the remaining people in Judah. It was a difficult period with two factions contending for political power. One party advocated continued submission to Babylon and the other wanted to join with Egypt and rebel against Babylon. Zedekiah was influenced by the anti-Babylon group and led a revolt in 589 BCE. The Babylonian army quickly invaded Judah once more (588 BCE), capturing most strongholds, with only Lachish and Azekah offering much resistance. Jerusalem was surrounded once again and finally submitted in 587 BCE after a long siege. Zedekiah tried to escape, but was captured and watched his sons put to death before he was blinded and deported to Babylon.

In Jerusalem, parts of the city were burned, the fortifications and the temple destroyed, and the temple vessels removed to Babylon. There was a second deportation of people, especially those members of the upper classes who had escaped the deportation of 597 BCE. The fall of Jerusalem marks the end of autonomy for Judah. It was the conclusion of a political independence that began with the days of conquest and achieved constitutional form in the unified kingdoms of Israel and Judah. The land was now completely under foreign control and there remained only the poorer people, without leaders.

Exile was a catastrophe for Israel that left its mark forever on its traditions and life. It is a miracle that the traditions formed before the exile were preserved and for this we can be thankful to those who were in exile in Babylon.

The Babylonians allowed the people to remain in their own community while in exile. They did not force mixed marriages nor did they try to break down the nation's identity. The Israelites were able to foster and actively keep alive their traditions, their identity as a people and their hope for the future.

The exiles were inspired to hear God's word again and to interpret the disaster in the light of God's justice and mercy. There were significant writings that took place during the exile—Ezekiel and Deutero-Isaiah (Isaiah 40 to 55)—and considerable rewriting of earlier traditions, including the Pentateuch and Deuteronomic history. In the writings of Deutero-Isaiah we have an understanding of grace that approaches what we find in the New Testament. It seems the experience of the exile made the people of Judah aware that they could not of their own accord remain in a right relationship with God, for they constantly strayed from the covenant relationship by their disobedience and blindness to the ways of God. In the end their only hope lay in the sheer mercy and love of God who was seen to be faithful throughout Israel's history, so the people only needed to respond to be in a right relationship with God. This concept of grace in Deutero-Isaiah is paralleled in the grace that we know in the New Testament when God sent his only Son that we might have life.

The exile lasted until the rise of a new Persian empire under Cyrus who defeated the Babylonians in 539 BCE. He allowed the Judeans to return to Jerusalem, but after fifty years in exile there was now a second generation that knew little of their homeland and were not enthusiastic about returning. In fact, there were only small groups of people who returned over periods of time and there remained in Babylon a significant group of former exiles. The exilic age is recognised as the beginning of the Diaspora; that is, from this point on, there were groups of people of Israelite descent who settled in various parts of the world and retained their own national and religious identity.

Restoration: 538 BCE

Although Cyrus was willing to let the people return to Jerusalem, the exiles were reluctant to leave what was now their homeland and it is not an inspiring picture we have of the return to Jerusalem.

There was no immediate start to rebuilding either the city fortifications or the temple. There was a great deal of apathy, and the irony is that they were granted their freedom to return for the purpose of rebuilding the temple. In fact the rebuilding was not begun until 520 BCE.

The impetus to begin rebuilding the temple was due to a number of factors:

1. There was a change in the ruling powers in the Persian empire causing upheaval and giving the returned exiles a new enthusiasm to start rebuilding. When Darius 1 gained control of the empire, he gave support to the project.
2. There was new political leadership in Jerusalem with Zerubbabel as governor and Joshua as high priest.
3. The prophets Haggai and Zechariah stood up and spoke the word of God to the people, so stimulating and confronting them with the need to rebuild the temple to the glory of God.

In 515 BCE Jerusalem finally possessed a temple again.

Reconstruction of the city of Jerusalem and the return to some internal order were also slow. The situation in Judah itself was quite depressing with periods of drought and bad harvest causing hardship. There was friction between the returned exiles and the people who had been left behind in the land. The exiles saw themselves as the purified remnant who were God's people, and this caused jealousy among those who had stayed. Any attempt at rebuilding caused further suspicion and resentment at the action of these upstart intruders.

After the temple was finally built there appears to have been half a century when the community lapsed into despondency and religious indifference. There was a very lax attitude to temple worship and sacrifices were not carried out in a proper fashion. Judeans began to marry people of the surrounding communities, a practice condemned because it was against the law. It was also seen as a threat to the identity of the people.

Nehemiah and Ezra came into this situation in the middle of the fifth century. It is disputed which of these men arrived in Jerusalem first, but we do know that each played a very significant part in the life of Judah at that time. Nehemiah was the primary force in the process of rebuilding the city walls and in providing stable administration and security. He had some opposition from the Samaritans who saw the fortification of Jerusalem as isolating the city from the province of Samaria. Nehemiah organised the economic system and brought the Levites back from secular employment to priestly duties. He enforced stricter observance of the Sabbath and replaced the high priest with another priest who adhered closely to the law.

Ezra came from Babylon as a 'commissioner for religious affairs' bringing the law-book with him. This he read to the people to remind them of right practices and to bring them back into line with the law of God. We are uncertain of the identity of the law book but many scholars suggest it could have been the Pentateuch. Nehemiah and Ezra had a tremendous influence in the consolidation of the Judeans as a pure race and for the improving political and religious conditions in Jerusalem.

Tension between the inhabitants in Judah and the returned exiles in Jerusalem continued. However, with the direction and guidance of leaders such as Ezra and Nehemiah, the small community continued to preserve its traditions and rebuild its worship life in Jerusalem. This community remained and grew during the years of Persian rule and into the Greek period (330 BCE onwards). It was during the Greek era that the people asserted their independence and from the rise of the Maccabees in 175 BCE, until Pompey's victory in 63 BCE, they had a period of self-rule. We have very little information about conditions in the period from 400 to 63 BCE. The writings that contain most references to this time come from the collection of literature known as the Apocrypha, which is included only in some versions of the Bible. Daniel is the main source in most information in the Bible.

Israel's history is such a series of upheavals and crises that it can only be claimed a miracle that Israel survived to be the cradle of Christianity and a continuing Jewish people.

Questions

1. What nations played a significant role in the life of Israel? How did they influence Israel's history?
2. Politics and religion were not separate in the ancient world. Explain.
3. What do you see as the major events in the life of Israel? Why were these events important?

Time chart

Major kings and principal historical events			Major religious figures and developments of literature
Judah		**Israel**	**Judah** **Israel**
640-609	Josiah		Jeremiah (called in 626) The Law book (part of Deuteronomy) found. (621)
597	Fall of Jerusalem	First Exile	Ezekiel deported to Babylon, where he received his call to prophesy.
586	Fall of Jerusalem	Second Exile	
582	Murder of Gedaliah		Jews flee to Egypt, taking Jeremiah. During exile the Law book is expanded into Deuteronomy. The Deuteronomic history is written — incorporating earlier traditions. The Priestly writing probably produced in this period.
539	Cyrus takes Babylon		
538	Jews allowed to return		
520-515	The temple rebuilt		Haggai and Zechariah
457			Ezra arrives in Jerusalem. (trad. date)
444			Nehemiah arrives in Jerusalem. Books of Proverbs and Job produced in this period.
397			Ezra arrives in Jerusalem (alt. date)
336-33	Alexander the Great conquers the Middle East		Ecclesiastes probably written at about this time; Ecclesiasticus (Jesus ben Sira) writes his book (about 180).
167	Outbreak of Maccabaean revolt		Book of Daniel published. Wisdom of Solomon written, perhaps about 100 B.C.
63	The Romans take over Palestine		

Time chart

Major kings and principal historical events		**Major religious figures and developments of literature**	
Before 1500 B.C.	Patriarchs	Individual stories handed down by word of mouth.	
1280 B.C.	Exodus	Moses) Traditions of exodus and	
circa 1250-1200	Settlement	Joshua) settlement preserved orally.	
circa 1200-1020	Judges		
circa 1020	Saul		
circa 1000-961	David	Samuel J traditions being collected Nathan at this time.	
961-922	Solomon		
922 Division of the kingdom		Ahijah	
Judah	**Israel**	**Judah**	**Israel**
922-915 Rehoboam	922-901 Jeroboam		E traditions possibly collected at about this period.
	876-869 Omri		
913-873 Asa	869-850 Ahab		
873-849 Jehoshaphat			
827-800 Joash			
	842-815 Jehu		
783-742 Uzziah	786-746 Jeroboam II	Isaiah of Jerusalem (circa 742-685)	Amos (circa 746) Hosea (circa 740-725)
735-715 Ahaz	732-724 Hoshea	Micah	
	721 Fall of Israel		
715-687 Hezekiah		Northern traditions probably brought south by refugees after the fall of Israel.	
87-642 Manasseh		The Law book (part of Deuteronomy) probably composed during this period.	

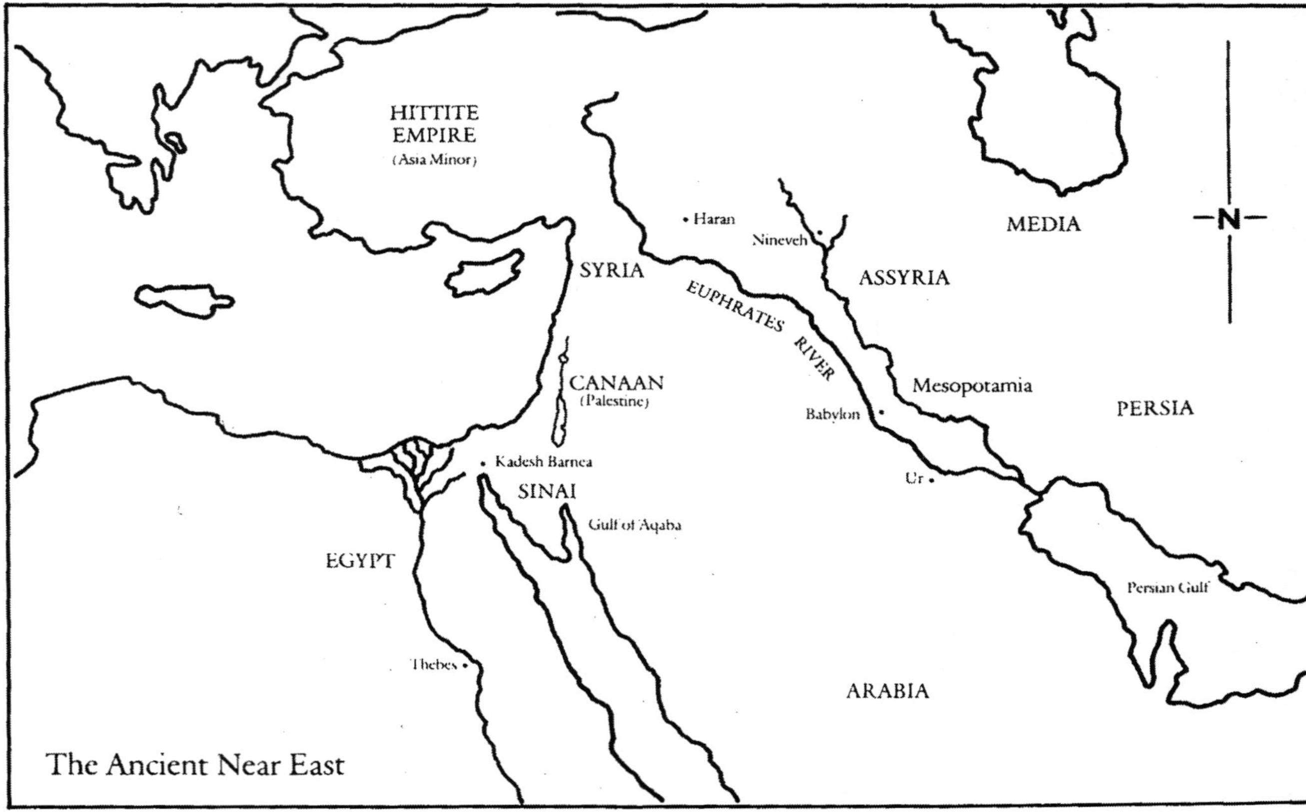

HITTITE
EMPIRE
(Asia Minor)
SYRIA
Haran
Nineveh
MEDIA
N
ASSYRIA
EUPHRATES RIVER
CANAAN
(Palestine)
Mesopotamia
Babylon
PERSIA
Kadesh Barnea
SINAI
Ur
Gulf of Aqaba
EGYPT
Persian Gulf
Thebes
ARABIA
The Ancient Near East

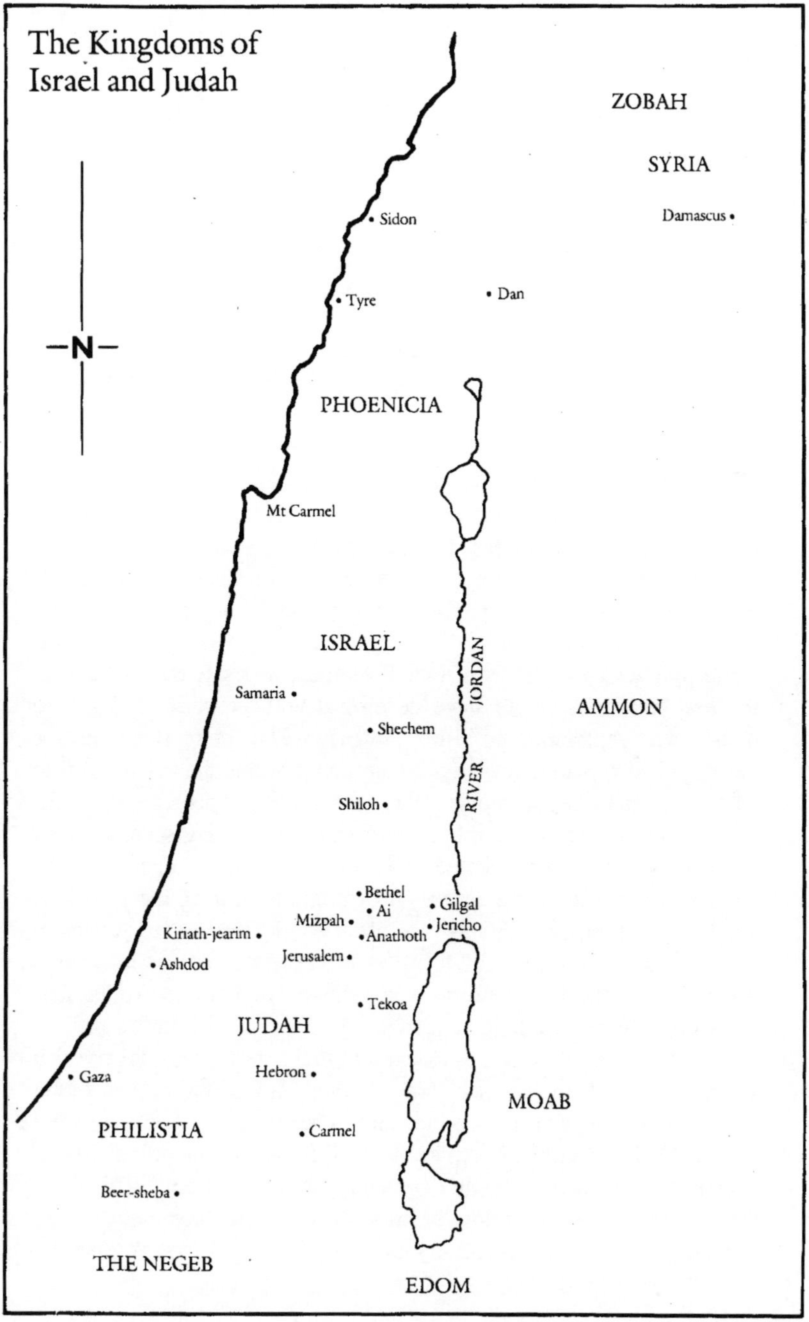
The Kingdoms of
Israel and Judah
N
ZOBAH
SYRIA
Damascus
Sidon
Tyre
Dan
PHOENICIA
Mt Carmel
ISRAEL
JORDAN
RIVER
AMMON
Samaria
Shechem
Shiloh
Bethel
Ai
Gilgal
Mizpah
Jericho
Kiriath-jearim
Anathoth
Jerusalem
Ashdod
Tekoa
JUDAH
Gaza
Hebron
MOAB
PHILISTIA
Carmel
Beer-sheba
THE NEGEB
EDOM

3

God Speaks to the People of Israel

Discussion of Genesis * Exodus * Leviticus * Numbers *Deuteronomy * the contents, characters, theology and traditions

Bible readings: Genesis 1–4, 6–9, 11–12, 15, 18–19, 22, 28, 32, 47, 50. Exodus 3, 11–12, 14, 19–24. Leviticus 5–6, 16, 19. Numbers 22–24.

The first five Books of the Old Testament (Genesis, Exodus, Leviticus, Numbers & Deuteronomy) are known by different names. Christian scholarship often refers to them as the Pentateuch and in the Hebrew Scriptures they are known as the Torah. These Books have a long a long history of growth and development. They began with oral traditions about the people's journey with God, which were remembered by the various tribes of Israel. As these tribes settled in the land the oral traditions would have developed with emphasis specific to their own experiences of that journey. The next stage in the development was the necessity to begin committing these traditions to writing, which didn't replace the oral tradition because only the learned would have been able to read and write. Many scholars think the first writings were created in written form in the middle of the tenth century BCE using earlier oral traditions. During the next four hundred years further writings took place among the various groups in Israelite society and the final form as we know it now, was reached in the middle of the fifth century BCE. These five Books were the first part of the Hebrew Bible to be recognised as sacred scripture.

We know in the New Testament that there are four gospels, which stand side by side and tell the story of Jesus Christ. Within each of the gospels there are both similarities and differences because they were written by different authors to speak to different communities. This is exactly the same in the Old Testament, but it is more difficult to discern the different traditions because they are often contained within the one Book. This is especially the case for the Books of Genesis,

Exodus and Numbers. Both Leviticus and Deuteronomy contain material from mainly the one author.

It was very common in Christian scholarship for these different tradition to be referred to as sources which were given names: the 'J' or Yahwistic writings, 'E' or Elohistic writings, 'D' or Dcuteronomic writings and 'P' or Priestly writings. They are not simply literary creations, nor the result of someone putting together pieces from larger works, but rather the creative and inspired work of faithful Israelites who want to make confessions of faith in new situations and at different times. They show that God speaks anew to the people throughout their journey. We will speak more about these after we have a brief look at each of the Books.

Genesis

Genesis is a fascinating Book, which begins with two creation accounts of the world in Genesis 1–3. It continues with stories about humanity in general through to the end of Genesis 11 before we come to the specific journeys of Abraham. Genesis 1–11 is often referred to as universal history or primeval history and is applicable to all of humanity. The genealogies trace Abraham descendants from Adam and Eve. Indeed, another purpose of the genealogies is to divide these eleven chapters as follows into a 5-fold division:

Genesis 2:4a heaven and earth—these are the generations of the heavens and the earth . . .

Genesis 5:1ff Adam: This is the Book of the generations of Adam.

Genesis 6:9 Noah: And Noah had three sons, Shem, Ham, and Japheth

Genesis 10:1 Noah's three sons: These are the generations of the sons of Noah . . .

Genesis 11:10 Shem: These are the descendants of Shem . . .

Creation of the world and humans is torn apart when the relationship between God and humans is told in Genesis 3 and between humans and humans in Genesis 4. One of the literary patterns which may be considered too not only be present in Genesis 1–11, but extend through into the remainder of the Book of Genesis is that connected with the command in Genesis 1:28—'be fruitful and multiply'. Not only does the phrase occur in a number of places, but the lists of genealogies show that indeed the people have been fruitful and multiplied—Genesis 5, 10, 11. The genealogies continue in Genesis 12-50 at particular points: Genesis 25:12 ('These are the generations of Ishmael'), Genesis 25:19 ('These are the generations of Isaac), Gen 36:1, ('These are the generations of Esau'), Genesis 37:2 ('These are the generations of Jacob'). The genealogies not only show that God's command in Genesis 1:28 has been followed, but the promises to Abraham in Genesis 12:1–3, Genesis 15:5 have come true. That is, Abram will have many descendants and become a great nation. At the point where each of the genealogies is listed we have the story of that person in the following chapters. Abraham in Genesis 11:27–25:18; Jacob in Genesis 25:19–36:43; Joseph, Judah and Jacob's family in Genesis 37:1–50:26.

In Genesis 3, the J writer recalls men and women's disobedience to God, and records the consequences of that disobedience. The narrator pursues the theme of disobedience and perversity, not against God, but against fellow beings. The story of Cain murdering his brother Abel (Gen 4) ought to be kept together with Genesis 3, for they complement each other. Disobedience against God, and crime against a brother, was seen to be equally sinful by these early writers.

The development of civilisation is portrayed in the chapter following the story of humankind's disobedience and God's punishment and mercy. This civilisation adopts agriculture as a way of life (Gen 4:2), founds a city (Gen 4:17), works with metal and develops music (Gen 4:18–22). The flood narrative deals with a community's disobedience as opposed to the individual's disobedience in the story of Adam and Eve. Again God's punishment was the result of the people's wickedness (Gen 6). God did not completely destroy either the whole of humankind or creation. Noah's family and all species of animals were preserved. The rainbow is a sign of God's grace and promise that the earth will never again be destroyed (Gen 9:12–1).

The stories in Genesis chapters 1 to 11 reflect the human experiences of life, work, pain, greed, disobedience, and in a sense arc giving an explanation for them. They show the human drive to acquire knowledge beyond the limits set by God. The result brings a separation from God but also portrays God's love and care for humanity (Gen 3:21). The need to be in relationship with God and with other human beings was part of God's purpose from the beginning of time. We note that these chapters speak of all humanity and are universal in that God created the world and everything in it. In the overall theology of Gen 1–11 this story, at its midpoint, tells again of humanity's inability to live in ways that mirror God's righteousness. And the people suffer the consequences, however God provides a remnant that will live in the recreation of God's world, a world, which includes all the animals in a covenant relationship with God (Gen 9).

This preview and summary of universal humanity now comes to the specific beginnings of Israel's history. It starts with the call of Abraham, shows Abraham's implicit trust in the promises of God and the account of Abram's travels into and through the land of Canaan. The story of Abraham's family covers four generations until the time spent in the land of Egypt. Behind this condensed version of the life of the patriarchs, was an era of nomadic tribes who eventually became the nation, Israel.

Genesis 12–50 tells the stories about Abram and his descendants as they move from Haran into the land of Canaan and begin wandering around the land and then into Egypt. These stories began as oral traditions passed down within the tribes long before they became part of the written tradition. It is the way many cultures remember their history, but in the Western world we became influenced by the enlightened definition of 'history', which understood 'history' as written facts from an objective viewpoint. This has caused many scholars to debate whether the Patriarchs can be proven to be true people through archaeological means. Other scholars say that this is not possible and therefore they cannot be historical people. If this argument was applied to Bedouin tribes or Australian Aboriginal people we deny them any history. History as oral tradition passed down is the history of a people, and does not need to be justified by Western values. The people are portrayed as very human with all their faults and strengths—they lie, deceive, steal, test God, they have courage, journey into the unknown, seek God, question God and are obedient. These traits apply to men and women, and many of the women (Sarah, Rebecca, Tamar) play a significant role in the working out of the promises of God.

After the story of Abram in Genesis11: 27–25:18 the next block, Genesis 25:19–36:43, tells us about Jacob and finally about Joseph in Genesis 37:1–50:26. At the end of the Book we are placed ready to begin the story of Moses, the release of the Hebrews from Egypt and their wanderings in the wilderness.

Genesis 11:27 and Genesis 25:1–18, enclose material which narrates the story of Abram and his descendants. When Abram married Sarai we are told in a stark way, that she was barren (11:30). This statement is crucial to the way the plot unfolds from Genesis 12 onwards. Genesis 12:1–3 becomes the guiding principle for the remainder of the Pentateuch (Genesis through to the end of Deuteronomy) and linked back to Genesis 1–11. The command to multiply in Genesis 1:28 has been fulfilled and now becomes specific to a people who will be a great nation. The earth is cursed because of Adam's disobedience in Genesis 3, but in Genesis 12 people will be cursed if they curse Abram, and conversely they will be blessed through him. Genesis 12:1–3 is an unconditional promise of descendants and blessing given by God to Abram. It does not say, 'if Abram does this, then I, God will do . . .' However, the story itself demonstrates in the response (vv 4–9) that Abram is obedient. The language of 'now' and the imperative 'go' (v 1) give immediacy to the story. The promise of a great nation in Genesis 12:2 will alert readers to a problem in view of the fact that we have been told that Sarai is barren—so how can Abram become a great nation?

Genesis 12:10 begin the journeys of Abram and Sarai into and around the land of Canaan. Genesis 12:10ff speaks of a famine that drove Abram and Sarai into Egypt, and we have the account of Abram passing Sarai off as his sister because he is afraid. She gets taken into the Pharaoh's house and Abram receives great numbers of livestock and servants in return for this sacrifice of Sarai. Somehow Pharaoh connects the onset of plagues with the realization that Sarai is Abram's wife. They are sent on their way much wealthier than when they went into Egypt. The narrative continues describing the various places visited and Lot is included now in the story. Because it is one continuous narrative we find connecting phrases at the beginning of chapters, which move us to a new time and incident throughout Genesis 12–25.

Very early in Abraham's travels, God made a covenant with him using the mode of a very ancient rite (Gen 15:7–18). In this covenant God reassures Abram that he will have descendants, and moreover, prophesies the time in Egypt before they come into the Promised Land. Because Sarai fails to conceive, she offers Hagar, her maidservant to Abram in order that he can have a son. This is quite normal practice in that time and many of the twelve tribes of Israel are descendants from maidservants of Leah and Rachel. Sarai is jealous and throws Hagar out of camp into the wilderness where she meets an angel who instructs her to return and call her child Ishmael. These descendants become Muslims of today. Another covenant is spoken of Genesis 17 introducing the practice of circumcision, which became one of the marks of identity for the Israelites. The names of Sarai and Abram (the father is exalted) are changed to Sarah (princess) and Abraham (father of nations) and they are told to call their son Isaac. Following the visitation of the messengers in Genesis 18 Abraham goes with the messengers to Sodom and the story of Lot and his wife interrupts the flow of the story about Abraham and Sarah (Gen 18:16–19:38). Part of its purpose is to explain why the Moabites and Ammonites were hated by the Israelites—they were conceived by incest. Abraham continues his journey into the Negev and for the second time passes Sarah off as his sister to a foreign king, this time the King of Gerar. God speaks to the king telling him Sarah is the wife of another man who had told him she was his sister. Abraham has two excuses for his behaviour (vv 11–12) and had instructed Sarah to say that Abraham was her brother. Again Abraham benefits enormously with more cattle, goods and money. We return then to Sarah and Abraham and finally there is a son born who has been promised back in Genesis 12. After the birth of Isaac, Sarah casts Hagar and her son, Ishmael by Abraham, out into the wilderness. There, God rescues them and promises that the descendants of Ishmael will become a great nation.

Several years have passed when we move forward into Genesis 22 and Abraham is commanded to take Isaac to offer him as sacrifice. Sarah has no part of this story and we have now idea whether she knew of Abraham's intention or what her feelings might have been. Sarah's death is recounted in Genesis 23 in which Abraham bought land, after some discussion, from the Hittites and the cave east of Mamre became the burial place of Sarah. Abraham is getting on as well and becomes concerned that Isaac marries from within the family and not a Canaanite woman. He makes his servant swear that he will travel and obtain a wife from his brother's family for Isaac.

Genesis 25:1–11 tells us that Abraham remarried and had several more children whose genealogies are named in Genesis 25:1–6. The names appear to belong to Arabian tribes and Keturah is the name of the 'Syro-Arabian desert east of the Jordan' (C Westermann *Genesis 12–36* (London: SPCK, London) 396). The genealogy of Abraham's son Ishmael is noted in vv.12-18, followed by the story of Isaac's sons (Esau & Jacob) in Genesis 25:19–33:20.

Isaac stays in the land of Canaan with great success in his farming ventures. This success caused the local King Abimelech to expel Isaac from his lands who moved to Gerar. When Isaac moves on to Beersheba, God speaks with him repeating the promise which was given to Abram in Genesis 12:1–3. Moreover, the reality of the promise is demonstrated in the following verses (Gen 26:26–33) when Abimelech acknowledges that God must indeed be with Isaac (seen in the success of finding water and reaping large crops). They seal a covenant together by joining in a meal. The final verses (Gen 26:34–35) provide the link, which will continue the story about the twins begun in Genesis 25. The story of how Jacob usurps his elder brother and the consequences is narrated in Genesis 27–33.

After the description of Jacob's encounter with God he arrives at Haran where like his father he met one of his future wives, Rachel, at the well. His stay covers a fourteen year period in which Jacob finally gets to marry Rachel only to finds that she is barren and Leah her sister continues to produce offspring for Jacob—four in all. Because Rachel was unable to bear children she gave her maid, Bilhah to Jacob who bore him a son named Dan. More sons are born to Jacob through the maids of Leah and Rachel, and two more sons by Leah after the curious story of the mandrakes (Gen 30:14–20). The final child by Leah is a daughter called Dinah. After this entire God suddenly remembers Rachel and she finally bears a son to Jacob named Joseph. These children born from Rachel, Leah and their maids become the patriarchs of eleven of the tribes of Israel. Benjamin is born later.

The story is gradually moving to the time when they will end up in Egypt. Genesis 37–50 tell us how Joseph arrived in Egypt and been sold to an officer of Pharaoh called Potiphar. Joseph's adventures see him accused of false seduction, time in prison and his eventual release because he is able to interpret dreams. Joseph becomes the person who controls all agricultural produce and dispersion in Egypt. He marries the daughter of a priest of On and has two sons named Manasseh and Ephraim. This points to the fact that some of the tribes are descended from mixed nationality. As a result of Joseph's careful administration the famine, which came upon Egypt after seven years, was averted. Furthermore, as the famine spread across the Middle East, Jacob and his sons learnt there was grain to be bought in Egypt and he sent ten of his sons to buy grain. The story of their journey and meeting with Joseph—the brother they tried to get rid of—is told in Genesis 42–46. The remaining chapters of the Book of Genesis tell us how well Joseph governed, the growing wealth of the tribes of Jacob, Jacob's blessing and speech prior to his death (Gen 48–49) and his final journey to be buried with Abraham and Sarah, Isaac and Rebekah. Joseph's death is recorded in the final verses of Genesis 50.

There is a number of covenants mentioned in the Book of Genesis all of which come into the category of unconditional or promissory. Unlike the conditional covenant in Exodus 19 in which God seeks a response of obedience from the people, God bases the covenants in Genesis on first person pronouncements. Moreover, Genesis 9 has a universal covenant with all living creatures, but once we move into Genesis 12 the covenants are specific to Abraham and his descendants. The relationship has been set up from creation when humans were created to be in special relationship with God (Gen 1:26–27).

We referred above to the idea of sources and attempts have been made since the 18th century to explain such things as: a different word used for God—Yahwist or Elohim: multiple versions of the same story —Abraham's pretence, Genesis 12:10–20, 20:1–18, 26:6–16: repetition within the same story—Genesis 6:5–7, 11–12: contradictions —for example, Exodus 20:24 gives permission to offer sacrifices at numerous altars while Deuteronomy 12:13–14 forbids this and restricts sacrifice to one place only or Gen 7:17 in which the flood remains for forty days and in Gen 7:24 the flood remains for 150 days and other examples. The classic theory suggests that the Pentateuch has a number of written sources as well as the early oral traditions, which account for the sort of differences mentioned above. In Genesis 1–11 there is the Priestly source which can be seen in Genesis 1: 1-2:4a, 6:9–22, some verses in Genesis 7–8, 9:1–17, 10:1–7, 11:10–27 and the remaining texts come from the Yahwistic source. Some characteristics of what is know as the 'P' source are: the use of the Hebrew term toledoth/generations, the writing is sophisticated and often in a liturgical style (Gen1: 1–2:4a), in the creation account God speaks and it happens, humans are made in the image of God, the covenant is unconditional and can be made with the animals, and an abiding concern to state numbers and years. The Yahwistic source uses myths and sagas to tell the story, God and animals speak (anthropomorphic) and the world is very small (Gen 2:10–14) compared with the universal world of the 'P' source (Gen 1:1–2:4a).

Exodus

The Book of Exodus tells how God took pity on the Israelites when they became slaves in Egypt (Exod 1). Exodus continues the story of their journey to nationhood as God chooses to liberate them from the Egyptians, and lead them in their consequent journeys in the wilderness. Moses becomes the focus for the remaining four Books of the Pentateuch as he guides the Israelites to the edge of the promised land—the land promised to Abram in Genesis 12:1–3. Moses is called by God to confront the Pharaoh who eventually allows the Hebrews to go free. After the crossing of the Red Sea the pivotal event in the Book is revelation of God to Moses.

In Exodus 18 Moses took the advice of his father-in-law and chose leaders to work with him, after which his father-in-law returned to his own home. At the beginning of Exodus 19 the people finally arrive at the foot of Mt Sinai. Moses goes up the mountain to have conversation with Yahweh who declares that IF the people are obedient and keep the covenant they will remain in relationship with God. This is called a conditional covenant (Exod 19:5–8). At the foot of the mountain all the elders and people say, 'we will do as the Lord asks'. After this it is difficult to know whether Moses is back up the mountain speaking with God or at the bottom of the mountain. He appears to come down three times (vv 7, 14, 25) and only go up twice (vv 3, 20). This sets the scene for Moses to give the Ten Commandments in Exodus 20. What is called the Book of the Covenant follows in Exodus 21–23, which expands the commandments with particular examples and their conesquences. Exodus 24 is a reaffirmation of the covenant and theophanies (appearances) of God. The next seven chapters of Exodus give detailed instructions to Moses on the mountain about how the people are to make a tabernacle in which God will dwell in their midst.

After Moses has come down from the mountain he confronts Aaron because the people have made a golden calf to worship. Aaron blames the people and said the calf came out of the fire (Exod 32:21–24). Moses calls all those who are loyal to God to stand with him and those who respond are the sons of Levi (Moses' own tribe).

Moses instructed them to slay all the men in the camp, after which Moses went back up the mountain to atone with God over their sin of apostasy (worshipping the image of the golden calf). God forgives them, but also forecasts that when a divine visitation occurs, they will suffer their sin upon them (Exod 32:34). After this Moses is told to lead the people to the Promised Land, but God will not be with them (Exod 33:1–3). This incident was symbolic of their whole life and the pattern of Israel's future relationship with God. The people constantly strayed from the covenant and God kept calling them back into relationship.

The Book of Exodus finishes with a further account of the actual building of the ark, which basically repeats the instructions from Exodus 25–32. Within the Book we are given the origins of such Festivals as Passover and Unleavened Bread (Exod 12–13).

Some people have tried to find evidence within the Egyptian chronicles that the Israelites were present in Egypt in this period, but the lack of written material from that era limits any discoveries. What has been found in general terms is that foreigners did serve in Egyptian households, there were building programs using 'apiru', and foreigners did attain high service in important households. Rather than trying to prove historical fact as in the old Western idea of 'facts', it is better to understand the Book of Exodus as 'historiography', that is, the remembered history of the Israelite people which is crucial to their identity as the people of God.

The Book of Exodus is a mixture of very early oral material, which has come from different traditions and been, joined together in the one Book. The wilderness is the time when the people look back and see how crucial it was for their development as a nation. The revelation at Sinai, the role of Moses as the Lawgiver is important in each of the tribes. Some people have tried to identify some of the traditions within the Book and named them as sources: a tradition that uses the name of Yahweh called 'J', another called 'E', the tradition written by the Priests called 'P' and the very easily identified 'D' tradition mainly found in the Book of Deuteronomy. It makes sense that different communities as in the NT had different memories and emphases, which had become important to them and so when the Scriptures are committed to writing there is a desire to incorporate the diverse memories of people and their experience of God within their lives.

Leviticus

Leviticus begins after the tabernacle has been set up. They are still close to Sinai and so the whole of the Laws and directives given in Leviticus are placed within the Sinai experience of God. Furthermore, while the emphasis is on priestly matters in the Book of Leviticus, it is Moses whom is the intermediator giving the instruction from God to the priests or people. The words 'the Lord spoke to Moses' occurs fifty-six times.

The emphasis in the Book is to enable people to live holy lives in relationship with God. The laws are the way in which people can achieve this. Furthermore, they are intended to be instruments of God so that grace is extended to others as in the Abraham blessing (Gen 12:1–3). Worship life is the centre of peoples' lives with the priests as the ones who have major oversight of this worship. The Book is very different from any of the other Books in the Pentateuch and gives clear and specific authority to the Priests. This is the major reason the authors are suggested as belonging to the priestly assembly. The instructions depict a temple set up, fully equipped and functioning.

Leviticus is not meant to be interpreted narrowly as a law code (and hence more easily dismissed by many) or as static statutes unrelated to Israel's ongoing life. Law is seen as another gift of God's graciousness for the sake of life and well-being rather than burden. It is a response to the story of all that God has done, which is why the Pentateuch needs to be read as a whole narrative beginning in Genesis 1. Indeed we can see theological links to the Genesis 1 account of creation. Some examples are:

* separating and priestly responsibility (Lev 10:10)
* creation of every kind (Lev 11:14–22)
* concern for seasons and Sabbath (Lev 25:2–3)
* fondness for number seven is modelled in the seven speeches in (Lev 1–7)

Although we are suggesting that the priests are the writers of the Book of Leviticus, most people would accept that it has very old and ancient laws within it. These ancient laws have been incorporated and as time goes by changed to meet new situations. There are clear sections within the Book: Leviticus 1–16 is addressed to the Priests and covers the following topics: Chapters 1–7 offerings and sacrifices; 8–10 priesthood; 11–15 issues of purity and Leviticus 16 Day of Atonement. Leviticus 17–27 focus on Priestly instructions to the people and these nine chapters are often referred to as the Holiness code which covers such matters as: seventeen to twenty-five ritual and moral matters, care of the land and a Jubilee year every fifty years.

The priests are in charge of the sacrificial system, which is set out in precise detail. The priestly writing has this has one of it characteristics. It is especially important for the instruction to be clear about the disposal of animal blood, which is understood as life-giving and cannot be consumed. There are offerings of animals or birds of which some parts are burnt and not others. Some such as the 'Burnt offering' was for the expiation of sins, entreaty to God or thanksgiving. Sin and guilt offerings were added later. Sometimes offerings consisted of flour mixed with oil accompanied by frankincense. Often some of this went to the priest because they did not get a stipend to live on. We must realise that not all these rituals occurred at one time. There was a gradual building up of the rituals as it seemed necessary. Because Christians have never worshipped in a temple and no experience of sacrifice it appears strange and may be even offensive. We need to remember that sacrifice was part of the ancient world and part of the life of Israel as it gradually journeyed toward nationhood. As they became a settled people and built the temple so the rituals became more sophisticated and complicated.

The purpose was always to do with the worship of God. Differences in wealth are acknowledged, and if one could not afford a goat or sheep then a dove was acceptable. Offerings were not regarded as magical, their efficacy was not inherent in performance of ritual, but took account that God provided the ritual and act of grace. The sacrifice was done in freedom, but contrition and confession were an essential part of the ritual. It was tangible means in and through which God acted in a saving way on behalf of the faithful worshipper. Other traditions in the OT do not have sacrifice as part of the act of forgiveness. The prophets stress the need for repentance and trust is enough. It is interesting that in Jeremiah and Amos there are texts that denounce sacrifice and the need for true worship of the heart (Jer 7:21–23, Amos 5:22). Most scholars agree this is not a total denial for sacrifice but to get one's proprieties right. Sacrifice in OT means a religious rite and not the present day meaning of giving up something of value.

The Book of Leviticus finishes with the statement that, 'These are the commandments which the Lord commanded Moses for the people of Israel on Mount Sinai' (Lev 27:34). This makes abundantly clear that all the previous laws in Leviticus are given by Moses with the same authority as the ten commandments. This Book has interrupted the flow of the journey through the wilderness. This is now taken up in Numbers.

Numbers

The Book begins with a census taken of the people who experienced exodus and who will not enter the promised land. However, the second census list is of those of the new generation, who will be the people to enter the promised land (Num 26). The Book of Numbers contains itineraries, statutes, ritual and priestly prescriptions, wilderness stories, including a murmuring tradition. Some quite peculiar elements are present: a talking donkey, bronze snakes which have healing powers, the earth swallowing up people, poetic oracles and a well-known benediction ('The Lord Bless you and Keep you', Num 7:24–26). The promise of land is ever present in the Book of Numbers and the journeys depict a gradual process of getting to the edge. Indeed, Numbers 26 assumes conquest of land.

The Priestly writer appears reasonably dominant in the Book of Numbers, especially in Numbers 1–10 in which there are more laws relating to tabernacle and sacrifice. The familiar references to 'generations' are present in Numbers 3 in which the generations are named since the time of Moses. It demonstrates in a very practical fashion how the promise to Abram of descendants like the stars (Gen 12:1–3) is coming true. The material in Numbers chapters 10–20 is connected directly with Exodus 16 to 18 and gives in greater detail some of the Israelites' experiences and their wanderings in the desert. All attempts to enter the land by their own power were frustrated by the Amalekites and the Canaanites.

We find the people have moved on from Sinai, first to Kadesh and then to Moab. The material in the Book reflects these different periods: Numbers 1–10 in the vicinity of Sinai: Numbers 13–19 in the wilderness near Kadesh: Numbers 22–36 on the plains of Moab. Before they move to Kadesh there is a repeat of the Passover ritual, which is first told in Exodus 12–13. New elements have been added which reflect concerns of a later writer. As the people are moving out we have what is often called the 'murmuring tradition'. This particular verb (to murmur) is quite rare in the Old Testament, used only in Exodus, 15:22–27–17:1–7, Numbers 11, 20 and 1 occasion in Joshua 9:18.

This not the first occasion that the people have murmured against God and Moses. In Exodus 15:22–17:1–7, the complaints are lack of water, lack of food, and lack of water. In response God provides water on two occasions, manna, and quails with conditions attached to the provision. The great affirmation of the people in Exodus 14, that they believed, having seen how God rescued them from Egypt, does not carry through for very long. The Israelites are not willing to trust God when things get hard (Exod 15:22–25, 16:1–36). Certainly, it would be scary in the wilderness if food was scarce, but it didn't take long for the murmurings to start with a very one-sided memory of Egypt. Moses confronts them with the fact that their murmurings are not against he and Aaron—they are nothing, but against the Lord. This is their greatest sin, their lack of trust in God and the ease, which they can murmur against Yahweh. Again, this provision of food from God will remind them who rescued them from Egypt (Exod 16:6).

However, it is a very different story in Numbers 11 in which the Israelites move out form Sinai and begin the journey towards Kadesh. They complain that they are missing the exotic foods of Egypt (Num 11:5) and they are fed up with manna. They very easily forget that they were slaves in Egypt. In Exodus 15 God answered their murmurings, but in Numbers God turns the food bad and they die from a plague. The first occasion on which the people murmured (complained) against God was before they received the Law at Mt Sinai. The second occasion happens after they know how to behave and with the revelation of God there ought to have been a growing trust. The theme of murmuring in the pre-Sinai material uses 'to test' as its strongest verb and has no judgment on the Israelite's behaviour. God's reaction is to hear and help. No mention of impatience or judgment in pre-Sinai, but we encounter both in the Number's material. Another story of complaint is that told in Numbers 12 in which Miriam and Aaron speak against Moses, supposedly because he was married to a foreign woman. His first wife, Zipporah was also a foreigner—a Kenite whose father was a priest. In Numbers 12 Miriam is punished with a leprosy type disease, but Aaron escapes. Moses is elevated to even higher authority in this story.

Apparently the Israelites spent about forty years around Kadesh before moving on and there are further stories about rebellious people in Numbers 13–16. The Israelites suffer defeat at the hands of the Amalekites and Canaanites because of their failure to be faithful. As the people moved northeast onto the King's Highway they began to encounter the inhabitants of those lands. The King of Edam refused to allow them to pass and this is mentioned later in the oracles against the nations (Jer 49, Ezek 25). The Israelites fought the Ammonites and won that battle (Num 21). From there they set out across the plains of Moab and because the King of Moab is afraid of the Israelites he sends for Balaam to curse the Israelites. In Numbers 22–23 we have this story in which Balaam's donkey can see the angel and refuses to move. There are contradictory instructions from God: Balaam is told to go with the messengers and almost immediately God is angry because he went (Num 22: 20–22). Balaam has three encounters with God and is true to what God tells him. He is unable to curse the Israelites much to the displeasure of the King of Moab. In the end we have the model of a foreign prophet who hears God's voice and is totally obedient. Indeed, the Spirit of God comes upon Balaam and at the end of his prophecy in Numbers 24:3–9 we find similar words to those spoken to Abram in Genesis 12:1–3. It is a timely reminder to us that we cannot control the Spirit of God: God is free to choose anyone to be a channel of God's word.

The Book of Numbers records the death of Moses (27:12–14), and the commissioning of Joshua which is then dealt with in more detail Deuteronomy 32:48–52, 34:1, 7–9. The Book finishes as the people are close to the Jordan with the city of Jericho on the other side. Before we get to the crossing of the Jordan we have the Book of Deuteronomy, which interrupts the move into the land and recounts laws for everyday living.

Deuteronomy

The Book of Deuteronomy is dealt with in more detail in Chapter Four because it acts as the final Book in the Pentateuch and the first Book in the Deuteronomic History. In 2 Kings 22 to 23 it is recorded that a law Book was found and was red before the king and then to the people. Many scholars believe this law Book formed the core of the Book of Deuteronomy as we now know it, that is, Deuteronomy 5–26. This body of material, though found during the reign of Josiah (621

BCE), was written some years before its discovery. So people believe it could have been composed during the reign of Manasseh (687 to 642 BCE.). The reasons given are two-fold. One is that the writers of Deuter-onomy feared that knowledge of God and Israel's past would be lost as the people turned to Assyrian gods. In writing down the traditions a hiding them, they were endeavouring to make sure that future generations would find the Book and remember who they were—the people Yahweh. The other reason for the compilation of such a Book was to call Judah back to the one true God and to turn away from wor-shipping idols.

Another suggestion for the date and purpose of this Book is that it written just prior to Josiah's reign and hidden in the temple. When found, it could be used to support Josiah's reforms because it declared that it was God's will for the temple to be cleansed. Furthermore, it announced that sacrifices could only take place at the temple in Jerusalem—the place God ahs chosen—and not at local shrines.

While we cannot be certain about the date, there is almost unanimous agreement that chapters 5 to 26 and 28 had other writings added to them, either just prior to the exile or during the exile. The Book of Deuteronomy became the first Book in a composition now called the Deuteronomic History:—Deuteronomy, Joshua, Judges, 1 and 2 Samuel, 1 and 2 Kings. However, while Deuteronomy is the first Book of the Deuteronomic History, it is also the last Book of the Pentateuch. This can be seen from the diagram below.

Genesis, Exodous,
Leviticus, Numbers [Deuteronomy]

Joshua, Judges,
I & 2 Samuel, 1 & 2 Kings

The Pentateuch **Deuteronomic History**

There are a few fragments of Deuteronomic writing within the Pentateuch eg Exodus 19:3–6), but the main writing is in the Book of Deuteronomy itself. It has a distinct language and theology, which will be discussed fully in the chapter on the Deuteronomic history. While the D writings will be looked at separately, it must be remembered that it was in this period (seventh century) in which the scholars were inspired to write their theological work. There is the constant proclamation of God's word speaking to new Generations.

Composition of the Pentateuch

Discussion of sources

We referred above to the suggestion that the Pentateuch is composed mainly of four sources given the names: the 'J' or Yahwistic writings, 'E' or Elohistic writings, 'D' or Deuteronomic writings and 'P' or Priestly writings. The early traditions would have been passed down by word of mouth. People who are nomadic don't have the materials or time to commit traditions to writing. This occurs when people are settled and have the means to produce the writing matter and implements. However, there is much evidence to show that people are able to remember and pass on traditions for hundreds of years.

The suggested times for the incorporation of the so-called sources are tentative. It is really not possible to be certain and one has to say this is the most reasonable option in light of evidence.

The first writer who is called the Yahwist had many oral traditions upon which to draw. There would have been a wide variety of stories passed down by word of mouth, and it may be by the time of the Yahwist that some of them had already become grouped into cycles of stories based around one particular leader, for example, Abraham or Joseph. The Yahwist then added bridging passages so that by the manner of construction and the theology of the joining passages he conveyed his own particular message to the people of his time. The writers of the Old Testament were theologians in their own right. As we preach the gospel and need to make it relevant for today, so the early proclaimers took their stories of God's journey and made it relevant for their situation.

The suggested time of writing is after the people have become settled with David as King (1000–961 BCE) and Solomon has begun his reign (961–922 BCE). Three things point to this period as the most likely time of writing. First, there is no mention of the conflicts that were part of David's reign, for example, the dispute with Saul. Second, the lands and people that David defeated are spoken of as already part of the kingdom; that is, the Philistines, Moabites, Ammonites, Arameans, Edomites, Amalekites and Canaanites. Third, there was the cultural flowering and literary environment of that time. Court annals, psalms and wisdom literature were all flourishing in this period and therefore the environment was conducive to literary arts.

We can ask the question—why did the Yahwist feel it was necessary to take the oral traditions of the past and create a faith statement from them? A brief look at the situation of the time may help us answer the question. The reign of Solomon was the height of Israel's power, wealth, prosperity and peace. Never again would Israel be in such an exalted position. There was now the time and cultural environment to begin writing and recording on scrolls their experiences of God. When the tribes were struggling to survive in the time of the judges there was not the time. A second reason may be that after a time of hardship people wanted to preserve the stories of their origins, to put in writing a more permanent record of their journey so far with Yahweh. Third, it is often true in a situation of prosperity, with peace and material gain, that the people of God need reminding of the one upon whom they are dependent. The people needed recalling to the very roots of their faith and not forget how they were once 'no people'—slaves to the Pharaohs (Exod 3). They needed to recall that it was only through the liberating power of God and his great mercy that they were now in their own land. The Yahwist places a lot of emphasis on this knowledge of God's liberating power—leading them out of Egypt and through the wilderness. It was a call to be faithful to their God.

There is a constant theme throughout the Yahwist's writings of God's promises having been fulfilled. The promise of God had come to pass in the life of the people. In the writer's time (10 BCE) the promise of the land given in Genesis 12: 1–3, had been fulfilled: Abram's descendents have multiplied and are the recipients of God's promises. The tribes of Israel are part of a large kingdom (950 BCE). However, part of the promise has still to be fulfilled. The promise that they will be a blessing to others: 'by you all the families of the earth shall bless themselves', (Gen12:3) has still to come true. It was correct to say that they had dominion over a number of countries, but this was not how the Yahwist saw the people of Israel as a blessing to others. In other words it is a call to reach out to others proclaiming the love of God to all people. God's blessing was not complete until all people were offered the freedom and life in God through Israel's outreach and witness. It was a challenge to the people of God to remember what God had done for them and that there was still work to do. They had to continue to be the people who will a blessing to all other nations of the world. It was a call to mission.

A large part of the contents of Genesis reflect the early traditions probably used by the Yahwist when he first began to put the blocks of oral tradition into a written proclamation. The narratives about Abram and Sarai show how God's promises can be trusted even when Sarai was declared barren (Gen 11:30). They became parents and the ancestors of the tribes of Israel. It seems quite feasible that the oral traditions had already formed around the major Patriarchs—Abraham and Sarah, Isaac and Rebekah, Judah and Rachel and Joseph.

In the Book of Exodus the narratives about the people's freedom from slavery and how it occurred are important part of this writer's theology. It was very important to him to retell in detail how that came about and of the resulting liberation. Interestingly there doesn't seem to as much interest in the traditions from the Sinai experience. The Passover festival is important and we have one of the earliest traditions in the Song of Miriam (Exod 15:21). There are no Yahwistic traditions present in Leviticus or Deuteronomy

Characteristics and style of Yahwistic writing

Even if the reader of this Book doesn't like the idea of sources and the gradual coming together of the corpus of material now called the Pentateuch, one can still identify with the writing characteristics that present throughout the five Books. This early tradition uses the name Yahweh for God, which is quite discernible when read in the Hebrew. So the source is called the 'Yahwistic' after the name of God used by the composer. The style of writing is primitive and action based. This is typical of oral traditions in which the method of remembering is not flowery or vastly descriptive, but action based using lots of verbs. Some examples are: Genesis 22, which focuses on the actions of Abraham, 'take, go, offer, rose, saddled, took, cut and went'. It stresses the actions rather the feelings of the people. The readers are carried along and are required to use their imagination to fill in details. In these early traditions God is spoken of in human terms (anthropomorphic). 'And they heard the sound of the Lord God walking in the garden' (Gen 3).

The writer used different literary forms to proclaim his message, just as Jesus used parables so this writer used familiar forms. A couple of these forms were myth and saga. Myth was common ii religions. It has come to have a negative sense in the modern world, but in the ancient world this form of imagery expressed the divine in terms of human life. They were stories used in worship to tell of their gods and the role they played in human existence. However, when the writer used this literary form, he was always claiming the truth about the God of Israel. It always dealt with God's activity which was not in the unseen world, but within the human world and relationships (Gen 1–3). Although the composer borrowed from other cultures, the material reflected the Israelite understanding of God. Myths in the Old Testament can best be described as the Israelite faith in narrative form (Gen 2–3). Another literary form used by these early writers was saga. This form is common in strong oral cultures because it tells the stories of those humans were important in knowing about their past. Legends are similar in form and purpose.

Saga is grounded in the world and has an historical base. It often centres around a person like Abraham who was important in their understanding of how the Israelite nation came into being. The story of Joseph portrays a person who was rejected because of jealousy, yet rose to fame in another country, brought blessing to that country and did not hold a grudge when his brothers reappeared asking for food. Indeed, there would have been no ongoing people for whom the initial promise of land was relevant, had it not been for Joseph's skills in management of the grain.

In the early writings, Yahweh is associated with particular sanctuaries that later in the people's history are important worship centres. For example, Abraham built altars at Shechem, Hebron and Beersheba where the Lord had appeared to him. Jacob built an altar at Bethel after his experience of God (Gen 35:14). These sanctuaries are mentioned frequently in the Old Testament. Unconditional covenants are another characteristic of these early traditions and writings. The primary covenant was that between God and Abraham in Genesis 12. It was initiated by God proclaiming a promise to Abraham that the land of Canaan would be given to his descendants. Abraham was quite passive on the whole incident, since there was no immediate demand by God for a response. The covenant was unconditional and had as its substance a promise. Similarly, the unconditional covenant in Genesis 8 between God and Noah was the promise that God would never again to destroy the earth, or its inhabitants.

These early writings are likely to be the core around and through which the remaining strata of material are built and interspersed. This growth took place over the next four hundred years.

The second source named by some is called the 'E' source of Elohist writings, which probably came form the northern traditions, after the division of the kingdom of Israel (north) and Judah (south) in 922 BCE. Scholars have been uncertain whether there was a separate body of written material from Israel or whether there were only the fragments of an 'E' that became attached to the J writings. It is highly feasible that writing was taking place in Israel in the early ninth century using the oral traditions of the northern tribes as a source. It is suggested that the crisis of 721 BCE, when the ten Northern tribes were taken away by the Assyrians, triggered the need to incorporate some of the northern traditions with those narratives of the south. It is almost certain that some people fled from the north and took up residence around Jerusalem before being captured and deported by the Assyrians. Since the people from the north had suffered annihilation, it was important to keep alive their understanding of God. Furthermore, their exile and demise as the nation of Israel it was a important message for the sister kingdom of Judah. God was speaking to the people of Judah and traditions from Israel were interpreted in the light of God's purposes for the people. The writings of Israel are never static always alive to speak God's word to the nation in new situations. Through the experience of Israel, Judah might hear the word of God in relation to her own situation and prevent a similar disaster befalling her.

This was especially the situation of Judah in the time of King Manasseh who was blatantly leading the people away from Yahweh to the worship of idols. The actions of the King may have given the impetus for God's word to be heard in such dire circumstances. There was a real fear that that the people might forget Yahweh altogether. In situations such as this, it becomes important for God's word to be heard and preserved in case there was a complete loss of faith in God. Furthermore, it could lead to a loss of their traditions, which expressed their experiences of God in the past. So the writing was an important way of preserving for future generations the experiences of God and this wayward people.

Because it is difficult to define precisely the Elohistic writings, there will be brief mention of some narratives that are accepted as 'E' by a significant number of scholars; for example, Genesis 20:1–17; 26:26–33, which have parallels in the Yahwistic writings and Genesis 22:1–19 has no parallels elsewhere and portrays striking features in content, style and theology. Another block of material, which may have come from this northern tradition, is based around the figure of Joseph: Genesis 40–41; 50:15–26.

Elohistic writings contain the call narrative of Abraham (Gen 12), Abraham and Sarah at Abimelech's court, the expulsion of Hagar and Ishmael, and the command to sacrifice Isaac. It carries on with several stories about Jacob, then Joseph, covers Exodus, the Sinai covenant, and a few passages about the wilderness wandering in the Book of Numbers.

Characteristics and style of Elohist writing

The composer uses the Hebrew word Elohim for God, hence the reason for this source named as 'E' or Elohist. The name is used widely (Gen 17:3, 9, 15, 18, 19, 22, 23) but it is not the only criterion for identifying this body of tradition. Accounts of God revealing self to the patriarchs are often depicted in 'E' as dialogues between God and that particular patriarch, as leader (Gen: 22:1–14).

> After these things God tested Abraham, and said to him, 'Abraham!'
> And he said, 'Here am I.
> He said, 'Take your son, your only son Isaac, whom you love, and go to the land of Moriah, and offer him there as a burnt offering upon one of the mountains of which I shall tell you.'
> So Abraham rose early in the morning, saddled his ass, and took two of his young men with him, and his son Isaac (Gen 22:1–3a).

These accounts of revelation have general pattern of call, command and action.

Further to this particular manner of revelation in 'E', the crises or turning points in Israel's history are marked by God's revelation to the patriarchs (Gen 28:10–22). Sometimes these revelations were part of a dream a Genesis 28:10–22. Dreams and visions were common features of God speaking to a person (Gen 46:2), and Joseph had the special gift of interpretation of the dreams and visions of others (Gen 40–41).

The 'E' writer altered accounts of tradition which, suggested unethical behaviour on the part of the Patriarchs. For example, in the parallel story of Abraham in Genesis 20:12, Sarah is said to be

Abraham's half sister so he is not the liar that is portrayed in the 'J' account in Genesis 12:13. According to the Elohist, it was partially true. This often happens in writings of different accounts about the same people. David is represented in the Deuteronomic History with all his faults, but in the later Chronicler's account, his faults are omitted. This is a common way for a nation to present its heroes. The farther away in time they get from flesh and blood people, the more ideally they are portrayed. When these characteristics are taken into account some scholars are led to the conclusion that a different tradition exists which we identify as 'E'.

When the Elohist added the various pieces he wanted say something about God which related to his situation. So he knew different stories about Joseph who was a very important figure for him. He shows that God was able to work through the misfortunes of Joseph because even these were important for the overall purposes of God. God's plans for the nation will never be threatened by the pettiness and jealousies of individuals (Gen 48:15–21). This was an encouraging message for the people of Israel to have in a time that was looking desolate. It gave hope that God would use the situation and be victorious to the end.

Joseph is portrayed as a very wise person who had a particular gift of interpretation, but who realised all his knowledge came from God. He recognised he was wholly dependent on God and it was because of God's power that he could discern the right action in particular situations (Gen 41:16). It was through him that God interpreted the dreams of Pharaoh's servants and of Pharaoh himself. People all through Israel's history needed reminding that they were dependent on God and were not self-sufficient.

Stemming from this northern tradition was a deep interest in prophecy and the word of God (Gen 20:7). Prophets often played a crucial role at crisis points in history. Abraham was a prophet in the eyes of the northern traditions as was Moses. In later history there were prophets such as Ahijah, Elijah, Elisha, Amos and Hosea who heard the word of God and were called to proclaim it to the people. The people did not always respond to the prophetic word but what the prophets said was always very important in the life of Israel. In retrospect they understood that the prophets were right and ought to have been heeded.

One of the elements that comes through the prophetic message is the continuous disparagement of foreign gods. It was a minor factor in the early material (Gen 31:25–42), but became a major contention in the later prophets—Hosea and Jeremiah. There was always the fear of Israel going after the Canaanite gods and worshipping them, but in the early eighth century it had reached a severe crisis. King Manasseh especially must have provoked a great deal of anxiety in loyal Jews with his overt encouragement to worship Assyrian gods and participate in Assyrian cult practices.

The Elohistic writings seem to be more reflective in the area of moral problems such as guilt and forgiveness (Gen 20:5, 6). In the 'E' narrative there is a more intellectual response. Obedience and testing were part of this tradition, which is so magnificently portrayed in the story of Abraham with his son Isaac (Gen 22:1–14).

When these aspects were added to the core of the Yahwistic writings, they enhanced the earlier message and added new dimensions to those already present.

We will briefly make some comments about the 'D' or Deuteronomic source. It is very easy to discern as portrayed in the Book of that name. It is the final Book in what we call the Pentateuch, but was probably written as the first Book of the Deuteronomic History. The writers of that history wanted to show the exiles why they ended up in Babylon and to put it simply—the Israelites disobeyed the first commandment: *You shall have no other gods before me* (Exod 20:3). The Ten Commandments were expanded in Deuteronomy 5–26 and all came from the mouth of Moses (Deut 5:1–5). Because the Israelites failed to keep the first commandment they lost the land and the Books of Joshua—to the end of 2 Kings demonstrates this theological point. It is very easy to discern both the style and theological position of the 'D' writer.

The final major addition to the core of writings, as already discussed, was compiled by the Priestly writers. Like the previous composers the writer takes very early oral traditions and writings and creates a new proclamation about God. This process began either during the exile (598–520 BCE) or soon after the Jews returned to Jerusalem. The experience of the exile and return called forth a new understanding of God. The main purpose of the 'P' writers was to give hope to a people who had experienced despair and the loss of all that gave meaning to their life, especially the loss of land which had been the promise of God to the earliest Patriarchs. The Israelites had taken over Canaan and under the leadership of David had acquired a great empire. This had gradually been lost over the next 400 years, with first the demise of the northern kingdom, and then the loss of land around Judah. The final humiliation came with the collapse of Jerusalem. This meant the destruction of the temple, the place where major sacrifices and festivals were celebrated. At one time it was thought that the temple was so holy (God dwelt there) it could never be destroyed, but even this last remnant of hope was lost. To complete their downfall, their king Jehoiachin, had been taken into exile. 2 Kings 25:27–30 tells us that he was released (in 561 BC) but there is no more information given about him, and no record of any further kings of the house of David. The Jews had lost land, temple and king and they were exiles in a foreign land. People in those circumstances need to hear a word of hope for the future.

One of the ways that the P writers give hope, is to show that God did not make empty promises. The creation was the result of God's spoken word. This was re-enforced by using other written traditions to show that the promise of God to give the people the land had been kept. The promise that Abraham would have descendants numbered like 'stars in the sky' was seen in the same way. God's promise had been fulfilled. If it can be shown to the people that God's word had come true in the past, then there was every reason to believe it would come true in the present and future. It was a way of giving hope. The 'P' writers intertwined their texts among the past proclamation of faith ('J', 'E' and 'D' writings), and this new document is a talented literary composition.

In the Deuteronomic writings, the people of Israel were given a reason for their exile experience and offered the possibility of turning again to God. The Priestly writer was faced with the task of giving people hope and encouraging them to stay in covenant relationship with God. If it was disobedience to the law that had brought their downfall and years of exile, then the 'P' writer had to show the people how they could stay in relationship with God. Consequently there was a strong emphasis on ritual and ways of correct worship (Leviticus). There were minute and exact details on the way people needed to make their sacrificial offerings, in order that there were no mistakes and no displeasure given to God. It was meant as a positive and helpful way of preventing a repeat of the disaster of the exile. The rituals themselves were understood as provided by God as a blessing and as a means of 'staying right' with God. They could gain forgiveness by ensuring the correct rituals of sacrifice and obedience to the law.

The law was regarded as a help to the Jews to enable them to respond to God's care for them. In the period following the exile, the law was a brilliant response which met a need for people to feel secure in their relationship with God. The difficulty that occurred over the next 500 years was the vast growth in laws and requirements which became a great mass of detailed obligations for the Jews to obey. It became so burdensome that the voice of God was smothered. Jesus, in his disputes with the Pharisees, suggested that while the law was good at times, it became a hindrance to people when it was longer appropriate or caused hardship (Matt 12:1–8)

The 'P' writings begin with the creation story in Genesis 1, and continue through to the point that Moses stands at the edge of the land looking from the west side of the Jordan (Genesis 1–Deuteronomy 34). It does not intrude into the message and work of the Deuteronomic Historian in the Book Joshua to 2 Kings, which deals with the conquest of the land, the settlement, the history of the monarchy and events leading to the subsequent loss of the land. In his work the Deuteronomic Historian gives a clear explanation for the exile and loss of the land. In leaving the Deuteronomic material intact the 'P' writer was using it both in a positive and negative fashion. Positively it showed how God gave the land once, in fulfilment of the promises to Abram, and therefore would give the land again. The exile was a symbolic second time in the wilderness, waiting to enter the Promised Land once more. Negatively however, if the writings are addressed to people in the post-exilic period they stand as a warning that once they regain the land, they must stay in covenant relationship with God. If they fail to do so the land can be taken from them again.

While the 'P' material is concentrated in Exodus 25 through to Numbers 10. This material includes the instructions on how to build the Tabernacle, then its actual construction after the rebellion of Aaron in Exodus 33. The Book of Leviticus, is the handbook for the priests and their function within the temple together with commands to the people on how to keep holy and pure. In Numbers, it tells of regulations concerning Levites, the death of Aaron, and the installation of Joshua. This block of material from the 'P' writer is in the centre of the five books of Pentateuch. Additional texts begin in Genesis 1 with the creation narrative, flood, a covenant with Noah, the list of the generations, which is the family tree of the Jews, and stories of the Patriarchs. In the Book of Exodus, the Priestly writer emphases the oppression of the Israelites in Egypt, the call Moses, the miracles of Moses in Egypt, the Passover and the Exodus, the crossing of the Sea of Reeds, and some events in the wilderness. The 'P' composer finishes with his comments about the death of Moses.

The whole composition of the Pentateuch is quite brilliant and it is hard to communicate the ways in which this composer has brought together very early oral laws, narrative traditions and the writings we have already spoken of above. I accept that the 'P' author took the Book of Deuteronomy and deliberately included it in his final composition, Genesis to the end of Deuteronomy.

Characteristics and style of Priestly writing

The writings are systematic and precise. There is a definite ordering of the material that runs throughout the whole work. The 'P' writer has a strong liking for lists of genealogies which are deliberately interspersed at strategic points throughout the narrative. 'P' was always concerned to add the exact date of a particular festival if other writers had omitted such detail (Exod 22:2b). This preference for genealogies and chronology make 'P' easy discern among the various writings. The method of sacrifice was elaborately described so that when a very early feast such as the Passover was mentioned in the 'J ' writing (Exod 2:23–27) the 'P' writer expanded the account to give precise instructions for its celebration (Exodus 12:1–10). There was a need to make sure that people knew the specific ways to offer a sacrifice and ensure it was all done in proper and correct manner.

A specific format of 'P's' writing is in Genesis in which God speaks a word and creation comes into being (Gen 1:1–26). When he commands, it happens. 'And God said, let there be light; and there was light' (Gen 1:3). This pattern is seen in other 'P' texts, for example, Moses is called by God to lead the Hebrews out of Egypt (Exod 6:2–7). The story unfolds and demonstrates that this indeed happens (Exod 12:29–32). God had made a promise and the narrative demonstrates how this promise will be fulfilled. It declares to the people that the promises of God can be trusted for the future as they were in the past.

Priestly theology has a high view of humanity, which is made in the image of God. Humans were given dominion over creation and all that was in it, which before the Industrial revolution did not lead to abuse of the earth. Since then the 'dominion' of the earth is slowing seeing its demise through technology and greed. To be made in the image of God implied a special relationship, which in turn meant a greater responsibility for the people of Israel, in proclaiming God's ways.

During the time of the monarchy, the stress had been on the conditional covenant as seen in the Deuteronomic and prophetic writings. The people had to keep right with God by keeping the commandments, especially those related to the Sinai covenant. The experience of the exile made the 'P' writers realise the futility of people trying to be faithful to God by their own efforts. Consequently the writers looked back to the early covenant with Noah (Gen 9:8–17) and Abraham (Gen 12:1–3), which portrayed God as the initiator, making promises that were not conditional upon the people's agreement. 'P' took these unconditional covenants and added further dimensions, such as, the proclamation of God's promises were everlasting (Gen 17) and with all people (Gen 9:17). In exile, the people's only hope was to rely on a God who would keep promises for evermore. They could look to the future with hope because God would not let them down. This understanding of the grace of God is how Christians see the love of God in the gift of his Son Jesus Christ. God so loved the world that he gave his only begotten Son that we might have life. We did not earn it. God chose to send Jesus freely for our salvation.

The blessing to Israel had begun for the Yahwist at the point of Abram's departure from Haran to the land of Canaan. In Genesis 12:1–3 we see this spelled out for the first time. The Priestly writer's experience lead him to believe that the blessing and God's purposes had begun at creation (Gen 1:1–28). It was a much wider understanding of God's purposes, stretching back to the moment of creation of the world God's power as Creator.

The Sinai covenant was acknowledged as part of God's purposes also, but the primary emphasis by 'P' was placed on the two covenants with Abraham and Noah. Both of these have a stress on the land. In the Noah covenant, the land will never again be destroyed and in the Abraham covenant the land was promised to his descendants. The record of these covenants assured the exiles that they would return to the land.

The promise of the land was dependent on the people's obedience to the covenant in the Deuteronomic material, which describes a land flowing with milk and honey to which Moses was leading his people. The account of the people in the wilderness, being led to the west side of the Jordan and left there, spoke to the exiles in Babylon. They were part of a second wilderness experience and were standing looking towards the Promised Land once again. The 'P' writer, by emphasising the integrity of God's promises, was telling the people that once again God would lead them from exile back into the land which had been promised to them. They had been disobedient and lost the land because of that, but now they were looking to God who was faithful the promises of their forebears to lead them once more into the promised land.

The 'P' writer was concerned to help the people stay in relationship with God. One of the ways, which they believed this would happen was through the correct and proper worship rituals. It is not difficult to understand the people's fear of punishment and the possibilities of a further exilic experience if God decided to stand in judgment over them again. Therefore, they saw rituals as the means of keeping right with God and a way t prevent any return to another Babylon.

The recurring lists of genealogies were a very practical way of showing God's command to *'be fruitful and multiply'*, had indeed come true (Gen 1:28; 8:17; 9:1). The lists in Genesis 10 and 11:10–26 testify to the fulfilment of these promises that were not thwarted by the sin and rebellion of humankind in Genesis 3. People were punished, as seen in the case of Noah, but a remnant was saved to begin again. Promises were also made to individual Patriarchs; to Ishmael, 'for I will make him a great nation' (Gen 21:15–21), and to Jacob, 'God Almighty bless you and make you fruitful and multiply you . . .' (Gen 28:3). It was a realistic way of demonstrating the faithfulness God's word, so that even exile, which was brought about by the people's rebellion and waywardness, did not in the end thwart God's promises.

Not only did God bless the creation of women and men and command them to multiply and fill the earth, but the Sabbath was also blessed and hallowed (Gen 2:3). The Sabbath was an important day for the Israelite worship, and as their day of rest. It became even more important in exile when it was vital for them to get together and remember their identity as a people. It was a time for remembering their past and their God who cared for them, and who had given them hope for the future. It therefore proclaimed hope for the future and was important in keeping God's people pure and undefiled as a race.

Associated with the need for identity was the emphasis on circumcision as a sign of the covenant. It became a mark of Israel's faithfulness as Yahweh's people. Their persistent behaviour in staying apart from the surrounding cultures and environments has brought the Jews persecution and ridicule throughout the centuries. It has also been their salvation for as a people they never succumbed to the pressure of becoming absorbed into the particular nation in which they were residing.

Throughout the 'P' material there unfolds a message and theology which was not only speaking to the Jews then, but, as the message became accepted as scripture, it was understood to be able to speak to the Jews in following generations. The Pentateuch as we have it now is a Priestly composition in which the immense diversity of God's dealings with Israel is brought together. The different traditions are honoured, complement each other and give a far deeper knowledge and understanding of God than if only one tradition had been retained.

Questions

1. What do the writers of the Pentateuch (apart from Deuteronomy) tell us about covenants?
2. How and why does the 'P' use the 'J' and 'E' traditions to proclaim a new message?
3. Give an outline of one main character in the Pentateuch. Pay attention to that character's relationship to God.
4. Compare Priestly law with Deuteronomic law.

4
Learning from History

§The situation, contents, sources, characteristics theology and message of Deuteronomy Its place in the Deuteronomic History* Discussion of Joshua, Judges, 1 and 2 Samuel, 1 and 2 Kings*

The proposal made by the German Scholar Martin Noth in 1941 gives the key for the interpretation of the Books Deuteronomy, Joshua, Judges, 1 and 2 Samuel, and 1 and 2 Kings. He proposed that these Books were created as one long history by a person or persons from a Deuteronomic school of writers. The writing was done over a number of years and, whilst the emphases may have changed as the word of God was interpreted anew, there was a strong continuity of thought and language in their work.

While this body of writings is referred to as a history, in fact the authors have used history to proclaim a message to the people. It is a theological work. It had a long history of growth before its final form was fixed, some time after 561 BCE, the date when King Jehoichin was released from prison in Babylon. The Books of Joshua to 2 Kings are referred to in the Hebrew tradition as the Former Prophets, but modern scholarship generally accepts that, with Deuteronomy, they form the Deuteronomic History.

Deuteronomy

Bible readings: Deuteronomy 5–8, 12–18, 30–31

The Book of Deuteronomy itself plays a prominent part, not only as the first Book of the Deuteronomic History, but also as the last Book of the Pentateuch. It may seem strange to the modern reader that a book can be positioned to serve these two purposes but the Old Testament writers were creative, though we may find their use of traditions difficult to appreciate today.

The work of the Deuteronomic writers may be identified by their use of distinctive words and phrases. The language is repetitive and has a clear preaching style. It was aimed at teaching and uses exhortation, long sentences, a distinctive vocabulary and frequent synonyms. A few of the common words and phrases used are:

testimonies, statutes and ordinances, abomination, high places, green hills, a land flowing with milk and honey, hear with your ears, with a mighty hand and outstretched arm, chosen, covenant, and a holy people. There are many other special words and phrases used which make it possible to identify Deuteronomic writings throughout the Old Testament.

The Book of Deuteronomy is the start of this large history and its theology is the basis of the ensuing message. During the reign of king Josiah of Judah, a book was found in the temple, which was undergoing restoration. This incident is described in 2 Kings 22 and 23. 'The Book of the Law', as it is referred to in 2 Kings, consisted of most of chapters 4:44 to 26 and 28 of Deuteronomy as we know it today, and is accepted by the majority of scholars as the core of that Book. When it was found in the temple, it was first read to king Josiah and then to the people and was presented as the motivation for cultic reform. In fact it probably supported a reform that had already begun. Josiah was cleansing the temple of items of Assyrian worship and enforcing tight restrictions on the worship life of Israel when the book was found. He decreed that Jerusalem be the center of sacrificial life of the people and he made provision for the Levites, who had officiated in the local shrines, to be cared for in other ways (Deut 12:12). Centralising of sacrifice had deprived them of their living.

The account of the discovery of the Book of the Law raises three questions: Who wrote the Book? When was it written? Who hid it in the temple? A number of answers may be offered. The Book could have been written just prior to the cleansing of the temple and placed there deliberately to give authority to Josiah's reforms. Or, the Book was written during the reign of Manasseh when he was enthusiastically following the ways of Assyrian worship and encouraging everyone to follow his example. Under the threat of the Israelites abandoning their own God, the Book was written so that the traditions of Israel would be preserved for future generations. It may not have been possible in that environment to preach against Manasseh's practices so this method was adopted for the sake of the future. How the Book came into the temple may never be known with certainty, but it was a great help to Josiah's movement to banish idols and bring back purity of worship.

The authors of this Book appear to have come from prophetic or levitical groups. Some suggest the Levites, because they were part of the cultic life of Israel and had access to the traditions of Israel. When there was need to write down the Law and proclaim its message, had both the knowledge and the gifts to do so. A slight variation of this suggestion is that a group of dissident Levites who had been expelled from the temple after Solomon became king, had taken up residence in Anathoth and, together with the prophets, had become the creative force behind the Deuteronomic History.

Another possibility is that religious leaders, either Levites or prophets, who had fled south after the destruction of Israel and settled in Anathoth were the authors of Deuteronomy and then became the nucleus of a school which developed the Deuteronomic theology through the next 150 years. They may have been writing at the time of Manasseh or later in the seventh century BCE. The theology and traditions in Deuteronomy reflect those of Israel (northern kingdom) and there is a strong emphasis on the prophetic role. There is evidence of prophetic schools that perpetuated the concept of the Mosaic covenant and the prophet as intercessor and spokesman of God's word. So there are reasons for proposing a group that was descended from the northern nation and arising within a school of prophets were the authors of the Book of Deuteronomy.

Who the writers of Deuteronomy were may be uncertain but the message reflects the northern traditions and ideas and was written either early or mid seventh century BCE.

Contents

The Book of Deuteronomy is presented as a speech by Moses, given at a point between Sinai and the occupation of the land. Moses was acting as mediator between God and the people and the lawgiver. He is depicted as preaching to the people and many of the chapters are expansions of the Ten Commandments. For example, in Deuteronomy 6:4–18, verses 5–18 are a sermon based on the first commandment (6:4). Deuteronomy 7 to 10 contains a preview of the conquest of the vast Jordanian region, with general warnings and admonitions in chapter 11. The Prologue (Deut 4 to 11), placed before the detailed requirements of the Law (chapters 12 to 26), impresses again and again the people's need to rely on the goodness and bounty of God.

The code itself (chapters 12 to 26) contains an extensive collection of laws put together rather haphazardly and covering all areas of the people's lives. There are laws dealing with the cult: centralisation of worship (12:1–18), offering of first fruits (26:1–11), offering of a tithe (26:12–15), and observance of feasts (16:1–13). There are laws concerning rank: the judge (16:18–29), the king (17:14–20), the priest (18:1–8), and the prophet (18:15–22). There are also martial laws (20:1–20; 21:1–14), prohibitions concerning food (14:1–21), and sexual prohibitions (22:13–29). There is a large part of the code concerned with humanitarian aspects of living as the people of God. This is an unexpected aspect of Old Testament Law and not found elsewhere in scripture.

Here are some examples of the humanity expressed in this code. Every seven years the creditor was expected to release all those in debt to him and grant them a full reprieve (Deut 15:2). There had to be the evidence of more than one witness at a trial to prevent injustice occurring (19:15). People were to help animals in distress (22:4) and, if an animal was found it had to be kept safe until it could be restored to its owner (22:1–2). A nesting mother bird was to be left but the eggs could be taken (22:6–7). Gleanings were to be left in the field for the widow and the sojourner (24:19–22). An ox was not to be muzzled as it trod out the grain (25:4). Women had a slightly raised status in the eyes of the Deuteronomist, who, in the tenth commandment, put the wife before the house and land (5:21). In the version of this commandment in the Book of Exodus, the home and land are more important than the women. The whole tenor of the Deuteronomic law is caring and concern, and reflected a settled farming community.

The original closing chapter of Deuteronomy (the Book of the Law) has the age old custom of blessings and curses used to ratify the law and was expanded to include definite announcements of prosperity (28:1–14) and calamity (28:15–68).

Moses is represented as expounding the covenant and the covenant law to the Israelite community. It is peculiar to Deuteronomy that Moses gives the interpretation whereas in Exodus, it is God who gives the law to Moses who, in turn, speaks to the people. The Book portrays Moses warning the people before their entry into the land of Canaan. If they kept all the commandments then they would be successful and God would give them the land, and they would stay in it.

Style

The language, as has already been mentioned, is distinctive and stands out clearly among other writings of the scriptures. There is also a prophetic type schema, in which a prophecy is proclaimed early in the writings and later it is shown to have been fulfilled. The oracle in 2 Samuel 7:12 in which Nathan prophesies that the offspring of David will become king, is shown to have come true in 1 Kings 8:2, where the Lord is said to have fulfilled the promise by the action of Solomon. Ahijah, in 1 Kings 11:20 prophesies the division of the kingdom, which is seen to have been fulfilled in 1 Kings 12:15.

The Deuteronomist shows a direct relationship between the word of God spoken by the prophets and events in Israel's history. God was part of the total life of the people. In the later writings this tradition was extended. God spoke through the words of the prophets and the prophecy was fulfilled, but the 'P' writer went back to creation, there God spoke and things were created. Therefore, whenever God spoke in the history of Israel, that word was fulfilled. Traditions were developed, changed and appropriated as the life of the people changed and as the revelation of God was seen and heard in new ways.

The literary form of the Book of Deuteronomy is similar to the treaty form used in surrounding cultures. These secular treaties have a preamble, historical prologue, statement of general principles, detailed obligations imposed on the people, direction for the deposit of the treaty and future reading of it, witness of the gods, curses and blessings. Deuteronomy does not follow this pattern exactly, but in its general form is very similar. The Book is not only emphasising covenant and what that means, but is itself set out as a covenant document. It is like the use of subliminal advertising on television —this literary device speaks almost to the unconscious, reinforcing what the words are saying on the surface.

The authors, writing in the seventh century BCE, used the literary device of putting words into the mouth of one of their heroes. This gave the whole message a lot more authority than if it was indirectly narrated. The language used to describe God and the geographical details are typical of seventh century BCE and therefore it is unlikely that Moses actually spoke what is written in these chapters of Deuteronomy. It would also have been difficult to have a written record in Moses' lifetime since writing did not become common to the Israelite people until the reign of Solomon. Many of the laws had been part of the oral tradition. However other laws reflect the current situation and the needs of the seventh century BCE (Deut 12:12).

Message

The creator of the Book of Deuteronomy used as the basis for his message, the Sinai covenant and especially the first commandment, 'You shall have no other gods before me' (Deut 5:7). He does not at this stage deny the existence of other gods, but clearly states that the people are to worship Yahweh only. It is exclusive worship and a call for the Israelites to recognise Yahweh in their lives and not to consider at any point worshipping other gods. Obeying this commandment became very difficult when the king was actively encouraging worship of foreign idols that were set alongside the Ark in the temple. During the seventh century BCE, when Judah was constantly under the dominion of Assyria, there was a great deal of tension arising from the pressure to worship other gods.

As the people were called to worship the one God, so they were reminded of the reason why they should worship God. It was not a message in a vacuum, but recalled to the people what God had done for them in the past (Deut 5:1–6). It was God who raised up a leader to bring them out of slavery into freedom when they were sorely afflicted in Egypt. They were reminded constantly of God's saving action, which was intended to bring further response.

God did not liberate the people and lead them into the new land because they deserved it, or that they were any better than other nations. It was purely grace and love that motivated God to act in this way (Deut 7:6–8). They were holy because they were chosen by God. The holiness came from the association and relationship with God and not because of the people's actions or that they were more pious than any other nation.

God not only chose them (7:6), but also provided a covenant to help them stay in the relationship God formed with them. God expected the people to be obedient, to keep their side of the covenant and to love God with all their heart, soul, and might (6:4). This strong emphasis on obedience comes through the law that Moses gave the people. The law in Deuteronomy's version of the Decalogue (5:6–21) came as general principles and is then developed in chapters 12 to 26 to show how it related to specific areas of the life of the people.

This law shows great care for people in all walks of life. For example the Levite who was displaced when centralisation of worship became law was to be cared for (14:27). Borrowers were to be released from their debt at the end of seven years (15:1–2). Fellow Hebrew slaves were to be freed after seven years (15:12). There were special laws related to accidental killing (19:4–7) and explicit laws concerning the relationships of men and women (22:13–20). The law was there to help people stay in relationship with God and with their fellow human beings. It portrayed a lot of care and reflects the era of settlement and the monarchical period in Israel's life.

The writer is deeply concerned that knowledge of God should be retained by the people. One of the ways to ensure that the traditions were remembered and kept alive by succeeding generations of Israelites was to teach the children. The people are reminded constantly to tell their children what God has done for them (6:20–5). The tradition will be guarded from dying out by the young people knowing of the past experiences of God and the law which they in turn could pass on to future generations. This emphasis on teaching the children was very important in an environment that encouraged worship of, and assimilation with, other gods.

The Deuteronomist proclaimed that if the people were obedient, then the result would be the gift of the land: 'You must follow exactly the path that Lord your God has commanded you, that you may live, and that it may go well with you, and that you live long in the land which you shall possess' (5:33). Beside the promise of the land was the proclamation that if they obeyed the commandments of Moses they would also live. The land is portrayed as synonymous with life. Possession of life and land are dependent on the people's obedience to the Law of Moses. The writer composed this Book when Judah still retained the land and therefore the promise of land had been fulfilled. However, there was the very recent loss of Israel, which the Deuteronomist believed was due to the people's disobedience. This message was a dire warning to the people of Judah that their disobedience and straying after other gods could well result in the loss of land and life for them also.

In summary, the message of the Deuteronomist was to call the people back to an exclusive relationship with God and to remind them of God's love for them revealed in their history. If they remained true and faithful and were obedient to the law, then they would have the land that God had promised them. If they were disobedient they would lose the land and life.

These themes recur through the whole of the Deuteronomic History, and underline its theology. The history is the story of a people who were not able to obey. Their disobedience is traced from the beginning of their settlement in Canaan right through to the final degradation in their removal from the land and the exile experience.

The Book of Deuteronomy, which was a seventh century BCE production, was then used as an introduction to a much larger body of material, called the Deuteronomic History. Deuteronomy had further chapters added to it (1:1 to 4:44; 27; 29 to 34), but it is not clear at precisely what time the various chapters or sections were supplied. The last verses inserted would be from the Priestly writer, when he chose to make it the last Book of the Pentateuch. This large body of material may have been written just prior to exile but after the death of Josiah (607 BCE), or written in exile. If it was started in the pre-exilic period, it was certainly given its final form during the exile itself, around the time when Jehoiachin was released from prison (561 BCE).

The Deuteronomic History is a document that in its final form gave both the reason why Israel was in Babylon and offered the possibility of turning to God and finding new beginnings with God. It was so designed to hold up the past history and behaviour of Israel to itself so the people would be able to see why they deserved the punishment they were suffering. Then it proclaimed the message that if the people turned again to God and repented, they would find restoration and renewal. There were stages of growth in the Deuteronomic History that are discussed in various commentaries, but it is very difficult to date the stages precisely. Because of this we will study the Deuteronomic History as we have it in its final form (Deuteronomy to 2 Kings) as it proclaims God's word to the people in exile.

Joshua

Bible readings: Joshua 1–6; 23–24

The Book of Joshua was arranged so that chapters 1 to 12 speak of the conquest of the territory west of the Jordan. The central section (13 to 21) tells of the distribution of the land among the tribes. The Book concludes with an address by Joshua (23), and the assembly of the tribes at Shechem (24).

The traditions and material that were used for the creation of the Book of Joshua were complex and drew on early oral traditions. Chapters 1 to 12 have material that was associated with the tribe of Benjamin and its sanctuary at Gilgal. Other traditions, whilst not originally part of the Gilgal stories, have been combined with them, indicating a long history of growth and augmentation in the formation of the present material.

The account of the conquest of Jericho is contained in chapter 6, and a history of other cities captured, Ai and Gibeon, in 7 to 9. The latter was by peaceful means and not by military conquest. The story then turns to the defeat of the Canaanite kings in the South (10), with a summary of conquests in 10:28–33. There follows a parallel account of the conquest of the kings in the north of Canaan (11:1–15).

The story of how the land was conquered is then followed by the account of the division of the land between the tribes. This central portion (13 to 21) was in fact the fulfillment of the promise to the patriarchs and then to the Israelites, 'To your descendants I will give this land' (Gen 12:7. See also Gen 26:3, Exod 3:8). This is offered again at the end of the Book of Joshua, 'Thus the Lord gave to Israel all the land which he swore to give to their fathers . . .' (Josh 21:43). The distribution of the land and the promise of God cannot be separated.

The second section makes use of traditions which list territories actually occupied or yet to be conquered, plus another source showing the division of Judah into twelve districts (Josh 15:21–62; 18:21–28). Some of the sources used in the construction of this section were very old and contained in them stories indicating that not all the territories were conquered in the same way (Josh 15:13–19; Jud 1:11–15). There is an acceptance that ancient materials have been incorporated here, but it is not easy to discover when and how they were separate entities in their own right.

The writer took these traditions and then, by placing them in a framework of his own creation, proclaimed his message to the people in exile. Chapters 1, 12 and 24 provide the theological interpretation of the accounts they surround.

Deuteronomy emphasises that Joshua was the divinely appointed and authenticated successor to Moses. 'Joshua the son of Nun, your assistant, he shall enter there, encourage him, for he is the one who will secure Israel's possession of it' (Deut 1:37–38. See also 3:28). He was installed by Moses (31:7) and commissioned by the Lord himself. 'Be strong and bold; for you shall bring the Israelites into the land that I promised them. I will be with you' (31:23). When he took up his task he was exhorted to be strong and of good courage (Josh 1:6,7,9) and to begin exercising his authority (Josh 1:10). There were many incidents in Joshua's life that parallel the life of Moses. Joshua, like Moses, crossed an important body of water (Josh 3:1) and was seen as a military commander with a reputation for success, who then had the authority to distribute the land. Joshua acted as intercessor, as did Moses (Josh 7:7–9; Deut 9:25). Before he died Joshua, like Moses, made two farewell speeches which follow the covenant form as in Deuteronomy 29 to 30.

Joshua is depicted as walking in the way of the Lord. He was obedient to the law in Deuteronomy and is thus portrayed as righteous and the perfect model for the people to copy. He was not only the person who was instrumental in leading them into the land and dividing it among the tribes, but he is portrayed as the ideal person, because of his obedience. In this he contrasts with the later kings of Israel and Judah who were judged because of their disobedience to the law. So the people followed Joshua as they had Moses. God was with Joshua (1:5–6) as God had been with Moses and there was a sense of continuity

There is a strong emphasis on the idea of God leading the people into the land. God guided them when it was the right time, and, because God was with them, they were victorious. His concept is sometimes referred to as Holy War, it was God's decision regarding when it was right to attack or to fall back and if they, the Israelites, obeyed God's command, they would be successful in their military venture, but if they did not wait until they had heard God, then the venture would fail.

The unity of all Israel was a concern for Joshua. The covenant was made with all Israel (Deut 31:1, 7; 34:12), and Joshua emphasised the union of the twelve tribes (Josh 23:1–13). In his last word to the people he exhorted them to follow the word of God, and be obedient in response to what the Lord God had done for them in driving out other nations, so that Israel could have the land of Canaan (Josh 23). He warned them about mixing with the local people and becoming corrupt in their religious practices. They would be driven from the land if they disobeyed the covenant. It is clearly stated at the beginning of the Deuteronomic history that if they did not obey the law, they would be deprived of the land. The people of Israel were warned from the very beginning of their stay in Canaan that there was always the possibility of judgment and punishment.

While Joshua 23 is a Deuteronomic expansion of Joshua 24, both are Deuteronomic compositions but from different stages in the growth of the Deuteronomic history. Joshua 24 does contain ancient material (24:25–27), which parallels that in the Book of the Covenant. The theme in Joshua 24, making and renewing the covenant, occurs in many of the bridging passages throughout the Deuteronomic history (eg 1 Kgs 8). The Covenant form of Joshua 24, which has similarities to the treaty form of surrounding cultures, is set out as follows:

Preamble	1–1a
Confession of faith	2b–13
Invitation to make a choice and people's response	14–24
Making the covenant	25-27,28
Various comments on the relics buried at Shechem	29–33

The theology of the Book of Joshua is dependent on ideas found in Deuteronomy, which supports the concept that these Books, plus the remainder of the Deuteronomic history were created by a group of people from the same school or holding to a consistent tradition and language.

Judges

Bible reading: Judges 2–3

The introduction to the Book of Judges, 2:6 to 3:6, leads into the main body of stories concerning the judges, which is divided into accounts of the major and minor judges. Other chapters have been added to this body of material; 1:1 to 2:5 is an extremely condensed and fragmented version of the conquest of Canaan as a whole. Judges 17 to 18 and 19 to 21 are two independent supplements, linked with Judges merely because they tell of events relating to this era.

The account of the conquest of Canaan in Judges 1 was written from a later point of view in which details of early victories have been simplified, but its purpose was to act as a summary and introduction to the ensuing events related in the Book of Judges. The account in Judges was connected to the end of Joshua by the statement in 2:6, 'When Joshua dismissed the people . . .', which is a clear reference to the assembly of people at Shechem renewing the covenant with God. This introduction (2:6 to 3:6) contains a brief summary of the people's experience in relation to God over the next generation. The people, now settled in the land, committed apostasy, 'the people did evil in the sight of the Lord . . .' (Jud 2:11); then there was oppression by the enemy as punishment for their sins (2:13–15), and the people cried to the Lord for help (3:9). The Lord raised up a leader (judge) to save them from oppression (3:9), 'The Spirit of the Lord came upon him and he judged Israel' (3:10).

The following chapters spell out in detail what was summarised in general in 2:6 to 3:6 and the narrative is dominated by stories of those judges who were the initiators of heroic exploits: Othniel, Ehud, Shamgar, Deborah, Barak, Jepthah, Gideon and Samson. They were the people raised up to rescue the tribes from crises and who gained public esteem and authority. Complex traditions surround some of the judges eg Ehud, while others, like Othniel, have only brief statements about their deaths. Minor judges—Tola, Jair, Ibzan, and Zebulun—were not associated with any great exploits but, because of family affinities, were said to have judged Israel. They could originally have been part of a regular office as their length of service and their place of work were recorded, giving in essence two different roles for a judge: one secular and regular, and the other charismatic and in response to a tribal crisis.

The pattern of apostasy, punishment and deliverance is reflected throughout the Book of Judges. The language in the theological explanation of 2:6–23 is closely aligned with that used by the Deuteronomic writers, demonstrating a continuity in thought and construction of the writings.

A charismatic judge was only associated with one tribe or a small group of tribes, and not as a leader raised up for all twelve tribes of Israel. The office was not a continuing one, but only came into effect to meet a crisis in times of oppression. The spirit of the Lord came upon the judges when they were called to act on behalf of God. It was this charisma that drew a number of the tribes together for an immediate purpose. The Deuteronomist portrays all the judges as following in sequence, but there may in fact have been some overlap.

The Deuteronomist was concerned to show seventh century BCE people that even their forebears at the time of settlement in the land were disobedient and had worshipped other gods. They stood in need of punishment but they repented and cried for help, and in mercy God raised up leaders and liberated them. This was Israel's story from the beginning. The people went their own way, but God wanted to draw them back into the covenant relationship. God loved these people and chastised them when they were disobedient that they might see their folly and return to the One who cared for them.

The supplement, Judges 17 to 18, is an early narrative which tells the story of a farmer who erected his own chapel, with graven images, and installed an itinerant Levite as priest in it. The chapel was stolen by the tribe of Dan and given a new location. Because of its association with idols it could not be regarded favourably by the Deuteronomic writers. Why then is the story incorporated here? It may be a sarcastic comment by the Deuteronomic composers to demonstrate that a shrine with such doubtful origins could not possibly be used for pure worship. Its heritage dictated that it would be used for unworthy practices, as we see in the example of King Jeroboam when he set up a golden bull to be the focus of worship at this shrine.

The next supplement, Judges 19 to 21, has two sources joined together. There is difficulty in assigning a reason for its inclusion at this point. It may be the role that Mizpah and Bethel play in the northern traditions, in which they are portrayed as important worship sanctuaries for the people of the northern kingdom.

1 and 2 Samuel

Bible readings: 1 Samuel 1–4; 8–18; 2 Samuel 6–8

These Books begin the narratives of the kings of Israel. 1 Samuel gives an account of Samuel's influence in the affairs of Israel (1 to 25), Saul's life and experiences (9 to 31), and the initial stories of David (16 to 31). Second Samuel covers the major part of the reign of David.

There are two traditions that run very close together through these Books. One is the historic experience of the monarchy and the other is the prophetic assessment of the monarchy. Many people today want to separate the prophetic role of the church from the state but in Old Testament times it was very clear that prophets were part of the state political scene. There are specific prophetic traditions concerning Samuel, particularly in regard to his childhood (1 Samuel 1 to 3) and his relations with Saul in later years (1 Sam 7, 8; 10:17–27; 12; 13:8–15; 15). Other prophetic traditions appear in the accounts of Nathan and Gad (2 Sam 7; 12; 24).

Besides the prophetic material that was used throughout these Books, various other sources were used. There are extensive literary compositions highlighting certain significant events, objects or people. The story of the Ark (1 Sam 4 to 6; 2 Sam 6), the history of the rise of David (1 Sam 16 to 2 Sam 5) and the account of the succession in the house of David (2 Sam 9 to 20), are all examples of these literary compositions. Into these compositions have been inserted brief reports, memoranda, and theological comments by the Deuteronomic authors. The theology of the Deuteronomic writers is proclaimed in their method of reshaping material and by the way they put the various parts together.

The Deuteronomic writers did not always handle their material in the same way. In Judges and Kings, the writings are tightly organised into a specific schema. However, in Joshua and 1 and 2 Samuel, the authors let the sources tell their own story with little editorial comment. This means that there are times when the story does not in fact represent the Deuteronomic viewpoint. This is quite peculiar in our way of thinking—to use intact material that has a different viewpoint from what is being presented in the remainder of the history. However, the final result when this contradictory material is surrounded by Deuteronomic comment means that it became part of the total message and theology of the Deuteronomist. An example of this occurs in the so called Succession Narrative (2 Sam 20 and 24), which portrays God as firmly in control of events and able to work God's saving purposes in spite of the unfaithfulness of the people. God is portrayed in the Deuteronomic material as one who will reward the faithful and punish the un-faithful. The reason for this black and white representation by the Deuteronomic authors was to make a definite point about God's dealing with the people but was contradictory to some of the other material used, for example, the Succession Narrative.

Summary of the contents

There are very few birth narratives in the Bible, but examples of these are found at the beginning of the patriarchal era (Isaac), national era (Moses), royal history (Samuel) and Christianity (Jesus). The story of Samuel's birth and call is recorded in the first chapters of 1 Samuel (1 to 3) and concludes with the establishment of Samuel as a prophet (1 Sam 3:19–21). Even here, a judgment is pronounced and is proclaimed against Eli because his sons did not carry out the proper manner of sacrifice (1 Sam 3:13–14). The corruption of worship was condemned time and again by the Deuterononic writers and was one of the major sins of the kings of Israel and Judah on whom judgment was passed.

This section is followed by the history of the Ark (1 Samuel 4 to 7:2), which describes the great defeat by the Philistines of the Israelites, the capture and eventual return of the Ark and its lodging at Kiriath-jearim. The conclusion to the history of the Ark is in 2 Samuel 6, which tells of it being brought into the city of Jerusalem by David and given its resting place in the tent as the focal point of worship and sacrifice. The defeat of the Israelites by the Philistines was instrumental in the call of the people for a king to lead them against the threat of annihilation by the Philistines. The scene is thus set for the following narratives concerning the kings of Israel and Judah.

The Ark had great power. It was the symbol of God's presence with the people in battle and its capture caused great distress among the Israelites. The Ark caused problems among the Philistines who captured it and eventually it was voluntarily sent back to the Israelites. It remained in the countryside until David brought it from its resting place into Jerusalem. With the arrival of the Ark the people were reassured that the presence of God was with them in their city. In David's time it was kept in a tent but it was later moved into the temple that was built by Solomon. In later traditions, the temple in Jerusalem became known as the dwelling place of God, and in the Book of Isaiah, is said to be immune from destruction. This was proved wrong when Jerusalem was destroyed in 587 BCE. While the people in exile still looked to the temple for inspiration and hope, they realised that God did not dwell there only, but was present with them in Babylon. The presence of God with them was signified by the glory of God so the people did not need the Ark or the temple to reassure them of that fact (See 1 Kgs 8:11; Ezek 1:28; 44:4).

1 Samuel 7 to 12 contains the account of the origin the monarchy, and within these chapters two quite clear points of view are presented.

There were some people who wanted a king and saw the monarchy as a positive move for Israel and a gift from God to the people (1 Sam 9:1 to 10:16). Another group felt it was demonstrating a lack of trust in God; the people were depicted as wicked to want such a thing (1 Sam 10:17–27). The second viewpoint is very close to that of the Deuteronomic writers, but it could easily have developed from an embryonic tradition of the prophets who were against monarchy.

Samuel is depicted as a seer, prophet, priest, judge and kingmaker. He anointed Saul who then led his people very capably into victory over the Philistines. Finally there is Samuel's farewell to the people, which marked the transition from the Judges style of leadership (charismatic) to the more institutional style of monarchy. It also gave a warning against the dangers of the monarchy (1 Sam 12:1–25).

Saul was very much in line with the charismatic leaders of the Judges period and, although he was the first king of Israel, he never had a government and state bureaucracy as did later kings. Saul's reign is seen as a transition role between that of judge and king. He was neither one nor the other. Chapters 13 to 31 of 1 Samuel describe the reign of Saul, the continuing battles with the Philistines, and the gradual personal disintegration of Saul. The Book goes on to recount the growing rivalry between David and Saul as David became part of the court, won Saul's daughter, befriended Saul's son, displayed heroic qualities against the Philistines and finally had to flee because of Saul's jealousy.

The ascension of David begins in the last chapters of 1 Samuel (16 to 31) and continues through 2 Samuel 1 to 5. It tells of David's anointing by Samuel and the events mentioned in association with Saul and his family. There is a great deal of detail about David's life as an outlaw when he had to flee from Saul to save his life. After the death of Saul, (2 Sam 1:1–16), David was declared king. He was still threatened by the presence of Saul's remaining son, Eshbaal, who had also been proclaimed king. However Eshbaal was murdered two years later and David was anointed king by the northern tribes and so became leader over all the tribes of Israel. There followed the capture of Jerusalem and the final victory over the Philistines.

This period of Israelite history was a time of great military and material gain. David was a shrewd and capable leader and politician. He was king over Judah (2 Sam 2:1–7) and the northern tribes of Israel (2 Sam 5:3) by the personal choice of the people. His choice of

Jerusalem as the capital for the kingdom was politically shrewd because it was on the border of the northern and southern tribes. It was also sound military strategy because the city had such strong fortifications against enemy attack.

The remaining chapters of 2 Samuel (6 to 24) deal with David's transfer of the Ark to Jerusalem and the promise of God given by Nathan to David in which he is assured that his royal house and kingdom will last forever. God says David will be his son, whom he will live forever and never be cast aside. Then follows accounts of the wars and David's adultery, finishing with the rebellion of his son and the story of Solomon's succession to the throne (1 Kgs 1:1 to 2:46). The heart of this account was David's transgression (which was omitted by the Chronicler). The story of David depicts a king who began his reign with glory and honour and ended in sadness, struggle and heartbreak.

There is supplementary material in 2 Samuel 8 and 21 to 24, which deals in great detail with David's military activities. It suggests that a number of sources were available to the Deuteronomic authors.

1 and 2 Kings

Bible readings: 1 Kings 8; 12–14; 2 Kings 21–25

The beginning of 1 Kings would seem to fit better into the end of 2 Samuel, as it deals with the final period of David's reign. Solomon's reign is dealt with in 1 Kings 1 to 11, and the history and judgment of the kings of Israel and Judah in 1 Kings 12 to 2 Kings 17. 2 Kings 18 to 25 tells the story of Judah's kings after the fall of Samaria in 721 BCE. There is as much written about the first two kings of Israel as there is about the rest of the kings of Judah and Israel. Saul and David were regarded very highly by the Deuteronomists in the light of God's plan for saving the people of Israel. The very brief comments on some of the kings who had long reigns demonstrates that the writer was not interested in giving details of their reigns, or the social and religious conditions of the time. Their intention was to survey each of the kings in the light of the Mosaic covenant as presented in Deuteronomy and judge whether each king had been faithful to God or not. If they had led the people in the way of true worship of God only, they were pronounced as good and walking in the way of the Lord (2 Kgs 18:3).

If they had set up idols they were condemned as walking in the ways of evil (1 Kgs 15:25–26).

Included in 1 and 2 Kings is a large complex of prophetic material based around the figures of Elijah and Elisha (1 Kgs 17 to 2 Kgs 9). Elijah was closely connected with the affairs of the state and was called upon by God to confront the false prophets of the court with their deceitful ways. In the test that took place on Mount Carmel, Elijah was vindicated as a true prophet of God (1 Kgs 18). King Ahab was warned by Elijah when he cheated Naboth of his vineyard. Elijah's words were seen to come true when finally Ahab and his wife Jezebel met their deaths—a just punishment for their wrong deeds.

Elisha was of the same school as Elijah, but his emphasis was in the area of miracles and healing. He was not a person involved in the politics of the state or one who passed judgments, but rather performed signs and wonders that occasionally bordered on the bizarre. Elisha was often mentioned as belonging to a band of prophets and on one occasion a school is clearly described (2 Kgs 6:1). Perhaps the purpose in presenting two very, different types of prophetic activity is to emphasise that each role is equally acceptable as a prophetic function.

The Books 1 and 2 Kings deal briefly with each of the kings of both Israel and Judah, and then, after the fall of Samaria, with kings of Judah only. Out of all the kings in both kingdoms there were only two, Hezekiah and Josiah, who were classified as good, and both of these were from Judah. It is hardly likely that all the kings were so bad but it is presented in such a way as to highlight the Deuteronomic message. The goodness of a king is measured only in respect of his attitude to God's word and purity or worship. Kings such as Manasseh and Ammon were judged more evil than others because of the extent of their apostasy. The Deuteronomist finished his history with the release of Jehoiachin in Babylon in 561 BCE, which suggests that the writing stopped at this point, or soon after.

Sources

There were many sources used in the composition of 1 and 2 Kings. The amount of material taken from each source varies, from a small extract from the Book of the Acts of Solomon (1 Kgs 11:14), to longer complexes like the Elijah and Elisha stories (1 Kgs 17 to 19; 21; 2 Kgs

1:2–18). Other sources were the Book of the Chronicles of the Kings of Israel (1 Kgs 14:19), the Book of the Chronicles of the Kings of Judah (1 Kgs 14:29), and accounts of Ahab's wars with Damascus (1 Kgs 20 and 22). There were four prophetic strands, the two mentioned above around Elijah mid Elisha, legendary material based around Isaiah (2 Kgs 18:13 to 20:19) and the traditions of Ahijah of Shiloh (1 Kgs 11:29–39; 12:15; 14:1–8; 20:29).

All these sources were used to serve the theological purpose of the Deuteronomic writers. The whole of the history was set down in the light of God's message and purpose for the people of Israel. There was to be no compromise with other gods or alien worship practices and, in particular, no association with the Baal cults. When the kings of Israel and Judah strayed from this command they were judged and condemned as evil. The loss of Israel was seen to be due to the fact that the kings had walked in the ways of other gods (2 Kgs 17:7–12), and the same judgment would befall Jerusalem (2 Kgs 23:27). God was not punishing them because of some whim but because of their own unrepentant behaviour.

The Deuteronomists

Noth suggests that there was one writer who created this Deuteronomic history in Judah after the fall of Jerusalem. Many scholars believe it had more than one production and that editing has taken place. Some proposed the Levites as the authors and others suggested a school of prophets. Because of the emphasis and use of northern traditions, such as the Mosaic covenant and the role of prophecy, it seems likely that it could have been from a group of people who fled south from Samaria after 721 BCE, settled in Judah, and wrote their history as crises arose. The Book of Deuteronomy was used as the first Book of the history, with the basic theological understanding contained in it as the standard for the following discourse. The material could have been written just prior to the fall of Jerusalem, but all agree that the final redaction (expansion/editing) took place during the exile either in Babylon or Judah.

Message

The message in its final form was addressed to the exiles in Babylon. The Deuteronomic writers held up the mirror of Israel's history to the people and showed them why they were in Babylon and why they were suffering such ignominy and disgrace. The cause was portrayed throughout as the peoples' own waywardness and disobedient behaviour. It was not God who had failed them but their disregard for the prophets' word and their inability to keep the covenant. There was a constant call to the people and the kings to be in covenant relationship with God. This covenant was the one given by Moses to the people (Deut 5), and spelled out in detail for them in Deuteronomy 12 to 26. The emphasis was on the disobedience of the people in not responding positively to God's commands.

The Books demonstrate that the people's apostasy began during their time in the wilderness (Deut 9) and continued as they settled into the land (Jud 2:11). This behaviour persisted and was seen to be the reason for the loss of first Israel and then Judah. It was the story of a land given by God, who raised up leaders to take the people from slavery, through the wilderness and into a new land. This was followed by the gradual deterioration of the relationship with God who punished them in the hope that they would eventually return to their God and be God's people.

Prophecy plays an important role in the whole unfolding drama of the Deuteronomist. Right from the beginning Moses had authority as the lawgiver but he was also portrayed as a prophet. The prophets spoke the word of God to the people and it came to pass in the life of Israel. Time and again, the truth of the prophecy was seen to be fulfilled. The prophecy of Nathan to David that God would raise up offspring after him (2 Sam 7:12–13) came true when Solomon declared that the promise of God had been fulfilled (1 Kgs 8:22). Other examples of prophecy coming true are found in 1 Kings 11:30-31, fulfilled in 1 Kings 12:15–16, and 1 Kings 14:7–11, fulfilled in 1 Kings 15:27–30. In the end the prophets spoke of the destruction of Judah because of its apostasy (2 Kgs 21:10–15). This was fulfilled when 'the Lord sent against him bands of the Chaldeans, and bands of the Arameans, and bands of the Moabites, and bands of the Ammonites, and sent them against Judah to destroy it, according to the word of the Lord which he spoke by his servants the prophets' (2 Kgs 24:2).

The prophets spoke of judgment but they also spoke of repentance and return to God. Noth suggested that the only purpose of the Deuteronomic writer was to show Israel why it was in exile. Many scholars think this was only half the purpose of the writings and there was also present the idea of renewal and return to God, and, therefore, hope. For example 1 Samuel 7:3 'If you are returning to the Lord with all your heart . . . he will deliver you out of the hand of the Philistines'. Renewal was present in their early days of apostasy, as it was in later times (1 Kgs 8:33–35). There was hope for the people if they turned to God from their evil ways. The fulfilment of God's word in regard to judgment had come true, so they could also rely on God's word of acceptance and deliverance if they repented. The word of God was certainly very important for the people in exile.

The people were in exile because they failed to repent, not because God's promises were not fulfilled. This emphasis on the possibility of the people turning to God and making amends by human behaviour was seen to be false in the later exilic writings. People are never able to be totally obedient and so keep covenant with God. A renewed relationship and the possibility of hope can only be dependent on the unconditional love of God for the people, which enables God to forgive. The exile forced the later writers to realise that their only hope lay in the unconditional promises of God, which had been present in the early covenants with Abraham and Noah.

Much of the specific Deuteronomic thought is displayed in speeches given by Moses (Deut to 3; 29 to 31), Joshua (Josh 1:1–18, 23), Samuel, (1 Sam 12), and Solomon, (1 Kgs 8), plus other bridging passages such as in Joshua (8:30–35; 12; 21:43–45; 22:1, 6, 9; 24:1–28), Judges (2:11–23), 2 Samuel (7) and 2 Kings (17:7–20). In these passages a conflict between the southern and northern traditions can be seen, with the southern traditions subordinate to those of the north. For instance, the Mosaic covenant takes precedence over the Davidic covenant and so the royal ideology becomes subject to the law. Where David had been supreme, now both he and his people had to follow the law of Moses (1 Kgs 1–4; 9:4–9). Even Hezekiah was portrayed as not only walking in the path of David but also keeping the commands of Moses (2 Kgs 18:1–6).

The tradition of Jerusalem as the place where God dwelt had to be re-thought because of the exilic experience. They could still look to Jerusalem for hope of return but now they were in Babylon it raised the question of God's dwelling place. Was God with them or left behind in the Holy City? An important concept that developed was that the name of God, when pronounced, was the place of God's presence. It was little help to the exiles to think of God dwelling in Jerusalem when they were far away in exile (for example, Ezek 11:14–16). This was the development of a tradition forced upon them by their exper-ience, that God was contained neither in an ark nor in the temple.

The Sabbath was another tradition that came to have a deeper significance in the period of the exile. It was important for the exiles to meet together to remember their past and to worship God. Teaching their children was a high priority in the need to preserve the traditions and keep them alive for the people in exile. These traditions took on primary importance as they helped to preserve both their faith and their identity as a people.

If the Deuteronomic writing had taken place prior to the exile, it could have acted as a warning to the people. When this was edited during the exile it was presented as the reason for the exile and presented the possibility of repentance and of renewal of the relationship with God. It still sounded a warning to the people in exile who were surrounded by the gods of the Babylonians, and could easily stray again. So the Deuteronomic history was not only a message about the past, it was a living call to the people in exile to repentance and faithfulness

When the Priestly writer appropriated the Book of Deuteronomy and added chapters 32 to 34, there was still that message of hope for a people who were preparing to go once again into the Promised Land. All the messages of the Deuteronomist still applied and were pertinent to the later situation.

The Deuteronomic history was a major theological work and must be regarded as written by people inspired by the Spirit to proclaim God's word to ongoing generations of Israelite people. Its genius and creativity is not only a message for past generations but still speaks to us today, especially in the areas of worshipping other gods and of our continued disobedience and waywardness.

Questions

1. Discuss the theological message of Deuteronomy.
2. Is Deuteronomy a unity? Discuss
3. How did the 'Law Book' help Josiah?

5
Building on the Past

*§The work of the Chronicler * The kings of David's line * Faithfulness and retribution * The sources, purpose and date of 1 and 2 Chronicles * Discussion of Ezra and Nehemiah*

Bible readings: 1 Chronicles 17; 23–29; 2 Chronicles 1–4; 34–36

It is generally accepted that the Books of 1 and 2 Chronicles, Ezra and Nehemiah, as we now have them, have the one final author. One of the main arguments for this conclusion is the continuity between the Books. For example: the story in Chronicles being continued in Ezra and Nehemiah, a similarity in the style of writing in all the books, the repetition of the last verses of 2 Chronicles 36 in the first verses of Ezra 1, and a close similarity of purpose. Indeed, the purpose of the Books is not to be seen in them individually, but when they are taken together. We may therefore, speak of the four Books being the work of the Chronicler.

The work of the Chronicler has the appearance of being a history and is in large part parallel to the Deuteronomic history. There are three major differences between the Deuteronomic history and the work of the Chronicler. First, the record of history extends from creation to the time of Ezra and Nehemiah in the fifth century BCE, second, there are differences in the way the material is presented and third, in the purpose of the two works.

Contents of the Chronicler's work

The first part of the work, 1 Chronicles 1–9, gives a summary of history from Adam to Saul, the first king of Israel. This section consists almost entirely of genealogies. The second part, 1 Chronicles 10–29, is an extended narrative dealing with the reign of David. The important idea of David as ideal king, so apparent in the Deuteronomic History, is given more emphasis here. Of particular importance is David's role in preparing for the building of the temple (1 Chron 17:28), and in making arrangements for music and singing in temple worship to be in the hands of the Levites (1 Chron 17:23). In this account there is nothing that would detract from the idea of David as the ideal king. So we have no mention of Uriah and Bathsheba, nor of the troubles experienced in the succession from David to Solomon.

Solomon is also dealt with in considerable detail in the third section, 2 Chronicles 1–9. His importance as the builder of the temple is stressed, as are his wisdom, his wealth, and his fame, which is proclaimed by the visit of the Queen of Sheba. The fourth section, 2 Chronicles 10–36, deals with the kingdom of Judah from the division into the separate kingdoms of Judah and Israel, to the destruction of Jerusalem and the temple, and the exile of the people to Babylon. The Chronicler does not deal with the kingdom of Israel because it had refused to acknowledge the Davidic line of kings and the temple in Jerusalem, both of which were essential to the people of God according to the Chronicler.

The Books of Ezra and Nehemiah record the decree of Cyrus, the return of the people from exile, and the rebuilding of the temple (Ezra 1–6); Ezra's arrival in Jerusalem from Persia and his dissolution of mixed marriages (Ezra 7–10); Nehemiah's commission to go to Jerusalem to rebuild the walls of the city and the accomplishment of this task against the opposition of Jerusalem's neighbours (Neh 1–7); Ezra's activity in reading the Book of the law of Moses to the people and making a covenant for the people in which they accepted obligations concerning worship and the priests (Neh 8–10); the re-ordering of the life of Jerusalem with a proportion of the people from the country areas of Judah being resettled in the city; the work of the priests and Levites established, and provisions made for worship in the temple (Neh 11–13).

The Chronicler's presentation

The area of parallel between the Chronicler's work and the Deuteronomic History is apparent from the outline of their contents; that is, the period from the beginning of the monarchy with Saul to the Babylonian exile. There are, however, important differences between the two. We have seen the way the position of David is highlighted in Chronicles. Besides omitting any negative features, a characteristic which is observed for all the 'good' kings of Judah, David's action in providing, in detail, plans for the building of the temple and contributing to the regulations for its worship, and his transfer of the throne to Solomon (1 Chronicles 22–29) have no parallel in the Books of Samuel and Kings. The inclusion of this material emphasises the importance of the temple and the line of Davidic kings who were heirs to the promise to David.

In the discussion of the monarchy after the death of Solomon the Chronicler is concerned only with the kings of Judah, that is, those who were descendants of David and who reigned from Jerusalem. This is made plain in the words of Abijah, king of Judah, to Jeroboam, king of Israel, 'the Lord God of Israel gave the kingship over Israel for ever to David and his sons . . .' (2 Chronicles 13:5. See also verse 8). 1 Kings 12:21–2 Kings 17 records the history of the two kingdoms in parallel. By the omission of the northern kingdom the Chronicler was stating plainly that the true Israel comprised those who remained loyal to David and the worship at the temple in Jerusalem.

This point is confirmed by the way the Chronicler treats the 'good' kings. Their main quality was their faithfulness, which is given particular emphasis. For example, Jehoshaphat, who is given qualified approval in 1 Kings 22:43–44,46, is shown in Chronicles to have been a king who was loyal to the ways of God, and who worked to establish the law of God among the people (2 Chron 17:1–9, 19:4–11). The result was that Jehoshaphat became rich, was honoured and 'God gave him rest' (peace); but the people did not turn to God (2 Chron 18:1, 20:30, 32–33)

Hezekiah and Josiah, kings who reformed worship in Judah, are given approval in the Book of Kings (2 Kgs 18:1–8; 22:1–2). In Chronicles the account of their deeds is expanded and they are shown to have been pious kings who worked hard for the cause of loyalty to God (2 Chron 29–32, 34–35). In addition to expanding the accounts of these kings, the Chronicler removed those parts of their stories that might discredit them in any way.

It is important to note the pattern of presentation of this narrative. The kings are shown to be faithful and unfaithful alternately. However, the faithful were not able to prevent the catastrophe of the destruction of Jerusalem and the exile of its people. Jehoshaphat is a good example of this. He was a good king, however 'the people had not yet set their hearts upon the God of their fathers' (2 Chron 20:33).

Another important difference is in the way the Chronicler points beyond the exile. In 2 Kings 25:27–30 the author records the release of Jehoiachin the king exiled to Babylon in 597 BCE. It seems reasonable to interpret this as a sign of hope to the people; that after a period of exile they would be released. It could also be seen as a sign that hope rested in one who was a descendant of David. But the Chronicler does not record this incident. Rather, he records the edict of Cyrus that the people return to their land and rebuild the temple of God. Thus he makes the temple the focus of the people's hope.

Finally, the Chronicler's understanding of retribution as a fixed and immediate order of life with God does not have a parallel in the Deuteromic History. The Chronicler shows that Saul's death resulted from his consulting a medium (1 Chron 10:13), and Josiah's untimely death came because did not heed a word from God (2 Chron 35:22). This also appears to be the explanation for the inclusion of the account of Manasseh being taken to Babylon by the Assyrians where he repented before God and returned to Jerusalem to reverse the policy he had previously encouraged (2 Chron 33:10–17). It gives the reason for the long reign of Manasseh; that is, there had to be some sign of faithfulness to God to explain why Manasseh had not been cut off by God as an act of retribution against him (2 Chron 33:10–20).

In applying this concept of retribution the Chronicler illustrated the prophetic word spoken by Azariah to King Asa: 'The Lord is with you while you are with him. If you seek him, he will be found by you, but if you forsake him, he will forsake you.' (2 Chron 15:2) His example demonstrated the truth and power of the prophetic word—disobedience inevitably brings judgment and punishment, while repentance and obedience bring the blessing of God. This was an important message to a people who had experienced the disaster of the exile because they had not heeded God's prophets, but who, by God's grace, were now restored to their homeland and in a renewed relationship with God. Obedience was of paramount importance.

The sources

The discussion of similarities to, and differences from, the Deuteronomic History raises the matter of sources used in the Chronicler's work. So much of the material is the same as that found in the Books of Samuel and Kings that it is clear that he had the Deuteronomic History available to him, or something very close to it. In addition to this, the Chronicler quotes other sources in his work. In his material on the Kings of Judah he refers to 'the Book of the Kings of Judah and Israel' (2 Chron 16:11), 'the Book of the Kings of Israel and Judah' (2 Chron 27:7. See also 1 Chron 9:1, 2 Chron 20:34, 24:27, 33:18 for similar references). When these sources are looked at closely it is seen that they are the one source and that it is the Books of Kings referred to in various ways.

Other sources quoted relate to prophets. For example, 'the Chronicles of Samuel the seer, and in the Chronicles of Nathan the prophet, and in Chronicles of Gad the seer . . .' (1 Chron 29:29); 'the history of Nathan the prophet, and in the prophecy of Ahijah the Shilonite, and in the visions of the seer Iddo . . .' (2 Chron 9:29. See also 2 Chron 12:15, 13:2, 20:34, 26:22, 32:32, 33:19). None of these sources is available to us, although some of the prophets are known from the Deuterononiic History. In 2 Chronicles 20:34, and 32:32 the impression is given that the prophetic writings were already to be found in a larger source and, once, again that is the work we have in the Books of Samuel and Kings. By making his references in this way the Chronicler is indicating his belief that the writing down, preservation, and transmission of the historical material goes back to the prophets of Israel. This agrees with the tradition that identified the historical Books, the Deuteronomic History, as the Former Prophets.

The Chronicler appears to have had other sources, not part of our Old Testament, available to him. By the use of these he was able to supplement his basic source and give more information about Judah's kings. For example, Rehoboam's fortifications to defend Judah (2 Chron11:5–10), Uzziah's war against the Philistines and other foreign powers, and the fortifications he built (2 Chron 26:6–8,10).

Identification of sources used in Ezra and Nehemiah presents more of a problem. It has been suggested that these Books are the free composition of the Chronicler, but this ignores the fact that some parts appear to be from official documents and Ezra 4:8–6:18 and 7:12–26 are written in Aramaic. (The remainder of these books are written in Hebrew). This suggests that the author had some official material available to him. The lists of names in Ezra 2, Nehemiah 7 and 11–12 also suggest some sort of source, perhaps from the temple archives. In addition, there is material that appears to have been taken from 'memoirs' of Ezra (7–9) and Nehemiah (1–7, 12 and 13). However, they too appear to be composed of sources and it is most likely that they were written by followers of Ezra and Nehemiah who wanted to honour these men for their great work on behalf of their people.

In Ezra and Nehemiah the Chronicler has used his sources to present a description of the organisation of the community and worship of the people in the fifth century BCE. It is important to see that the account has an historical basis, but the purpose, as with the Books of Chronicles, is clearly theological.

The Chronicler's purpose

From what we have seen so far it is clear that the Chronicler was not attempting to produce a history that would rival the Deuteronomic History. Chronicles, Ezra and Nehemiah are more of a supplement to the earlier work and something of an exposition of it. The Chronicler's work not only deals with the experience of the people up to the Babylonian exile and gives reasons for the exile, it also carries on to present the basis for the re-establishment of God's people in Jerusalem after the exile.

In his work the Chronicler established a number of things related to the people of Israel and their experience of God. First, the exile was the result of the disobedience of the people, and, in particular, their failure to heed words of warning from the prophets whom God persistently sent to them (2 Chron 36:15–17a).

Second, the basis of God's dealing with Israel before and after the exile was the promise to David. He and his descendants were the legitimate kings of Israel who were to maintain the cause of God on earth. This promise applied to the community in Jerusalem, but for it to continue, it required of the people obedience to the law of God (2 Chron 36:15–16, Neh 8–9). A major expression of obedience was faithful worship at the temple, which, in a real sense, continued the effectiveness of the promise to David after the exile.

Third, the role of the temple was of great importance. This is highlighted by attributing the organisation of its building and the arrangements for music and singing to David, the first in the line of promise. David was also responsible for giving the Levites responsibility for music and singing in temple worship. Then, instead of the statement about the release of Jehoiachin found in 2 Kings 25:27–30, the Chronicler has the edict from Cyrus that the temple be rebuilt (2 Chron 36:22–25, Ezra 1:1–4). This is an important sign of God's grace and purpose for Israel. God, through Cyrus, returned the people from exile and gave them the temple and its worship as the means of remaining faithful to their God. For the Chronicler, the opportunity to worship God in the sanctuary at Jerusalem was of primary importance. Even more important than the possibility that the line of David might continue.

Fourth, much of the work of Ezra and Nehemiah, after the law was read and the covenant made, involved proper organisation of officials and supplies for the temple (Nehemiah 10–13). It is clear that, for the Chronicler, the temple at Jerusalem was the legitimate temple and could withstand the claims that might be made for any others. Recent archaeological evidence has shown that other places where God was worshipped were in existence in Judea in the post-exilic period. For the Chronicler the place for orthodox worship was the temple at Jerusalem. However, he is not especially anti-Samaritan as some have claimed. It is unlikely that antagonism between the people of Judea and Samaria arose until some time after the Chronicler completed his work. However, when that antagonism did arise, the work of the Chronicler strengthened the claims for the temple in Jerusalem.

The community pictured by the Chronicler is one which is centred in its worship at the temple in Jerusalem, zealous in its observance of the law of God and protected from outside interference by the city walls and the prohibition of mixed marriages. The Chronicler made a great contribution towards the development and preservation of Judaism.

Date

It is most probable that the Chronicler's work was completed soon after the events recorded in Ezra and Nehemiah, but not so soon that the author did not have to rely on sources. The most likely date is about 350 BCE; that is, about two generations after the latest date suggested for Ezra's journey to Jerusalem, 398 BCE (Ezra 7:8 says that Ezra went up from Babylon in the seventh tear of Artaxerxes, king of Persia. There were two kings of that name: Artaxerxes 1 (464–424 BCE) and Artaxerxes 2 (404–359BCE). (For a discussion on the question of when Ezra went to Jerusalem see a commentary on Ezra and Nehemiah.)

Questions

1. 1 and 2 Chronicles have no history of the northern Kingdom. Why?
2. In what way is the picture of David in 1 and 2 Chronicles different from that in the Deuteronomic history?
3. In your own words say why the Chronicler wrote his work and what traditions were important to him.

6
Being Responsible to God

*§The prophets * The historical situation and their response * The source of their message * Their aims * Discussion of Amos, Hosea, Isaiah 1 to 39, Micah, Zephaniah, Nahum, Habakkuk*

Bible readings: Isaiah 6–9, 31–35

Almost one third of the Old Testament is devoted to the books of the prophets. This emphasises the importance of the material, which derives from the prophets and their disciples. They were significant in the development of the understanding of God's relationship between God and the nation Israel. This importance is confirmed by the fact that the prophetic writings were the second major section of the Old Testament to gain authority as Scripture, around 200 BCE. The Torah was first around 444 BCE followed by the books Joshua to 2 Kings (known in the Hebrew division of the scriptures as the Former Prophets), Isaiah to Malachi (Latter Prophets), and last were the writings around 100 BCE. Each of these major divisions contained very early material gathered over the centuries.

Before we discuss the prophetic books we will look briefly at the prophets—who they were, the period in Israel's history when they were active, their place in Israel's life, and the relationship between prophet and Book.

The prophets

The first thing for us to notice is that Israel had many more prophets than the fifteen whose names are preserved in connection with the prophetic books. The books which talk about Israel's history after they enter the land, tell us of others who performed important tasks at various times in Israel's history. People such as Gad (2 Sam 24:11–14) and Nathan (2 Sam 7:1–17; 12:1–15; 1 Kgs 1) who were prophets in David's court: Ahijah of Shiloh (1 Kgs 11:26–9) who rejected Solomon and designated Jeroboam to be king over ten of the twelve tribes of Israel: Micaiah ben Imlah (1 Kgs 22) who spoke God's word of judgment on Ahab: Elijah and Elisha (1 Kgs 1–2 Kgs 13) who opposed the apostasy of the kings of their time and so influenced the course of Israel's history. In addition to these, Abraham (Gen 20:7), Moses (Deut 18: 15–22) and Samuel (I Sam 3:20) are called prophets. Indeed, Moses is presented as the model of what a prophet of Israel should be like (Deut 18:15–19). When we look at the prophetic role of these three great characters of the Old Testament we see the main tasks of the prophet—to speak the word of God as it was communicated to them (Moses, Deut 18:18–22; Samuel, I Sam 3:19–4:I) so that Israel would know what God required, and to intercede with God when the people were in need (Abraham in Gen 20:7,17; Moses in Exod 32:11–14, 31–4; Samuel in I Sam 12:19). The first task is illustrated many times in the prophetic books, while the second appears in Jeremiah 37 in which Jeremiah was requested by the king to pray for the people in a time of great trouble (Jer 37:1–10), and in a negative sense in Jeremiah (11:14–17) and Ezekiel (14:3) where the prophets were forbidden by God to pray for the people.

The title 'prophet' should not make us think that all prophets were the same. Each was an individual who retained their individuality as they exercised their prophetic ministry (there were male and female prophets). The prophets were committed to the task of helping Israel to know God's way and walk in it: each prophet brought to the task elements of their own personality and background. We must not jump to conclusions about the details of a prophet's life, but it is clear that Hosea was familiar with the ways of prophets and priests (Hos 4:4–10), and bakers (Hosea 7:4), while Amos knew rural life and the market place (Amos 7:14, 8:4–6). Jeremiah was from a priestly family from the tribe of Benjamin in the area around the village in Anathoth (Jer 1:1). He knew of his ancestor Rachel and therefore it was quite natural to use the tradition of Rachel's weeping (Jer 31:15). Rachel was the mother of Benjamin, the youngest son of Jacob. Ezekiel was also from a priestly family and was among the first group of people deported to Babylon in 597 BCE (Ezek 1:1). These prophets knew the traditions of their people, which played an important part in their proclamations.

There were many more prophets than these who are named in the Old Testament. In addition, there were bands of prophets who behaved in unusual ways, such as those who met Saul when he was searching for his father's asses (I Sam 10:10). In the time of Ahab and Jezebel when Elijah was active, there were prophets of Baal and prophets of

God, and between the two groups there was bitter competition (I Kgs 18 4, 20–40). 1 Kings 22 tells us about the kings of Israel and Judah consulting 400 prophets of God on the advisability of going to war with Syria. Micaiah ben Imlah was also consulted and he gave the kings a different word from God. Micaiah's word was shown to be the true word because it was fulfilled (I Kgs 22:28, 34–4.0). When Elijah handed over his prophetic duties to Elisha they visited Bethel near Jericho, where they were met by the 'sons of the prophets' (2 Kgs 2:2–5).

Hosea and Jeremiah condemned false prophets (Hos 4:5; Jer 23:9–22), and Jeremiah was in disagreement with prophets who said that the exiles would soon return from Babylon (Jeremiah 27:14–22 See also Jer 29:1, 29–32). The oracles we have in the prophetic books are those that came from prophets who were recognised as people who spoke on behalf of God. This recognition came through demonstration that the word spoken by the prophet was fulfilled by God, for example, in Jeremiah's case, he prophesied the death of Hannah which occurred within the year as Jeremiah had proclaimed (Jer 28:15–17).

Another important characteristic of the prophets is that they were called by God to be special communicators of God's word. An account of the call is given in the case of some prophets and not others (Isa 6, Jer 1:4–10, Eze 1:1–3:15, I Sam 3). The account in Amos 7:14–15, which is not so detailed, almost certainly refers to a call experience. Hosea 1–3 may refer to such an experience, as may Habakkuk 2. From these examples we see that the prophets did not seek to become prophets. They were overawed by the experience and the responsibility, but they were, as a result of the experience, convinced of their call and filled with an overwhelming sense of God's presence with them (see especially Jer: 8 and Ezek 3:10).

The time of the prophets

It will be seen from what has been said that people who were called to be prophets, appeared over a wide time span in Israel's history—from Abraham right through monarchy, during and after the exile, with Haggai, Zechariah and Malachi. However, the major period of prophetic activity was that of the monarchy, the exilic and early post-exilic periods.

During this time Israel faced many problems as she struggled to maintain a place in the land of Canaan. The major problem, as the prophets saw it, was loyalty to God. They understood that the relationship with God depended on Israel remaining loyal and obedient to the God who was constantly gracious and faithful. The problem presented itself in two ways—religious loyalty and political loyalty, although it is often hard to separate the two.

The temptation to worship other gods was always present. Israel was surrounded by people who worshipped other gods and who made claims for their gods which were attractive to the people of Israel. In particular, the gods of the Canaanites, the people who were in the land before Israel, presented a special attraction. They were gods of agriculture who, if properly worshipped, it was believed, guaranteed the produce of the land. For Israel the temptation was to take over this worship and incorporate it into to worship of God. Its prophets rejected this and proclaimed God's judgment on the people. However, the people succumbed to the temptation to worship local gods. The basis of the prophet's message was that God, was Creator and God over the whole earth. It was God who provided all that Israel had by way of food, clothing and wealth. Therefore, Yahweh was the only one to be worshipped. Hosea 2:8–9 gives a plain statement of this in a passage in which Israel is charged as a faithless wife who has gone after other providers, and so forsaken God. See also Jeremiah 2: 26–8.

The prophets proclaimed that loyalty to God meant worshipping Yahweh alone. God was not replaceable with any other forms of divinity, nor would other gods be tolerated as part of the people's worship life. The relationship with God could be maintained only as long as Israel accepted Yahweh as her only god (see Exod 20:3–6). The method of expressing this loyalty was very important to the prophets. It was not just a matter of worship at shrines or temples, it was also a matter of living in accordance with God's laws and commandments. For Israel the relationship with God was intended to be reflected in the people's relationship with each other. So Hosea condemned the people because 'There is no faithfulness or kindness, and no knowledge of God in the land; there is swearing, lying, killing, stealing and committing adultery; they break all bounds and murder follows murder' (Hos 4:1b–2. See also Exod 20:13–17; Amos 2:6–7). The consequence of this, the prophet proclaimed, was God's judgment and punishment on his people (Hos 4:3; See also Isa 1:24–26).

Political loyalty involved Israel's trust in God. Israel was placed between the great the powers and wealth of Egypt and the African continent, and [between] Mesopotamia and the riches of the east, so that nearly all trade and military forces passed through her land. Thus, for most of her history, Israel was under threat from some powerful neighbour. In order to protect herself from these threats Israel made treaties with other nations. The prophets condemned these treaties for two reasons. First, by making an alliance with a foreign power Israel was showing her lack of faith in God, who was her provider and protector. So Isaiah took God's word to Ahaz that he should not seek Assyrian aid against Syria and Israel who were threatening Judah. Rather, he should trust God (Isa 7:1–17). Hosea pictured Israel as a silly, senseless bird, calling to Egypt and Assyria; but this will not save her for she had betrayed her God (Hos 7:11–13. See also Ezek 16:24–29). One form of faithlessness was characterised as 'playing the harlot' with Egypt and Assyria. Alliances and treaties were not just inadequate means of dealing with their problem, which was a denial of God and would be treated as such by God.

The second charge the prophets made was that Israel did not understand her situation. She thought of it as a purely political problem involving the power play of the nations. The prophets saw the threats posed by the nation as the work of God, therefore no treaty could save Israel. God had raised up the threatening power to be an instrument of punishment because of Israel's faithlessness and disloyalty. Even the nation with whom the treaty was made would be God's instrument of punishment (Jer 21:3–14; Isa 3:1–3).

When the pre-exilic prophet's words were fulfilled and Israel was taken into exile in Babylon, the prophetic task was one of reconstruction. First, they had to help Israel understand the exile both as punishment [both] for past disobedience, and an opportunity to repent. If Israel repented God would forgive them and renew the relationship with them (eg Jer 3:12–14; Ezek 34:11–31). Another task was that of convincing the people that God was in control and that God would restore them to their homeland (Isa 40–55). Finally, those who returned to Jerusalem needed the stirring words of the prophets Haggai and Zechariah to persuade them to rebuild the temple destroyed in 587 BCE (Hagi 1–2; Zech 1–8).

The source of the prophets' message

It was abundantly clear that these prophets, whose records we have in the Scriptures, believed they received their messages from God to communicate to the nation. God inspired them and enabled them to understand not only what was happening in the world round about them, but also to see its significance for their relationship with Yahweh. Two important factors were involved in this.

First, the prophets were well aware of what was happening in Israel and the world about them. They perceived how the people of Israel behaved from day to day. They saw extortion, greed, and ill-treatment of the poor (Amos 2:6–7; 4:1-3; 8:4–6), religion practised as a duty to be fulfilled at the cult places, but denied in relations with others (Jer 7:1–Is; Amos 8:4–6; Mic 6:6–8). People were involved in worship which had no place in the religion of God (Hos 4:12–14; Jer 2:26–28): injustice in the law courts (Isa 1:23, Mic 3:9–11): intrigue in the selection of kings (Hos 8:4): the leaders of Israel sought alliances with foreign powers (Isa 7:1–17, Hos 7:11–13), and finally a despondent people in exile (Isa 40:27). Furthermore, the prophets were well aware of what the nations about them were doing. Amos and Hosea knew of the threat posed by Assyria. Consequently, their statements about the coming destruction were made with confidence. Isaiah could see that the alliance between Syria and Israel posed no real threat to Judah because both nations would be swallowed up by Assyria. He also saw that Assyria posed a threat to Judah, which could only be averted by trust in God.

Second, the prophets were well aware of the traditions of their people, which told of the relationship with God and its requirements of the people. God had been faithful, throughout their journey from the time of Abram. This faithfulness and care was known in all the acts of God in the provision of progeny to their release from Egypt. Prominent are the traditions related to creation (Amos 4:13, Isa 40:12-31; Jer 31:35–37), the exodus from Egypt (Amos 3:1-2; Hos 11:1, Isa 11:16, Ezek 20:5–10, 34-36), wilderness wandering (Amos 2:10, Isa 40:3–8; Jer 2:2–3, Ezek 20:10-24, 35-36), settlement in the Promised Land (Hos 1:4–5, 7:3–7, 8:4, 13:10–11, Ezek 16:1–14) and the monarchy (Hos 8:4; Ezek 20:3–3). The message of the prophets, whether of judgment and punishment (Hos 4:1–3), or hope (Isa 40:12–31), came when they considered the situation of the people in terms of the knowledge of God conveyed in these traditions.

Another source of the prophets' message was the words of prophetic predecessors. We can see that what a prophet said was remembered and preserved. The books we have in Scripture demonstrate this, as do the accounts concerning the prophets in the Deuteronomic

History, for example, those of Elijah and Elisha. Some of this material, the work of a proven prophet, was taken up by later prophets and applied to new situations. A good example of this is the use of the terms adultery and harlotry in the proclamation against apostasy. It begins with Hosea (2:1–13, 3, 4:11–18), and is taken up and developed in Jeremiah (2:20–25; 3:14, 6–10), and further developed by Ezekiel (Ezek 16 and 23). Similarly, Jeremiah takes up Hosea's other understanding of the relationship, that of parent and child (Hos 11:1–7; Jer 3:21–22).

We must not think of the prophets as unimaginative copiers. If we look at how they used the traditions that came to them, we will see that the traditions were applied with imagination and skill at the direction of God.

The aim of the prophets

It is easy when reading the prophetic books to get the impression that the prophets were negative people whose main aim was to enjoy the suffering of their people, both present and future. Even worse is to see them as people who represented a vindictive God whose triumph would be achieved in the destruction of Israel. Neither of these views does justice to the prophets or to God. The prophets' aim was to be positive—to help their people to continue their part of the relationship with God, not to see it ended by the destruction of the people. The prophets' hope was that the people would recognise the truth of what was said and repent. From their point of view, fulfilment of their prophecies would be repentance. Because the people did not repent, fulfilment had to be in the destruction the prophets said must come.

The major task of the prophets was to get the people of Israel to make a decision—to decide to accept the gracious gifts that God had given them and to respond with obedience and faithfulness. The prophets could not make the decision for the people, but they used all their persuasive powers, skill, and imagination to enable the people to make the best decisions for their well-being. They were not naive, as Isaiah 6:9–12 shows, but they were called by God, and even though the cry, 'How long, 0 Lord?' (Isa 6:11) may have been wrung from them, they did as God commanded them.

The prophet and the prophetic books

It is clear from the form that is present in the prophetic books that much of the material in them was first delivered by spoken word. This is especially the case with the material in poetic form. In some instances these sayings were written down by the prophet, or written by a disciple. Isaiah and Jeremiah record instances in which, because their words were not heeded, they had them written down. The purpose in doing this [action] was to ensure that the prophet's word stood as a witness to the people that God's word had been delivered to them and they would recognise it when it was fulfilled (Isaiah 8:16–18, Jeremiah 36:1–8). In this way small collections of prophetic sayings came into existence.

There is evidence that the prophets had friends and supporters who preserved their words thus ensuring that the prophets' oracles would continue to influence the life of the people. The prophetic groups associated with Elijah aid Elisha are the most natural sources for the material about those prophets. Isaiah mentions the disciples among whom the prophet's words were 'sealed'. Baruch, who wrote at Jeremiah's dictation, may have been a public scribe, but it is more likely that he was a friend and disciple of the prophet. His writings may have supplemented those of the prophet himself, or the two may have existed independently.

Collections of prophetic material preserved in this way became the inspiration for further prophetic words. We have seen this in the use of Hosea's words by Jeremiah and Ezekiel. At other times, the new prophetic words became part of the tradition of the original prophet. To some extent this is true for all the prophetic books. The process may have gone on for generations. During and after the exile, the separate collections were brought together into four books—Isaiah, Jeremiah, Ezekiel, and the books of the Twelve. At this point in the process the material was collected into blocks of texts that were focused on a particular area. For example, oracles concerning foreign nations were placed together (Isa 13–23, Jer 46–51, Ezek 27–32), and an initial decision made about the ordering for the collection of the Twelve Prophets. The latter is not in chronological order. It is probable that the 'hope' oracles were placed in their present positions at this time. Their incorporation highlights the point that in spite of, or perhaps because of, the judgment, which had befallen Israel there was still hope for the people: God still had a purpose for them.

The purpose of the books is therefore different from that of the original prophetic delivery. As complete collections they bear witness to the fulfilment of the prophetic words, and they explain the disaster, which came upon Israel. The major reason given for their time in Babylon was the people's own disobedience. Within the covenant terms of a relationship with God, it meant that God had to try to bring them to the point of repentance. The extraordinary feature was God's grace, which had delayed the end for so long. The prophets demonstrated that God warned them over and over again, and so the words of the prophets, as we have them in these books, make the past intelligible in a theological sense—in terms of the relationship between God and Israel. The books now serve both as an explanation for the exile and as a warning for the future. The hope passages point them to the continuing purpose God has for them if they will turn to and obey God (Hos 14, Amos 9:9–14, Mic 7:18–20). Consequently, the word of judgment in Ezekiel 1–33 turns to promise in chapter 34 and concludes with a description of a restored and renewed Israel. This restoration makes the temple its centre, to which God's glory has returned, indicating the presence of God is once more in Jerusalem. (Ezek 40–48).

Amos

Bible reading: Amos 3–8

Amos was the first of the prophets about whom an independent collection of writings was made. The traditions and sayings of earlier prophets have been preserved in the Deuteronomic History. It is clear that those concerning Elijah and Elisha had an independent existence, but they have not survived in that form. It is interesting to note that apart from the references to Isaiah in 2 Kings 18:13–20:19 (parallels Isa 36:1–39:8); the Deuteronomic History does not mention the 'writing' prophets. However, since the Deuteronomic Historian was vitally interested in prophesy and its fulfilment (1 Kgs 21:23–2 Kgs 9:36), it suggests that he was aware of the prophetic collections, which he considered complementary to his own work.

Although we have a Book which bears the name of Amos, we do not know very much about him as a person. As with the other prophetic books, the purpose of the Book was not to present a biosgraphy of the prophet, but to present a message that he proclaimed.

The emphasis is on 'the words of Amos' (1:1). Such personal comments as we have are intended to help communicate the message. They place the prophet in a period of Israel's history, which shows him as a man who was called by God to speak Yahweh's word to the nation, Israel.

Amos described himself as 'a herdsman, and a dresser of sycamore trees . . .' (7:14) when challenged by Amaziah, the priest of Bethel. In the heading to the Book it is said that he 'was among the shepherds of Tekoa . . .' (1:1). Amos is portrayed as a man of the land who was called especially to be a prophet. There is probably some recollection of his call in the words 'the Lord took me from following the flock, and the Lord said to me, "Go, prophesy to my people Israel."'(7:15). However, it is not the developed 'call' that we find in the later prophets such as Jeremiah. It was that call and commission which impelled Amos to prophesy to Israel. That he was neither a prophet nor the son of a prophet (7:14) was not important but God said 'Go', and he went. In the period before the exile the Northern Kingdom was known as Israel, which came to be the name adopted by the Babylon returnees to Jerusalem after 538 BCE.

The second thing we note is that Amos came from Tekoa, a small town to the south of Bethlehem in Judah. This is significant because his only recorded prophetic activity was confined to Bethel, in the northern kingdom. Therefore, he was to some extent a foreigner, telling the people of the north that God had judged them and would soon punish them. Although the two kingdoms had much in common, they were separate kingdoms and in many instances—rivals. Something of this can be seen in Amaziah's advice to Amos to return to Judah and prophesy there, not in Bethel (7:12–13). Amaziah was telling Amos that he did not belong in Bethel. Furthermore, he claimed that the true way of serving God was experienced in Israel, not in the kingdom of Judah, which was ruled by the house of David.

Alongside this difference, is the relationship both kingdoms had with the God who brought them out Egypt and into the land. Amos was able to speak to Israel in terms of this knowledge of God because they shared similar traditions of the God who chose this people, gave them the land in which they dwelt, and expected them to respond with obedience.

Third, we are told that Amos prophesied in Israel: 'in the days of Uzziah, King of Judah and in the days of Jeroboam the son of Joash,

King of Israel, two years before the earthquake' (1:1). We do not know exactly when the earthquake occurred, but it was toward the end of the reigns of these two Kings, around 750 BCE. Both Israel and Judah had enjoyed almost fifty years prosperity and freedom from the interference of powerful neighbours. Many people in Israel had grown wealthy, but at the expense of the poor. In addition, they had become complacent in the observance of their religion, with cultic activity divorced from the life of business, commerce and pleasure. But all this was about to end, said Amos. God would soon judge and punish the people of the Northern Kingdom and sweep them away into oblivion. Amos did not refer to the Assyrians by name, but they were regaining their strength, which had waned in the previous century. Soon, they would move west and become a mighty empire once again. Amos saw them as the instrument of God's punishment.

The Book

When we look at the Book of Amos we see its focal point is a number of visions that came to the prophet. These provided the point of commencement for the oracles of indictment and judgment against the Northern Kingdom. These indictments call on those traditions about God that were well known to the people.

The visions which the Lord showed to Amos—locusts eating the ground bare (7:1), the land devoured by fire (7:4), a wall with a plumb line against it (7:7), a basket of summer fruit (8:1), and the Lord standing beside the altar (9:1)—are central to the proclamation of the Book. Each of these visions proclaims the end of the Northern Kingdom as a people. After each of the first two visions, the prophet intercedes with God on behalf of the Northern Kingdom, and the judgment is turned aside. In the first two visions God judged the people but, because of God's compassion, the people's punishment was reversed: God repented (7:2b–3, 5–6). After the third and fourth visions God refuses to turn back another time, instead the stark terms of the punishment are pronounced (8:2b–3, 9:1). The vision of the summer fruit (8:1–2) gives the theme for the Book. The Hebrew word for summer fruit is similar to that for 'end', which suggested to Amos that the end would soon come for the ten tribes in the North. God will judge and 'the end has come upon my people Israel' (8:2). Amos was called to be a prophet to announce this end.

The reasons why God will bring an end to the ten tribes in the Northern Kingdom are given in the oracles that make up the major part of the Book. These oracles analyse Israel's life as response to God. The method is to portray Israel's life in such a way that a mirror is held up before the people so they can see their image, which is in stark contradiction to that of a righteous people.

The oracles begin with a series of eight statements of judgment against the nations—seven against Israel's neighbours and one against Israel herself (1:3–2:8). They say two things: first, that Israel is considered to be like the sinful nations that surrounded her, and therefore liable to the same judgment and punishment (9:8): second, the nations are subject to God. God is Lord not only of Israel, but of all nations. Although they do not acknowledge Yahweh they are still to be accountable to the God of Israel. (9:7). A further sign of this is God's action in bringing up an unnamed nation to surround Israel and plunder her (3:11).

The main part of the Book contains oracles against Israel. These are concerned with the public life of the people. They show a society divided into two classes of people—the wealthy, who had all the power, and the poor, who, being at the mercy of the wealthy, were downtrodden. This was seen in the way justice was administered, the way the two classes lived, and the way in which religion was practised.

The statements against injustice in the courts are very bitter. The court was the place where all citizens should have their rights upheld. This was especially so for the poor who had no other means for redress of wrongs and the demonstration of justice. However, it was not like that: there was little evidence of justice. The courts were corrupt and an instrument of oppression in the hands of the wealthy and powerful (5:7,12). They were used as a means to rob the poor and enslave them (5:10–12). One of the conditions set by God for the future was the need 'to establish justice in the gate . . .' which was the traditional place for legal proceedings to be conducted.

The responsibility of the wealthy for the condition of Israel's society is shown in graphic pictures. They 'sell the righteous for silver, and the needy for a pair of shoes—they trample the head of the poor into the dust . . .' (2:6b–7a, 8:6): 'you who trample upon the poor' (8:4); 'you who oppress the poor, who crush the needy' (4:1). In contrast with the poor and needy, the wealthy lived lives of selfish indulgence. They had ivory beds, drank wine in bowls, ate lambs and calves, sang idle songs, anointed themselves with oil, and went about unconcerned with the ruin of the nation (6:4–6). But the prophet said 'they shall now be the first of those to go into exile,' (6:7). Wealthy women (the 'cows of Bashan') indulged themselves in luxury at the expense of the poor. They too had been judged and would be punished (4:1–3).

The religion of the people is also condemned. It had become a celebration of security for the wealthy, but by its very practice it was a further self indulgence (4:4–5) and an affront to God (5:21–23). The people were told to seek God, but not at the shrines of Bethel, Gilgal or Beersheba (5:4–5). Their attitude to religion is shown in their desire to get the festivals of the new moon and Sabbath over quickly in order that they could get back to oppression and making money (8:5–6). The charge stated that the people had misunderstood the very foundation of their religion, which was based on a relationship with God. Within this relationship God not only required worship, but also right conduct and responsible action by everyone. Consequently, when the day of the Lord came, it would bring, not blessing and fulfilment, but mourning and lamentation (8:10).

There are two elements of hope in the Book. The first is that, on hearing the prophetic word, the Northern Kingdom will heed the warning and respond to God with faithfulness and obedience (5:4,6,14–15). As they stand, these are words of judgment on the cult of Israel, but they have implicit within them the possibility of returning to the covenant relationship with God. The overwhelming negative character of the remainder of the Book (except for 9:11–15) makes such hope only a theoretical possibility.

The hope offered in 9:11–15 is genuine. It is an expression of God's purpose for the nation. It looks forward to a time when the relationship would be renewed and the people would live in rebuilt cities and a replanted land. This passage belongs to the last stage of the development of the Book. Its purpose is to point beyond the destruction that has come upon Israel, in order that those who remained may put their trust in God.

The traditions, which underlie the oracles in this Book, are those of the relationship between God and Israel. There is no mention of a covenant, but there is explicit reference to the traditions associated with the choice of Israel by God who brought the people out of Egypt, led them through the wilderness, and gave them possession of the land (2:9–10). In addition, God is referred to as 'your God' (4:12), which brings with it the responsibility to be obedient, 'You only have I known of all the families of the earth; therefore I will punish you for all your iniquities' (3:2, 9:7–8).

These traditions, which tell of God's actions in forming Israel and establishing the tribes in the Promised Land, become the basis of indictment and judgment on Israel. Every statement of what God did in the past becomes a reminder of how they had betrayed the relationship by immoral activity toward their own community, and meaningless worship to God. A faithful and righteous response was required of Israel, which they refused to give.

The traditions of prophetic warning are recalled (2:11–12). As we have seen, Amos was not the first prophet to be called by God. Other prophets in Israel's history had warned the people of the consequences of their failure to accept responsibility as the people of God. This too becomes a charge against the people who denied prophets and Nazarites the opportunity to fulfil their calling (2:12).

Another important tradition is that of 'the Day of the Lord' (5:18–19). Its origin and exact nature are unknown, but from what we can gather from the various references to it in the prophet literature, it was seen as a great day of glory and triumph for God, and, therefore for the nation. Consequently, the people longed for 'the Day of the Lord' to arrive. In Amos the tradition is taken and turned against the Northern Kingdom. The triumph and glory of God would be at Israel's expense, rather than for its benefit, for it was unfaithful to God. We see here an example of a significant literary function in the work of the prophets—they change the understanding of an accepted tradition so that it spoke in a new way to Israel. The Day of the Lord became a day of judgment rather than a participation in God's glory.

The Book of Amos presents us with prophetic judgment on a people who were unfaithful in their relationship with God. Their faithlessness was shown in their neglect of God's requirements for their lives. Their relationships with others were governed by selfishness and greed, which resulted in perverted justice, oppression and robbery of the poor. Their worship was false. The only possible end for such a people was destruction, which would take place in a military catastrophe at the hands of a neighbouring power.

However, this would not be the end. Those who had been through the punishment could trust God there would be a remnant who would be renewed. The Book is thus a warning to the generations down the ages that God requires a response of obedience. Furthermore, it is a word of hope to those who are suffering judgment that God will indeed restore a remnant of those in exile.

Hosea

Bible reading: Hosea 1–4, 11–13

Hosea was active as a prophet during the years of rapid decline of Israel. The heading to the Book puts his activity in the period from King Uzziah to King Hezekiah in Judah, which would be from about 750 BCE–725 BCE. King Jeroboam of Israel is also mentioned, which may mean that Hosea's activity was concentrated in the period of his reign. We are told that his father was named Beeri, and that he was active in Northern Kingdom, which was probably his home nation.

Our knowledge of the prophet's life ends there although many attempts have been made to reconstruct the story of his marriage from the material in chapters one to three. It must be said that the information is inadequate for such an attempt. Hosea may have been drawing on the experience of his own marriage, but we cannot be certain of that. Even if he was, we cannot assume that the woman described as an adulteress in Hos 3:1 is Gomer, whom he married in Hos 1. What we can say with certainty is that the idea of the relationship between God and the nation is paralleled to that of a marriage and is used with particular literary force in Hosea.

The Book

The Book of Hosea divides naturally into two parts. Chapters 1 to 3 deal with the God–Israel relationship by means of symbolic actions related to marriage, and chapters 4 to 14 are a collection of oracles, which contain mainly messages of judgment and threat against Israel.

Of major concern to Hosea is the faithfulness or unfaithfulness of the people in the relationship with God. The basic expressions of the relationship are in terms of a family: husband and wife (Hos 1–3) and father and son (Hos 11). Accordingly, the relationship is not only a legal one, but also a very personal one. This brings it into the area in which such terms as love and forgiveness may be used. It also heightens the sense of betrayal when one party is disloyal to the relationship.

To a large extent the Book of Hosea complements that of Amos. We have an emphasis of social justice in Amos while Hosea has less focus on this aspect of the relationship, but is very concerned with the worship life of Israel. He condemns the nation's attempts to solve its problems by political means. Because Israel has been faithless in all areas of her relationship she will suffer judgment and punishment.

The judgment and the rejection of Israel are given in the symbolic naming Hosea's children in Hosea 1. The first is named Jezreel because God would punish the house of Jehu for the massacre of the house of Ahab at Jezreel (Hos 1:4–6). This judgment is on both the dynasty of Jehu, which ended with the assassination of Zedekiah, the son of Jeroboam, and on the monarchy as a whole. There is in this statement a reversal of the traditional interpretation of the action of Jehu who wiped out the house of Ahab and removed the Baal gods from worship areas (2 Kgs 10:4–5), actions viewed with approval and as a fulfilment of the prophetic word of Elijah in 2 Kings 10:10. Furthermore, by naming his son Jezreel, Hosea judged and condemned the Northern Kingdom's sad record with its kings, many of whom were assassinated.

The second child is named 'Not pitied', because God will no longer have pity on the monarchy of the Northern Kingdom, refusing to forgive them (1:6), and the third child is named 'Not my people', for they are no longer God's people (1:9). The naming of these two children can be compared with the vision Amos had of the final days of the Northern Kingdom because of the nation's betrayal of the relationship with God. Through these symbolic actions God pronounces the end of the relationship. The name, 'Not my people', with its explanation, is a reversal of the traditional statement of the relationship 'You shall be my people, I will be your God' (Exod 6:7; Jere 24:7, 30:22, 31:1,33).

Most of the remainder of the Book sets out the charges and judgments that have brought about the end of Israel. First, the ten tribes, which make up the Northern Kingdom, do not know God. The evidence for this is stated a number of times in the Book. It is seen in the lack of faithfulness and loving kindness by the people (4:1), and in the way in which people acted toward one another with swearing, lying, killing, stealing, committing adultery and murder (4:2). The priest and prophet had rejected the knowledge of God and forgotten the Torah. This would lead to the rejection of the priests and prophets, and the destruction of the people because they did 'know God' (4:4–6).

This 'knowledge of God' is not some theoretical or philosophic 'knowledge'. Rather, it is a disposition toward God, which is brought about by knowing God through experience. The people know who God is and what God has done for the nation. The term explains the traditions that conveyed to Israel the very basis of their relationship to God. Therefore, it was fundamental to their existence. To have lost this knowledge, and forgotten their God, resulted in a betrayal of that relationship. Part of the tragedy seen by Hosea is that Israel did not recognise their betrayal and loss.

According to the charge by Hosea it was Lack of knowledge of God that led Israel to practise the cult associated with the baals, the gods of the Canaanites, who were thought to be responsible for the fruitfulness of the land. In Hosea 2, as part of the symbolic actions related to marriage, Israel is charged with being an adulteress and a harlot. She has gone after lovers (the baals) because she thought they gave her the things of life—bread and water, wool, flax, and oil (2:1–6). She did know that God gave her these things, as well as her silver and gold (2:8). Like an adulteress Israel will be punished by the loss of her husband's (God's) gifts, by exposure to her lovers, and by the removal of Baal worship (2:9–13).

Charges of harlotry and playing the harlot are found in other places in which Israel is accused of association with the cult of Baal. A series of short oracles in 4:7–16 shows how the 'spirit of harlotry' had led them astray (4:12, 5:4). They were involved in the fertility cults of the Baal religion in which excess wine was consumed, they sought oracles from things made of wood and sacrificed and made offerings at places where Baal was worshipped.

Use of the terms 'harlotry' and 'forsaking God to play the harlot' express vividly abhorrence of the Baal fertility cult, which denies the close relationship that ought to exist between God and Israel. So many aspects of the Baal cult, with its sexual rites and other acts of sympathetic magic, were an attempt to manipulate God, but were contrary to the way of God. By their participation in these practices Israel was unfaithful to the God who had given so much to the people of Israel. The Ten Commandments stated they had to worship Yahweh alone and expressly forbade worship of images (Exod 20:3–4). To worship anyone or anything other than God was the most heinous of sins.

Israel's disloyalty is also portrayed by a father and son relationship in the beautiful poem in Hosea 11:1–7. This brief poem recalls the history of the relationship between God and Israel. God loved the child who was rescued from slavery in Egypt, but instead of gratitude and loyalty Israel turned from God to Baal. This occurred in spite of the way God called and cared. God's affection for Israel was shown by the caring treatment of the child when young: Yahweh taught Ephraim (another name for the Northern Kingdom) to walk and led them with cords of compassion and bands of love (11:3–4). But such love could not ignore the betrayal by Israel. God had to act against them in order to try to make them return to faithfulness, otherwise they would be returned to slavery (11:5–7). The poem acknowledges the great tradition that God formed Israel when the people were brought out from Egypt. Now, by proclaiming Israel's return to Egypt, the tradition is reversed, Israel no longer belongs to God.

Condemnation of the political activity of Israel was also based on betrayal of the basic structure of Israel as God's people. Israel had a tradition of involvement by the prophets in the designation of kings, who gave God's word to the kings, as the accounts of Elijah and Elisha show. This tradition was ignored in the last years of the northern kingdom, at least in the designation kings. For this Israel was condemned (8:4). Those who surrounded the king received special condemnation because they were not loyal (7:3–7,16). Finally, the monarchy itself is condemned because it caused Israel to trust in kings and princes, arms and warfare (13:10–11, 10:13–15).

Alliances with foreign powers were also condemned as a betrayal of God because of their ignorance and refusal to trust God. Again Israel's actions show lack of knowledge. Israel saw the answer to its problems in political actions and sought alliances with those who could strengthen and protect it. But the truth was God had turned against the Northern Kingdom and no alliance could protect it from God's this wrath (8:10, 5:13–14; 7:8–11; 12:1). The betrayal of God is again is demonstrated by reference to marriage and personal relationship, in which hiring allies is the same as hiring lovers (8:9).

The means by which judgment would come to Israel is given only in general terms. It could certainly be military assault as the descriptions of Hosea 5:8–13 and 10:14–15 indicate. Assyria is mentioned in connection with this (5:1, 11:5), but so too is Egypt, and in particular a return to Egypt (9:3, 11:5), which suggests that punishment by destruction and loss of freedom is the important factor, and not the identification of the instrument that God may choose.

It is not possible to say with certainty when the statements of hope became part of the Book of Hosea. They were probably added later, but they have an important place in the Book (1:10–11 2:14–23, 3:1–5, 11:10–11, 14:1–9). Hosea 2:14–23 speaks of renewal coming to Israel when God returns her to the wilderness, which reminds her that her initial response was one of faithfulness to the covenant with Yahweh. In response to this reminder the people of the Northern Kingdom will return and be faithful to the one God. She will renounce Baal (Hos 2:16–17) and, in a reversal of the divorce proceedings (Hos 2:1–13), she will become betrothed to God and will live in faithful relationship (Hos 2:20). There follows in verses 21–23 a reversal of the symbolic names in chapter 1. God will have pity on 'Not pitied' and 'Not my people' will become my people (Hos 2:23). We see in these verses how traditions, which spoke about the end of Israel have been taken up and reinterpreted to speak now of renewal. It will be noted that the important factors are the initiative and action of God which are consistently portrayed, and to which Israel will respond.

Chapter 3 envisages a name of deprivation, which God will impose on Israel to cause her to return (repent), and so be restored. Again this is a reinterpretation of the oracles, which charge Israel with adultery and harlotry. It shows that God continued to care for this disobedient people who must be punished, but who will be restored and renewed if they repent. The Book concludes with a call to Israel to return to God (repent) and an assurance that God will renew them (14:4–9).

Hosea draws heavily on the traditions of Israel in reminding the people of the special relationship with God, its requirements and the consequences of failure to observe those requirements. The choice of Israel in the deliverance from Egypt is of special importance. It was in Egypt that God took the initiative (11:1, 12:9,1), and because of Israel's disobedience Israel will return Egypt (9:3, 11:5). The punishment is a reversal of the blessing.

The covenant tradition is also important in Hosea. It underlies the idea that the relationship is both like a marriage, and like that of father and son. It reinforces the statement, 'you are not my people and I am not your God', which is given in positive form in Hosea 2:23. In addition the word covenant is in Hosea 6:7 and 8:1. This is unusual in the prophets. In Hosea it is a reminder that the relationship was formed by God, but Israel had broken it (8:1), and the punishment to come was inevitable as a result of that break.

Hosea called on the wilderness tradition. The wilderness was the place where Israel knew God in a close relationship (13:5), and where it may return to God. It was in the wilderness that the people realised their total dependence on God and it is in this realisation that the relationship may be renewed (2:14).

Traditions about the monarchy in Israel are an important part of the charges made against the nation. They are drawn on to highlight the disobedience of Israel in placing its trust in kings and alliances (1:4–5, 7:3–7).

Finally, Israel was reminded that the prophets had been active in its history, attempting to direct it in the way of the relationship with God. The words, 'By a prophet the Lord brought Israel up from Egypt, and by a prophet he was preserved.' Hosea 12:13 takes up the tradition that Moses was the great prophet who led the people out of Egypt and mediated the law to them (Deut 18:15–22). Many prophets came with God's word of judgment, but Israel did not heed them (6:5, 12:10), therefore judgment on Israel did not come without fair warning. The message of the Book is that God cares for the people, and because of that care their unfaithfulness and their disobedience cannot be ignored. It is for this that they will be judged and punished by Yahweh. However, the care will continue, and if they repent God will forgive and restore them into full covenant relationship. The Book of Hosea is both a warning and a word of hope.

Isaiah 1–39

Bible readings: Isaiah 1, 5, 7, 9, 11, 30, 31

The Book of Isaiah presents us with a good example of bringing together prophetic sayings and traditions round the name of an important figure. It has long been recognised that a change takes place in the Book at the end of chapter 39. The basic point of reference in chapters 1 to 39 is Judah in the second half of the eighth century BCE. From chapter 40 the focus is the exiles in Babylon and the community in Jerusalem in the years immediately after the exile. It has become customary to refer to First Isaiah (1–39), Second Isaiah (40–55), and Third Isaiah (56–66).

Our approach will deal with the three sections in their historical context. First Isaiah is thus placed here, along with the other eighth century prophets. Isaiah 40–55 will be dealt with in connection with the exilic period and 56–66 in connection with the post exilic prophets

The prophet Isaiah of Jerusalem

There is little direct evidence on which to construct a 'life' of the prophet Isaiah, which means we are forced to rely on incidental remarks in the Book. The Book says that his 'vision' extended over the reigns of kings Uzziah, Jotham, Ahaz and Hezekiah, which identifies for later readers the extent of his prophecies. His call to be a prophet of the Lord came in the year of Uzziah's death (Isa 6:1). The exact date of Uzziah's death is unknown, but it was within a few years of 740 BCE. The last events in which Isaiah was involved related to the campaign by Sennacherib of Assyria against Jerusalem in 701 BC His prophetic activity thus extended over a period of at least forty years.

Isaiah's entire prophetic activity was carried out in Jerusalem. The period was an important one for Judah as it saw the decline and fall of Israel (721 BCE) and the extension of Assyrian influence in the area. From 735 BCE onwards, Judah had to contend with the might of Assyria and for much of the time paid tribute to the Assyrians. The situation was difficult for Judah, and Isaiah was called to speak God's word into these times.

From his statements on national affairs and his apparent easy access to the king, it is thought that Isaiah was a person of noble birth and a member of the King's court. Some scholars have suggested that he was a priest based of the account of his call in chapter 6. Isaiah was married and had at least two sons (Isa 7:3, 8:1–4).

The Book

The Book is in a number of parts, which give the impression of being separate collections of material. Isaiah 1–12, and 28–33 consist of oracles and sayings concerning Jerusalem and Judah; Isaiah 13–23 contain oracles against foreign nations; Isaiah 24–7, 34–5 are poems of final judgment and deliverance; Isaiah 36–9 is an historical extract from 2 Kings 18–20 in which Isaiah plays a prominent part.

The main point that comes through each of these sections is that God is sovereign over all the nations of the world, and is in control of all events. This may be seen in many places, but especially in the speeches, which require the people to trust God. That is, they have a choice—either accept God's care for them and God's way, or seek their own way by trusting in themselves or their neighbours. This is especially clear in Isaiah 7:1–14. In the face of a threat from a coalition between Syria and Israel the wise thing to do politically was to seek a powerful ally, such as Assyria. But the wise thing for Judah, who believed in the relationship with God, was to accept that God was with her (Emmanuel, which means God is with us—Isa 7:14, Matt 1:23), and, with trust in God, seek no outside help. In fact, Judah chose to seek Assyrian aid, which brought suffering (2 Kgs 16:5–20).

Such lack of faith brought the charge that Judah was a rebellious nation that sought alliances without regard for God or God's will for them (Isa 30:1–2). The utter futility of their policy is shown in a contrast between the Egyptians and God: 'The Egyptians are human, and not God; [and] their horses are flesh and not spirit' (Isa 31:1–3).

The people were also rebellious when they disregarded God's ways in their dealings with one another. The whole of Isaiah 1 charges the people with rebellion. The nation was so bad that it was called Sodom and Gomorrah, notoriously wicked cities of the ancient world (Isa 1:10, Gen 13:13). Their rebellion was in their false religion. Sacrifices and offerings, observance of festivals, and hands lifted up in prayer were not enough when their hands were full of blood (Isa 1:10–15). What God required was that they should 'cease to do evil, learn to do good, seek justice, rescue the oppressed; defend the orphan, plead for the widow' (Isa 1:16–17).

There is an echo of Hosea when the rebellious city is called a harlot because she is full of injustice and harbours murderers. Her princes were corrupt, and they failed to defend the orphans or take up the cause of widows (Isa 1:21–3). The judgment of God is on this rebellious people. Those who repent will be redeemed, 'But rebels and sinners shall be destroyed together, and those who forsake the Lord shall be consumed' (Isa 1:28).

The theme of judgment and punishment comes through when the tradition of Israel as a vineyard is used in Isaiah 5, in which the yield was only worthless grapes. Because of this the vineyard will be destroyed. In the conclusion, Israel is identified as the vineyard. She will be destroyed because God, 'looked for justice, but, behold, bloodshed; for righteousness, but behold, a cry!' (5:7).

A series of 'woes' in the latter part of chapter 5 shows the condition of society in Judah. There is greed over the desire to gain property (v 8), indulgence in strong drink and no regard for the works of God (vv 11–12), that is, they are unable to discern what God is doing with them. They scoff at God (vv 18–19). They confuse good and evil (v 20). They rely on themselves for wisdom, and not the wisdom of God (v 21), the judges are drunken and they pervert justice (v 23). Not only is this a picture of a society that has broken down, but also it is the denial of God's requirements in the relationship between *God* and Israel. Those who behave in this way cut themselves off from God. They have 'rejected the law of the Lord of hosts, and have despised the word of the Holy One of Israel' (v 24b). They are judged, and in anger God will destroy them (v 25).

In speaking of judgment Isaiah uses the term 'the Day of the Lord' which was also used by Amos. Amos changed the understanding of the term from an announcement of blessing, which the people sought, to the day of God's visitation and punishment. Isaiah uses the term in this latter sense, but he extends it. The Day of the Lord is not only the day of judgment for Israel (Isa 3:18–26, 7:18–25), but is the day of judgment for all that would exalt itself; both in humanity and in nature. In addition, the Day of the Lord is a day of judgment for other nations, for example, Babylon (Isa 13:1–13), and Edom, (Isa 34:8). In this use it takes on a positive sense for Judah. For on that day God will judge those who have afflicted God's people. It will be a day of blessing for God's people (Isa 34:8). This positive sense of the term is a later return to the tradition, which was current in the time of Amos.

The form of punishment for Judah, which is envisaged in Isaiah, is that it will fall to a great army in the future. Judah will be attacked by a great power, which will devastate it, but the initiative for this action is with God. God will call a distant nation and it will come quickly to do this bidding (Isa 5:26, 10:1–4). Assyria is named as the power that will act as God's agent against Judah. It will devastate the people and plunder the land, and leave it like a body shaved with a razor (Isa 10:5–6, 7:20).

Furthermore, God's sovereignty is seen in the oracles against foreign nations. They may have been powerful, and at different times a threat to Judah, but God has proclaimed their end. For example, 'And Babylon, the glory of kingdoms, the splendour and pride of the Chaldeans, will be like Sodom and Gomorrah when God overthrew them.' (Isa 13:19). Interspersed among the oracles about the nations are words addressed to Judah. There is a proclamation of God's judgment upon the people and the destruction of their land, because they have been unfaithful (Isa 17:4–11), but in the main they are words of hope for Judah, as in the scattering of the peoplės who oppress Judah (Isaiah 17:12–14). Return and renewal of the people is proclaimed (Isa 14:1–2)

Hope has an important place in the Book of Isaiah. There are limited passages in Isaiah 1–39. However, there is the hope that is fulfilled when the people recognise that their ways are not God's ways, repent and the punishment is averted (Isa 1:16–19, 27). This is the strong desire of the prophets, but with their knowledge of the people they recognised that hope for Israel had to rest with God, and would be fulfilled only after punishment and repentance.

The return of a remnant is another expression of hope in Isaiah. The original meaning of the term is a 'threat' to Judah, as can be seen in the encounter between Isaiah and Ahaz (Isaiah 7:1–9). The prophet had his son with him whose name, *Shear-yashub*, means 'a remnant shall return'. If Ahaz persisted with his intention to seek the aid of Assyria in view of the threat from the Syria-Israel coalition, Judah would be left with only a remnant. The concept of 'remnant' is used as a threat in oracles against the nations, for example, Babylon, (Isa 14:22), Philistia (Isa: 30) and Moab (Isa 15:9). It is used in both senses of threat and hope, in Isaiah 10:20 and Isaiah 14:22–3. Even when God destroys Judah there will a remnant spared, who will return to God. The hope presented here is based on the recognition that disaster must come to Judah, but not everyone will be destroyed. The remnant will be small, but God will give opportunity for repentance, and God will receive this repentant people (Isa 4:3)

The house of David is a source of hope for Judah. The kings of David's line were of particular importance in the relationship between God and the people, as we see in 2 Sam 7:1–17, 23:1–7, and many of the Psalms (Ps 20, 21, 89). The understanding of this tradition, which the prophet Isaiah inherited from his Jerusalem background, was that, with the everlasting covenant, the king was obliged to maintain the righteousness and well being of his people, and was assured of divine protection and victory. This did not blind the prophet to the deficiencies in the kings of Judah, as the treatment of Ahaz (Isa 7–8) and Hezekiah (Isa 39:1–8) show, but it did lead to the belief that God would use the house of David to save the nation.

The two famous passages which take up this point, Isaiah 9:2–7 and 11:1–9, appear to have been adapted from a liturgy associated either with the birth of a prince, or the enthronement of a king. As they now stand they point to a future king of David's line through whom

God will bring all those things necessary for the well being of the people in their relationship with God. Once again the note of hope comes through the knowledge that judgment must come. The shoot will come 'from the stump of Jesse . . .' (11:1). The house of David will be judged with the people but, when the judgment is accomplished, God will send a descendant of David who will be a true king, and through him the remnant will be blessed.

The city of Jerusalem (Zion) is the other source of hope. The importance of the city as the place of God's dwelling and action is seen in Psalms 46:4–7, 48, 76:1–3. This tradition of God's presence in Jerusalem is doubtless behind the statements that attacking powers may devastate the areas surrounding Jerusalem, but the city itself will be left unscathed (Isa 1:8, 10:28–34, 31:1–8). But this is not an unconditional hope. The same city will be judged because it has become like a harlot, and only those who repent will be redeemed (Isa 1:21–31). Sacrifices and prayers were of no effect without a change of conduct (Isa 1:10–17), and an end must come (Isa 28:14–18). But even then there is hope — not for the rulers, but for those of God's people who had been afflicted (Isa 14:32) and were purified (Isa 1:25–27). Then 'out of Zion shall go forth the law, and the word of the Lord from Jerusalem' (Isa 2:3, 2:2–4).

The traditions on which Isaiah 1–39 are based are different from those found in Amos and Hosea. The traditions associated with the Exodus, wilderness, and conquest of the land are almost ignored. (Note: the return of the remnant from Assyria will be like Israel 'When they came up from the land of Egypt.' 11:10). The relationship between God and Israel is fundamental to the message of Isaiah, and from that relationship follows the responsibilities which are expected of the people. While the relationship is the same as that in Amos, Isaiah appeals to the traditions related to Jerusalem, the temple, and the Davidic kingship. Jerusalem is the seat of government and the place in which God's people would be safe. As we have seen, the conditional aspect of these traditions was emphasised by Isaiah.

The tradition of the vineyard is used in a new way, as is the Day of the Lord. The latter is used both as a day of judgment for sinful Judah and a day of blessing for the remnant that will be restored after the judgment.

Prophetic traditions from other books have been taken up in Isaiah. From Amos has come the attack on the women of Jerusalem (Isa 3:16–4:1; compare Amos 4:1–3, 'cows of Bashan'), but with the focus changed from social injustice to arrogance and social pretentiousness. The notions of the remnant and the Day of the Lord probably derived from Amos, but they have been transformed in Isaiah 1–39 in order that they serve the purpose of both judgment and hope. This transformation is an indication of the development of traditions, which continued right down to the exilic and postexilic periods. The exile was seen as a corrective punishment for disobedient Israel and traditions were interpreted with that understanding.

An especially important tradition used in Isaiah1–39 is the concept of the Holy One of Israel. God is holy and different from everyone. In the temple vision Isaiah was aware of this difference, which he could only explain as his uncleanness (Isa 6). When Isaiah was cleansed he was aware that he had been forgiven, and that holiness and righteousness had been brought together (Isa 6:1–8). This is the dominant thought in Isaiah 1–39. The Holy One of Israel required the people to be righteous. Isaiah saw they were not righteous, so he proclaimed judgment and punishment on them—punishment that would purify so that a remnant would return to God in penitence and faith, and God would bless them.

Micah

Bible reading: Micah 1–6

The prophet Micah was a contemporary of Isaiah. He was active from before the fall of Israel until the reign of Hezekiah of Judah (Mic 1:1). Micah's activity during the reign of Hezekiah is confirmed in the reference to his judgment against Jerusalem in Jeremiah 26:18. Furthermore, we are told that Micah came from Moresheth, a town about forty kilometres southwest Jerusalem. It has been suggested that he prophesied away from his hometown, probably at Jerusalem The speeches which may be confidently attributed to him suggest the setting was Jerusalem: he speaks to those who have power and authority (Mic 2:1–2), to the priests (Mic 3:11) and prophets (Mic 3:5–), and others whose office place them in Jerusalem.

Micah shared the concern of Isaiah for the ordinary people who were suffering under the exploitation of their leaders. He condemned those who acquired property by making others poor (Mic 2:1–2, also Isa 5:8), who denied justice to the poor (Mic 3:1–2, also Isa 1:23, 10:1–2) and misled them (Mic 2:8–11, also Isa 3:12). However, his message is narrower than that of Isaiah. Isaiah reflected his Jerusalem background and consequently, spoke of Judah's international policy and the royal court in Jerusalem, as well as local affairs. Micah is limited to the effect of changes in Judah's social and economic life that took place during the reign of Uzziah. These changes increased the power of the officials and the wealth of the business class at the expense of the poor. Society as Micah saw it, did not reflect Israel's relationship with God, therefore Micah pronounced judgment and punishment on Judah (Mic 2:3–5).

Similarities with the oracles of Amos, Hosea and Isaiah suggest there was a tradition of prophetic teaching by the time Micah was active. Micah condemned the seizure of property in similar terms to Isaiah and Hosea (Mic 2:1–2, Isa 5:8–10, Hos 5:10), perversion of justice (Mic 3:9–11, Amos 5:7, 12, 15, 6:12, Isa 3:14–15), lack of respect for human life (Mic 3:1–3, Amos 8:4–6, Isa 3:14–15), and the comfortable words of the prophets (Mic 2:6–7, Hos 4:5).

The Book

The Book of Micah shows a long history of tradition in which the message of Micah has been preserved, interpreted, and extended to meet the needs of the people over a period of about 200 years. It appears to be in two parts, Micah 1–5, 6–7, with a new introductory statement in 6:1, 'Hear what the Lord says . . .'

The basic message of the first part is one of judgment on those who oppress the poor, deny justice, and live in luxury. This is limited to Micah 1–3 and does not envisage any hope for Israel. It concludes with a description of the ruin of Jerusalem (Mic 3:12).

A collection of salvation/hope oracles has been added to the judgment oracles. There are two themes in these oracles. The first is the restoration of Zion to its place as the centre of God's reign (Mic 4:8–5:4). This restoration occurs through suffering because the punishment is exile in Babylon, but God will rescue the people from there and return them back to the Zion (Mic 4:8–10). Zion/Jerusalem is in the midst of many cities that are assembled against her, but God will judge those who come against her (Mic 4:11–13). Though her king has been humiliated, God will raise up another ruler who will reign in Zion (Mic 5:4), and in him God's reign will be made known in all the earth (Mic 5:4). These oracles show that God's purpose for Israel was not completed with judgment and punishment. Israel, once judged, punished, and restored, will achieve God's purpose by establishing Yahweh's reign on earth from Zion. In addition, God will raise up a leader who will be a shepherd to Israel and help the people to live in the security of God's covenant (Mic 5:4). The traditions of Zion and David are used to promote hope for a people in exile.

The second theme is God's relationship to the nations and which is found in the introduction and conclusion to the restoration theme. This theme promises peace among the nations as they learn the ways of God at the mountain of the Lord (Mic 4:1–4), and includes security for the remnant of Israel (5:5–8)

The last two chapters consist of a number of sayings that express both confidence in God, and the requirements of God. It concludes with the well known response to God, 'He has showed you, 0 man, what is good; and what does the Lord require of you but to do justice, and to love kindness and to walk humbly with your God?' (Mic 6:8). The conclusion to the Book is a song of praise to God, which celebrates the compassion and willingness of God to forgive the nation, and recalls the promises to Abraham, Jacob, and the fathers old (Mic 7:18–20)

The Book calls on the basic traditions of Israel. The oracles of condemnation and judgment assume the traditions of God's relationship with Israel and in particular, those aspects of the tradition, which require care within the community. The tradition of the promise to Zion is dominant in Micah 4–5. This is a reversal of the position in Micah 1–3 in which the oracles of judgment contain an implicit denial of this promise. Jerusalem is the place in which the iniquities of the leaders and rulers are practiced. Therefore, it will be destroyed. Chapters four to five proclaim that Zion will again be the city of God, after she has been through the travail of exile in Babylon (Mic 4:10). She will become the sign of the restoration of God's people. Zion will also be a blessing to the nations (Mic 4:2–3).

The traditions of the exodus from Egypt and the wilderness wandering (Mic 6:4–5; 7:15) are recalled to remind the people of God's willingness to save them when called upon. The remnant tradition is taken up with the sense of promise, which is developed in Isaiah. Its use in Micah assumes the scattering of the people and their rescue by God to receive God's blessing (Micah 2:12–13, 4:6–7). In Micah 5:7–8 there is mention of a remnant that will be gathered from among the nations to become a great nation. This remnant tradition has undergone a further transformation. It began as a threat in Amos

5:3, became promise in which a remnant will survive and grow in Isaiah 37:31–1, and then became the name for the remnant community saved by God (Isa 11:11, 16). In Micah the remnant is created by God's saving act rather than judgment. 'Remnant' has become the name for the final goal of God's action with Israel. This understanding is the result of many scholars who considered and developed the tradition

The Book of Micah presents a warning to those who disregard the requirements of the covenant relationship with God. They will be punished. On the other hand, it gives hope to those who have suffered punishment in the Babylonian exile, they will be redeemed by God. The Book also points to the future, in which God plans that those who will return to an exalted Zion will be the source of a new life of peace for the nations. The note of hope balances the judgment and suffering, which is very strong in the Book of Micah.

Zephaniah, Nahum and Habakkuk

Of the remainder of the minor prophets (The Twelve) it appears that only Zephaniah, Nahum and Habakkuk are from the pre-exilic period. It is not possible to give precise dates for them, but from their content it appears that they originated in the last quarter of the seventh century BCE.

Zephaniah

The heading to Zephaniah gives the only direct pointer to this period when it says that the word of the Lord came to Zephaniah 'in the days of Josiah the son of Amon, King of Judah.' (Zeph 1:1). The earlier part of Josiah's reign is suggested by the prophet's condemnation of idolatrous worship (Zeph 1:2–6). Josiah stopped this when his reforms took place in 626 BCE. Following this condemnation there are sayings about the 'Day of the Lord', which describe things that will happen on that day (Zeph 1:7–18). This leads into a call to the people to seek the Lord and his mercy (Zeph 2:1–4).

After a series of oracles against foreign nations (Zeph 2:5–15), the prophet turns back to Jerusalem and condemns the ruling classes for their neglect of God's way (Zeph 3:1–5). Judgment will come. The land will be devastated (Zeph 3:6–8), but a remnant—those who find refuge in God—will be preserved (Zeph 3:11–13). The Book concludes with a message of hope for Jerusalem, for God is with her (Zeph 3:14–20).

The Book has similarities to Amos in its condemnation of cultic practices, the unjust actions of the rich and powerful, its understanding of the Day of the Lord, and the concept of a remnant. It appears that Zephaniah re-presented these themes from Amos to his people at a time of transition from the reign of Manasseh, when Judah was under the strict control of Assyria, to the time when Assyria was weaker, and Judah was asserting her independence. Zephaniah called for renewed faithfulness to God in cultic and social practice.

The Book of Zephaniah proclaims judgment and punishment on the faithless, but triumph and victory for those who are faithful to God. God will care for the city of Jerusalem and its people. God is in her midst like a warrior to keep her safe (Zeph 5:17).

Nahum

The major emphasis in Nahum is on the expected destruction of the Assyrian capital Nineveh. This occurred in 612 BCE, and it is usual to date the material of the Book around that time. The presentation of the material suggests that it was compiled for use in celebrating the fall of the hated enemy.

The celebration of Nineveh's fall is presented with a grim realism, which leaves little to the imagination for the way such proud cities and empires were treated by their conquerors (Nah 2–3). This begins with words of comfort and encouragement for Judah and Israel (Nah 1:12–15, 2:2). Assyria had defeated the Northern Kingdom of Israel with its capture of Samaria in 721 BCE, and had effectively controlled Judah's fortunes until 626 BCE. Now, with Assyria soon to he completely vanquished, the prophet looks for the restoration of both kingdoms, that is Israel and Judah. Indeed, Josiah had already taken action to bring this about (2 Kgs 23:15–20, 2 Chron 34:3–7).

The first part of the Book is an introductory poem describing God's vengeance on his enemies (Nah 1:2–8), followed by an address to Israel's enemies generally (Nah 1:9–1l). This effectively gives the Book as a whole a general application, which celebrates God's triumph and assures Judah of the care for all who trust Yahweh and are truly faithful. The Book is now well adapted for cultic use.

Habakkuk

The Book of Habakkuk also appears to have been arranged for cultic use. It has two statements which raise questions of why the people's prayers have been unanswered for so long (Hab 1:2–4) and why such violent means are used to accomplish God's purposes (Hab 1:12–17). These questions are answered by two prophetic statements. The first, tells the people to look at what is happening about them and points to the use of the Chaldeans who will overcome the Assyrians (Hab 15–11). The second has the prophet promising to be alert for God's reply. God is neither dead nor distant. God will reply, and when that happens, the prophet has to write down what is said by God, in order that the way of the righteous and faithful is maintained by God (Hab 2:1–5).

The second major section is a series of 'woes' against those who do not heed God's ways (Hab 2:6–20). These 'woes' condemn those who incur large debts (Hab 2:6–8), those who make unjust profits (Hab 2:9–11), those who build a town by violence or fraud (Hab 2:12–14), those who are involved in riotous living (Hab 2:15–17), and those who resort to idols (Hab 2:18-20). Similarities with other prophets can be seen in these denunciations.

The final section is a prayer in the form of a hymn or psalm (Hab 3). It celebrates God's work in the world as God battles with the forces of primeval chaos (Hab 3:8–11) and overcomes those who oppose God's ways (Hab 3:12–15). The psalm concludes with a cry of trust in God. Whatever happens the writer will trust in God, for God can be relied on at all times (Hab 3:16–19).

The major thrust of the message in Habakkuk is that Israel should trust God and be faithful at all times. The psalm in Hab 3 makes this especially clear as well as being declared in Habakkuk 1 and 2. The whole Book makes a worthy celebration of confidence in God as the hope of Israel.

Questions

1. Who were the prophets and what part did they play in the life of Israel?
2. Compare the message and theology of Amos and Hosea.

7
Recovering Faith

§A brief overview of the prophets: Jeremiah, Ezekiel, Second Isaiah, Third Isaiah, Obadiah, Haggai, Zechariah, Malachi Joel, Jonah

Jeremiah

Bible readings: Jeremiah 1–3, 7, 12, 27–9, 31, 36

Jeremiah was a prophet in Jerusalem in the last years of the Kingdom of Judah. His prophetic activity began in 627 BCE, the thirteenth year of the reign of Josiah (640–609 BCE) and ended after the commencement of the exile. It is believed that he died in Egypt where he was taken by a group fearing reprisals for the murder of Gediliah, the governor of the province of Judah (Jer 40–1). The heading to the book tells us that Jeremiah was the son of the priest Hilkiah who lived in Anathoth, a village approximately five kilometres, north of Jerusalem.

At the beginning of his work Judah appeared to be about to recover some of her former strength and influence under king Josiah. The opportunity for this came with the decline of Assyria as a power in the area. However, recovery did not eventuate, Josiah was killed in battle by the Egyptian Pharaoh Necho, who sought to secure the area of Palestine for himself. Judah came under the rule of the Egyptians for a short time and following Josiah's death had two kings who were unequal to the task of securing Judah's position in a time difficult politics. The emergence of Babylon as the new power in the area not only prevented recovery of the land, but also led eventually to the end of Kingdom.

The call of Jeremiah shows that his function was to make known the word of God (Jer 1: 4–10). His task was 'to pluck up and break down, to destroy and to overthrow, to build and to plant' (Jer 1:10). That is, the prophet Jeremiah was in the line of prophets who proclaimed judgment on God's people.

Furthermore, the call shows Jeremiah's reluctance to become a prophet. He protested that he was too young, and did not know how to speak. However, God promised to be with him and to give him the words to say (Jer 1:6–8). This tradition of reluctance is confirmed in the so called ‘confessions’, which show the struggle Jeremiah had with the overwhelming task of proclaiming God’s word of judgment and destruction to a people who would not heed what he had to say (Jer 11:18–23,17:14–18).

Jeremiah suffered persecution for the work he did as a prophet. His sermon against the temple, in which he spoke of its imminent destruction, brought a threat of death which was only averted when the words Micah spoke against Jerusalem were recalled by the princes who were gathered to judge him (Jer 26:8–19). He was put in prison for advising surrender to the Babylonians who were, he said, doing the work of God in punishing this sinful nation (Jer 38:1–13).

The book

The book is made up of three major collections:

1. Jeremiah 1–25: Judgment announced against Judah.
2. Jeremiah 26–45: Sayings and stories of the prophet’s ministry.
3. Jeremiah 56–51: Oracles against foreign nations.

Within these collections there are oracles and statements of judgment and punishment together with messages of hope. The book concludes with an historical appendix (Jer 52), which is similar in content to 2 Kings 24:18–25:30. Within these collections there are oracles and statements of judgment and punishment together with messages of hope.

The oracles of judgment centre in the main on the faithless activity of Judah in worshipping other gods (apostasy), and in putting its trust in alliances. Underlying these charges is the understanding that there was a relationship between God and God’s chosen people. As in Hosea, the relationship is understood to be like that which exists within families, between husband and wife, and between parent and child, Judah’s apostasy is likened to faithlessness in marriage and lack of response of a child to its parent.

Jeremiah uses the themes of ‘harlotry and adultery’ to describe vividly the cult practised in Jerusalem. He used the imagery of wantonness to impress on the people not only that they had gone after other gods, but also, in doing so they betrayed a relationship of love and tender care. The tragedy for the people was that they did not appear to realise they were unfaithful. When they protested that they had not been unfaithful, Jeremiah said that the evidence was all around them in the things they did. He compared Judah with a wild camel that cannot be restrained. She was determined to go after other gods (Jer 2:23–5)

The officials of the king's court and the temple led the way in forsaking God. They sought help and guidance from trees and stones. Jeremiah asked, 'what help will they be in time of trouble?' (Jer 2: 26–8). Even from the earliest time the people had refused to serve God, but rather worshipped at the centres of Baal worship, the 'high hill', and the 'green tree' (Jer 2:20, 13:27). Why were God's people like this? To answer this the prophet compared Israel to a vine. God planted good seed, but when the plant grew it was a wild vine. Israel had started well, but had turned away from God (Jer 2:21). There is in this comparison a strong recollection of the song of the vineyard in Isaiah (Isaiah 5:1–7). By presenting his message in this way the prophet reminded the people that their apostasy went back at least to the time of Isaiah, and that Isaiah had pronounced judgment on his faithless people. That judgment was soon to be fulfilled.

The gravity of Judah's betrayal of her relationship with God was shown when Jeremiah charged Judah with adultery. She had acted like an unfaithful wife (Jer 3:20), and her children had followed her example by forsaking God, even though God was the one who provided for them (Jer 5:7, 5:7–9).

The priests and prophets bore a heavy responsibility for Judah's condition. The priests did not seek God, nor did they know him. The prophets prophesied by Baal instead of by God (Jer 2:8, 5:31), and gave the people a false confidence instead of warning them of the judgment that was to come upon them (Jer 6:13–15). Jeremiah recalled that the prophets in Samaria had contributed to that city's downfall when they prophesied by Baal and led the people astray (Jer 23:13). But the prophets of Jerusalem were worse. They were involved in all kinds of wickedness and their ungodliness was spread over the whole land (Jer 23:15, 23:9–15).

Furthermore, the formation of alliances with foreign powers was a betrayal of the relationship with God and an expression of the lack of faith in Yahweh. To turn to Assyria or Egypt was to seek 'lovers'. Here again Judah did not appear to understand the significance of what she was doing. She proclaimed innocence, but sought an alliance with Egypt (Jer 2:33–36). Such faithless actions would bring punishment—the punishment of exile (Jer 2:37).

Indeed, the people showed their rejection of God by rejecting God's instruction (Torah/ law) by which they were to live with one another in response to God's love for them (Jer 6:10). This rejection, along with their attention to the Baals, rendered their worship and sacrifice unacceptable to God (Jer 6:20), and led to a rejection of their worship in the temple, and even more so the temple itself (Jer 7:1–15).

Injustice in Jerusalem was of such a high order that Jeremiah did not expect a search of the city to find one single person of justice for whose sake they may be spared (Jer 5:1. Compare with Gen 18:22–33, where God promised Abraham that he would spare Sodom if ten righteous men could be found in the city).

As with earlier prophets, injustice is seen most clearly in the action of the rich and powerful against the poor. They grow rich by enslaving their fellow human beings (Jer 5:26; 22:13, concerning King Jehoiakim), and by perverting the course of justice so that the fatherless and needy are denied their rights (Jer 5:28). False dealing was common, even among the prophets and priests (Jer 6:13).

In summary, Jeremiah charged his people with forgetting God (Jer 13:25; 18:15) and with not knowing the ordinances of the Lord (Jer 8:7). They were estranged from their God. The consequence of this situation was judgment and punishment.

The message of judgment and punishment is present in many places after the oracles that charge the people with faithlessness. Alliances will be turned into punishment by exile (Jer 2:37 'with your hands upon your head . . .' signifies being led away into captivity). Judah and Jerusalem will be set upon by a foe from the north who will bring destruction, laying the land waste and leaving the cities in ruins (Jer 4:5–8; Jer 6, especially verses 22–6). Mourning women will lament and wail over them (Jer 9:10,17–2). All this would happen because the people would not return to God (Jer 2:20–2; 8:4–6).

The prophetic method of taking up and applying the words of previous prophets to a new situation is well illustrated by these statements of judgment in Jeremiah. The closest connections are with Hosea. Jeremiah uses the language of betrayal of the marriage relationship, and, like Hosea, charges his people with adultery and harlotry in their association with other gods and in seeking alliances with foreign powers. In addition, Jeremiah adopts Hosea's father-son image for their relationship. God provided for the nation as a father provides for a son and expected them to acknowledge the relationship and respond with faithful love. But they did not respond in this way and God was left to keep calling them back to the relationship (Jer 3:19, 22, compare with Hos 11:1–7).

Hosea charged Israel with not knowing God (Hos 4:1, 6). Jeremiah takes this image and sharpens it by charging Judah and Jerusalem with forgetting God (8:7, 13:25). The phrase, *'upon every high hill and under every green tree'*, used in Hosea (Hos 4:13) to describe pagan worship, is picked up also by Jeremiah (Jer 2:20; 3:6; 17:2).

There are two significant references to Isaiah. In Jeremiah 2:21 the prophet takes up the old tradition of Israel as the vine of God in such a way that it points to the Song of the Vineyard in Isaiah 5:1–7. The description of the choice vine produced from pure seed, which became a degenerate wild vine brings to mind the disappointment of God over the people of Israel who became like the degenerate vine. Jeremiah's description of the people as those who have eyes, but cannot see, who have ears but cannot hear stands at the beginning of a charge against Judah (Jer 5:2), and parallels Isaiah's call when he is told by God that his words will dull the people's senses 'lest they see with their eyes, and hear with their ears . . .' (Isa 6:10).

In using the words of his predecessors, Jeremiah was making plain to the people that the words of judgment spoken long ago to a different group of people still applied to them in their time. Hosea's words against the northern kingdom had been fulfilled in that the ten tribes had been taken away by Assyria and lost forever. Therefore, their potency was thus demonstrated. Jerusalem should heed the warning and return to God (Jer 6:8).

Jeremiah's understanding of the relationship between God and Israel was derived from the traditions of his people. He makes reference to God as the creator and provider beside whom idols are a false hope and of no consequence (Jer 10:12–16). The relationship was based on God's action in bringing Israel out of Egypt, in leading the people through the wilderness, and in the gift of the land of Canaan (Jer 2:6–7). Jeremiah looked back to the time of the wilderness as one of particular devotion by the people (Jer 2:2–3).

In addition to the poetic oracles of Jeremiah, which we have been considering, there is a large amount of material in prose form, much of which came from a group of teachers who were active during the exile. Their intention was to apply the words of Jeremiah in order that they were God's word spoken to the people suffering in exile in 586 BCE.

An examination of the prose material shows that it is very close in both style and vocabulary to Deuteronomy and the Deuteronomic History. Furthermore, It is apparent that the theological emphases in the prose material are different from those in the poetic oracles of Jeremiah. They are close to those found in the Deuteronomic History. It is probable, therefore, that the group that produced the prose material was a school of Deuteronomists living in the exilic period who were concerned to show that God still had a purpose for the nation Israel, and wanted to give them hope for the future.

The process involved here is very similar to the one used by Jeremiah in applying the words of his predecessors to his own time. The material was re-presented and adapted to the requirements of the new situation. The authors of the prose material expanded and developed some of the sayings of Jeremiah so that they related to the needs of the people in exile. It was not their intention to replace Jeremiah's words, but to extend their application to a later period.

As we saw in the discussion of the Deuteronomic History, the aim of the Deuteronomists was to explain the catastrophe of 587 BCE, both to indict the people for their unfaithfulness and to give hope to the exiles. The catastrophe happened because of the disobedience of the people. They did not obey God's law, nor did they heed the warnings given through God's messengers, the prophets. This explanation helped the people to see why they were suffering in exile, and was an exhortation to return to their God in penitence and obedience. If they turned to God a new relationship would be inaugurated. An example of this material is seen in the temple sermon (Jer 7:1–15). This is based on an incident in the life of Jeremiah and words he spoke at that time. The reference to the 'temple of the Lord' (Jer 7:4), the list of offences (Jer 7:9), and the likening of the temple to a 'den of robbers' (Jer 7:11) are the nucleus of the prophet's address on which the sermon is constructed. We note that the sermon sets out the law of God (Jer 7:5–6), charges the people with rejection of the law (Jer 7:8–12), and announces judgment on the people (Jer 7:13–15). Other examples of sermons using earlier words of Jeremiah are found in Jeremiah11:1–17, 17:19–27, 34:8–22.

There can be no doubt from these sermons that Judah's disobedience brought about destruction and exile, and that Judah deserved her punishment. But they did more than explain the past;

they showed that God required obedience from those who were his people. The sermons were intended to bring about a renewal of the people's relationship with God.

Along with the word of renewal, the authors of the sermons proclaimed hope for the people beyond judgment and punishment. If the people returned to the relationship, God would bring them back to Jerusalem and restore the nation. Again, in proclaiming this message, the authors developed and supplemented the statements of hope, which are found in Jeremiah's oracles. This process and message is seen in Jeremiah 24:4–10. Verses 1–3 contain an account of a vision the prophet had received, which was used to counter the hope that those taken into exile in 597 BCE would soon be restored to Jerusalem. Jeremiah, with the other prophets, said that punishment was not only inevitable for disobedient Judah; it was also the way to renewal. So the exiles must remain in Babylon, for in them was the hope of renewal for the people of Israel. This has been taken up and extended by the authors to give hope to the exiles after 587 BCE. The sermon says that God will restore them to their own land, renew them and give them a heart to know their God. In addition, it shows that what God had planned for the people of Israel would be achieved through the exiles, who had been judged and purified by exile, and not through those who remained in Jerusalem. Other examples of this type of sermon are seen in Jeremiah18:1–11, 29:1–32.

Another sermon (Jer 32) is based on Jeremiah's purchase of a field at the beginning of the siege of Jerusalem, which has an extended section, which dwells on the things God will do for those who have been given into the hand of the King of Babylon (Jer 32:36). Yahweh will gather them from the countries where they had been driven, bring them safely back to Jerusalem, and give them one heart and one-way: he will make an everlasting covenant with them. They will buy fields and God will restore their fortunes (Jer 32:36–44). There is a marked similarity between this and the 'new covenant' passage in Jeremiah 31:31–34. Of particular significance in both passages is the action of God in renewing and providing the way of response.

The traditions about how this relationship began are of particular importance in the sermons. The authors were concerned with a renewed relationship, which was based on the old one, yet different from it. There was therefore some adaptation of the traditions so that they applied to the new situation, but there was also, essentially, continuity.

The exodus from Egypt is the foundation of the relationship. It was by God's action that the people came out. Yahweh chose Israel, and the relationship began (Jer 7:22, 25, 31:32). It is the basis for judgment and for renewal. The tradition is also transformed when referring to the returning exiles. The return will be like the Exodus, a great event, which will mark the beginning of the renewed relationship (Jer 16:14–15; 23:7–8).

The tradition of the covenant made by God with Israel after the Exodus on Mt Sinai, is appropriated to explain the reason for the judgment and punishment in exile. This happened because Israel did not obey the 'words of this covenant which I commanded your fathers when I brought them out of the land Egypt . . .' (Jer 11:3–4). The words of the covenant were the laws, which laid down the manner in which Israel should respond to God within the covenant relationship. They were the laws such as we have in Exodus 20:22–3:19 and Deuteronomy 12–26. The continuation of the relationship depended on Israel's obedience to the law.

There is an important change in this understanding of the covenant tradition in the proclamation of the new covenant (Jer 31:31–4, 32:40). Israel had proved unable to fulfill the requirements of the covenant. Did this mean it would always be under the covenant curses? (Deut 28) The new covenant passage in Jeremiah 31 announces that God will bring the necessary change to people's nature by setting the law within them and writing it on their heat so that everyone will know God's self. The old covenant was made on God's initiative, to which Israel was expected to respond. In the new covenant God's initiative extends to giving the people the will and ability to obey. Continuity is maintained, but the tradition is extended to give hope to the people in exile. In the development of the new covenant the authors have taken up the promise of renewal, which Hosea gave to Israel (Hos 2:14–2).

The remnant tradition is used in two ways to make the same point. The remnant of God's people, in whom the true Israel continues, is those people whom God has driven into exile. This is presented in a positive way in Jeremiah 23:3–4. God will gather the remnant of the nation from all the countries where they have been driven, and God will bless them. The negative use is in Jeremiah 40–4 in which the term is used of those left in Judah after the exile of 587 BCE. These people would not be the remnant as demonstrated by their disobedience especially when they fled to Egypt. They are condemned in stronger terms in Jeremiah 44, and therefore denied any hope for the future. That hope lay with the exiles.

The overall message of the book of Jeremiah is one of hope. It first gives warning that within the relationship there is the responsibility to respond to God. Where that response is not forthcoming, the relationship is broken and punishment must follow. However, the punishment is aimed at restoring the relationship. If God's people will repent and return to the relationship, God will receive them, renew the relationship, and restore its benefits to them. Not only this, God has taken the further initiative by giving those who return to the covenant the will and ability to be obedient.

Ezekiel

Bible readings: Ezekiel 3, 4, 15, 16, 20, 34–7

The prophet

The only information we have about Ezekiel comes from the book bearing his name. We are told he was a priest and was in the first group taken into exile by the Babylonians in 597 BCE (Ezek 1:3). His call to be a prophet came in 593 BCE. According to the dating in the book he continued as a prophet until 571 BCE. He was therefore a contemporary of Jeremiah whose work he knew, though he does not refer to him by name. Ezekiel was married and loved his wife. He mourned her when she died, but as a sign to the people he was not permitted to show his grief (Ezek 24:15–18. This was one of a number of signs and acted prophecies he employed to convey his message to his people (further examples, 4:1–2, 9–10, 5:1–3).

Ezekiel was a person of importance among the exiles. On three occasions officers of the people came to his house to consult him (Ezek 8:1; 14:1; 20:1). It is doubtful that he ever returned to Jerusalem although some people have suggested this because so many of his statements are addressed to Jerusalem, and he appears to have known what was happening there. Others have suggested he was in Jerusalem all the time and that an editor altered the book to give it a Babylonian context. A further suggestion is that he had a double ministry, first in Jerusalem and then in Babylon, or that he was allowed to visit Jerusalem. None of these suggestions is necessary if we accept that communication happened between the two centres, which were parts of the same empire.

Three things dominate the prophet's call. First, the glory of God, which is elaborately described (Ezek 1–3) and second, the commission to proclaim the word of God. He was given a scroll to eat, on which were written words of mourning and lamentation (Ezek 2:8–3:3). Third, that Ezekiel had speak God's word to a rebellious house (Ezek 3:4-1).

The book

The book of Ezekiel has some similarities to the book of Jeremiah in that it has been compiled in a similar way to Jeremiah. The oracles against Jerusalem apparently before the fall of the city in 587 BCE (Ezek 1–24); oracles against foreign nations (Ezek 25–32); oracles apparently describing the coming restoration of the exiles to Jerusalem (Ezek 33–9); a vision of the restored Jerusalem, with a plan for the new temple, its priesthood and worship (Ezek 40–8).

The development of the material is also similar to Jeremiah. There are oracles from the prophet, which have been expanded and adapted to new situations at later times. It is, however, more difficult to identify the oracles of the prophet among the expansions. It has been suggested that this is because the prophet himself undertook the expansion process. That is, he adapted some of his oracles of doom delivered before the fall of Jerusalem to oracles of hope after the fall of Jerusalem. Another possibility is that those who were responsible for the later work rewrote the oracle on which their adaptation was based. Perhaps it is a combination of both. Certainly we must reckon with a group, which worked on the Ezekiel material for the benefit of the exiles. Similarities in expression and theological outlook to the Deuteronomic literature and the Holiness Code (Lev 17–26) show that the influences on the group were complex. In addition, it shows a coming together of different emphases to meet the needs of the moment among the exiles.

The oracles of judgment and threat brought against Jerusalem are based on the accusation of disobedience to God through involvement with other cults. This is most clearly seen in the long statements in Ezekiel 16 and 20. In chapter 16 the prophet makes use of a popular story to bring a charge against Jerusalem. He tells of a king who found a young child whom he adopts and cares for. When she grows into a beautiful woman he marries her and gives her all she would need by way of food, clothing, and jewelry. But she was not faithful. She played the harlot, lavishing her favours on any passer by (Ezek 10:15). She built a 'vaulted chamber' in every square, and a 'lofty place' at the end of every street, and there carried out acts of harlotry (Ezek 10:24–25). The reference here is to shrines that were built for worship of local gods. The practices at these shrines are designated harlotry, partly because of fertility rites which were practised there and partly because worship at the shrines was a faithless betrayal of the relationship with God. This faithless activity will bring judgment and punishment on the wife. She will be punished as an adulteress. All her fine things will be taken away, she will stripped bare and left as the foundling that she was before taken into care by the king (Ezek 16:39). The city will be destroyed (Ezek 16:40–1).

In this charge and judgment the prophet drew on and developed the oracles of Hosea and Jeremiah. Hosea charged Israel with adultery because she was involved with Baal cults, and Hosea saw punishment in terms of that for an adulterer (Hos 2:4–15). Jeremiah used the idea of marriage to describe the relationship between God and Israel (Jer 3:1–5, 19–20). Harlotry is again the charge against the faithless people. Ezekiel's statement also recalls Isaiah's charge that Jerusalem *'the faithful city has become a harlot . . .'* (Isa 1:21). Ezekiel has taken up the theme of these earlier passages, combined points from them, extended them, and presented a new statement. By this means he applied the word of God from earlier prophets to the situation of God's people in the days before the catastrophe of 587 BCE.

A similar charge and judgment is given in Ezekiel 20, but it is presented in a survey of Israel's history. Ezekiel emphasised the actions of God in choosing Israel and bringing the people out of Egypt (Ezek 20:5, 9), but Israel was rebellious from the beginning, and worshipped idols (Ezek 20:7–8). God intended to punish Israel, but, for the sake of his name, 'that it should not be profaned in the sight of the nations among whom they dwelt, in whose sight I made myself known to them in bringing them out of the land of Egypt'. God did not act in this way (Ezek 20:9). What he did was to bring them out of Egypt and give them his statutes and ordinances so they would know how to act (Ezek 20:10–11). This pattern was repeated in the wilderness until God swore to them that he would send them into exile because they were disobedient, failing to observe his statutes and ordinances, and profaning his Sabbaths (Ezek 20:13–24).

Charges of cultic apostasy are also to be seen in Ezekiel chapters 6 to 14. The charge reaches its climax in chapter 8, where, in a vision, Ezekiel saw the way Israel profaned the temple (Ezek 8:1–18). The abominations committed there drove the glory of the Lord out of the temple (Ezek 10:18–19). God's presence was no longer with the people in Jerusalem.

The charge of unfaithfulness through alliances with other powers is made, in Ezekiel 23. Two sisters who represent Samaria and Jerusalem are charged with harlotry because they have consorted with Egypt and Assyria (Ezek 23:1–21). As with Ezekiel 16, the punishment will be administered by the 'lovers' (Ezek 23:22–3). The story told is similar to that found in other ancient literature. Ezekiel took it and used it to show the terrible nature of Israel's betrayal of the relationship with God. There are similarities to Ezekiel 16:1–43, as well as the Hosea and Jeremiah material noted above. Particularly close parallels are with Jeremiah 3:6–12.

Judgment is spelled out clearly in Ezekiel. It is usually presented in terms of siege and military catastrophe. Acted prophecies leave the people in no doubt that terrible things are in store for the disobedient city of Jerusalem. Ezekiel portrayed a besieged city on a clay brick (Ezek 4:1–2), collected a variety of seeds in order to demonstrate how scarce food would be become (Ezek 4:9–11), shaved his face and head, and divided the hairs to symbolise the ways in which the people would be punished. When the Day of Judgment came the city would be afflicted with the sword, with pestilence and with famine (Jer 7:10–27). The judgment proclaimed in Ezekiel 16 and 23 is also in terms of military catastrophe (Ezek 16:40–41, 23:22–7). There was no doubt Jerusalem would be destroyed. Ezekiel likened the city to a piece of vine wood, which as wood is useless. When it has been charred in the fire it is of even less use, so it will be given up to the fire (Ezek 15).

Hope for Israel is a prominent feature in the book of Ezekiel, but it is hope for the exiles. Those who remained in Jerusalem after the catastrophe of 587 BCE claimed they were the continuing Israel. The land was given to Abraham, to one man; but they were many and the land was now their possession (Ezek 33:24). The prophetic response to this was judgment and the promise of destruction (Jer 33:27). Hope was for those who had been judged and who were suffering exile. Consequently, in the hope passages (Ezek 33–7), words of judgment are still important. The shepherds (leaders) who should have cared for and protected Israel are condemned (Ezek 34:1–10), before the statement that God would search out his people and gather them from the nations where they had been scattered (Ezek 34:11–16). Similarly in Ezek 36:16–20, 22–32, judgment precedes the message of return. In response to God's actions, Israel would repent (Ezek 36:31–2) and God would put a new spirit within her and give her a new heart (Ezek 36:26 Compare Ezek 11:19). God's whole operation with Israel would be like raising to life a heap of bleached bones (Ezek 37:1–14). The land to which the people return will be like the Garden of Eden (Ezek 36:35).

Other hope statements have been added to oracles of judgment in the earlier part of the book. After the charge and judgment of the faithless foundling and the two sisters in Ezek 10, it is said that God will remember the covenant and establish an everlasting covenant (Ezek 16: 59–63). To the judgment, which is delivered after the review of Israel's history (Ezek 20:1–31), is added the promise that the return of the exiles will be like a second exodus (Ezek 20:32–44).

In all of these statements of hope the emphasis is on God's action in saving and renewing his people. Israel is required to repent, but it is only God who can save them. God will establish the covenant with the people (Ezek 16:60, 62). God will bring them out from the countries where they were scattered (20:34, 38, 42). God will search for his sheep and seek them out (Ezek 34:11–13, 16).

In this we see again the work of development and adaptation of the word of God delivered by a prophet to a new situation. The author of the passages of hope did not want to deny the threat and judgment oracles. They applied not only to Israel before the fall of Jerusalem and the exile, but to any who were disobedient to God. They also applied to the exiles in that renewal could come only through judgment. Consequently, to those in exile, who had been judged, came the specific word of hope. God was still the God of Israel. God was still faithful. God would renew the people and restore them to their own land.

The book concludes with plans for the temple and the distribution of the tribes of Israel when the people are restored to their homeland. The importance of the temple for the restored and renewed Israel is stressed in this section. God reveals to the prophet the arrangements for the temple area (Ezek 40:1–42:20), the altar (Ezek 43:6–27), ministry in the sanctuary (Ezek 44, the sons of Zadok will be in charge of ministry), contributions to the temple (Ezek 45:10–46:18), and the allotment of land to the tribes of Israel (Ezek 47:13–48:35). All of these elements centre on the temple. Even the allotment of the land is arranged so that the temple is in the centre of the tribal areas. In the restored Israel, all life will centre on the temple where the glory of the Lord resides (Ezek 43:1–5)

In this book a number of traditions are drawn on or taken up and expounded. The traditions of the earlier prophets, particularly Hosea and Jeremiah, were important. The understanding of the relationship with God using the metaphor of marriage is particularly important and extended to give a new sharpness to the denunciations of apostasy. Other traditions that were basic to Israel's life are drawn on. For example, the promise of the land to the descendants of Abraham was used by those who remained in Jerusalem after the destruction of the city to claim the land (Ezek 33:24). In denying their claim the prophet made it plain that the promise was conditional upon Abraham's descendants being faithful to God (Ezek 33:29).

The exodus and wilderness traditions are taken up in the charge in Ezekiel 20:1–31. God chose Israel in Egypt (Ezek (20:5), brought them out of Egypt (Ezek 20:6, 9), and led them through the wilderness (Ezek 20:10–23). God's action and care for the people of Israel, and the reality of the relationship, are clearly portrayed here. However, the prophet goes beyond what is usually drawn from the tradition when he charges Israel with disobedience in Egypt, even before the law was known (Ezek 20:7–8a, Compare with verses 11–13a), and they are said to have been rebellious in the wilderness (Ezek 20:13–24). The tradition is thus extended to make plain to Israel that they were always disobedient, even in the earliest days of greatest dependence on God. (Compare the apparent idyllic situation in the wilderness in Hos 2:14–15 and Jer 2:2–3)

The exodus and wilderness traditions are used in the promise that God will return the people to their homeland (Ezek 20:42). In using these traditions the author adds a new element to them. The time in the wilderness would be a time of judgment and purging, so that only those who are obedient could enter the Promised Land in this second exodus (Ezek 20:33–6).

The law tradition is important in Ezekiel. The statutes and ordinances of God are the basis of obedience for Israel. The law tradition contained in the Holiness Code (Lev 17–26) is close to Ezekiel and it appears that parts of Ezekiel are an exposition of that law (For example, compare Leviticus 26: 4–13 with Ezekiel 34:25–31).

In addition, we find the Day of the Lord tradition, which is a day of woe and destruction when God brings wrath on the disobedient people (Ezek 7:10–27), and the vine tradition (Ezek 15). In the latter tradition of Israel the vine tradition is reduced to absurdity when the people are likened to the wood rather than to the fruit. The prophet used the tradition because the people knew it not only in its positive form, but also in its judgment forms in Isaiah 5: 1–7 and Jeremiah 2:21. The judgment tradition is re-applied in Ezekiel.

The purpose of the book of Ezekiel is to show that God requires the response of obedience from people. Where that response is not forthcoming the relationship must end with the people swept away. But God is faithful. If the people will repent God will forgive them and gather them in again, and provide them with a renewed way of life. The book makes plain that this renewal is entirely the work of God who will give a new heart and spirit so that the people may be able to respond and observe God's law (Ezek 11:19–20, 36:26–7). Furthermore, God will establish the renewed Israel with the temple at the centre of the people's life so that they may know God's presence always with them (Ezek 40–8). The glory of the Lord is important here. It departed from the temple in Jerusalem as a sign of God's rejection of the people who committed abominations against Yahweh (Ezek 10:18–19). In the renewal, the glory of the Lord will return to the temple (Ezek 43:1–5) and Israel will know that God is with them.

A further purpose of the book is that God may be known by Israel and by the nations. The phrase 'that you (or they) will know that I am the Lord' occurs many times in the book (for example, Ezek 6:14, 7:27). All of God's actions toward Israel, whether they were judgment and punishment or forgiveness, renewal and restoration, are directed toward Israel acknowledging God as their Lord. These actions are intended also to have the nations acknowledge God as they see the way God deals with this people whom God brought out of Egypt (Ezek 20:9, 14, 22), and who judges the nations for their actions against Israel (Ezek 25:7, 26:6, 35:4). The book looks forward to the time when all people will acknowledge that God is Lord.

First Isaiah (40–66)

Bible readings: Isaiah 40–46, 49, 50, 52–55

The second major part of the book of Isaiah consists of two collections of prophetic material. The first, chapters 40 to 55, is concerned with the period when Israel was in exile in Babylon, and is addressed to the exiles there. Almost all the oracles come from the one prophet. The second section, chapters 56 to 66, is related to the period after the exile, and consists of oracles concerned with the restored community in Jerusalem after 538 BCE.

The suppression of the prophet's personality, which is apparent in differing degrees in the other prophetic books, is almost complete in Isaiah 40–66. It is possible we have a reference to the call of the prophet in what is called Second or Deutero-Isaiah (Isa 40–55) in Isaiah 40:6–8, but there is no certainty of that. The important thing for those who preserved this material was the word of God spoken by the prophets. The persons who spoke the word were not important.

For convenience we will look at the material in two parts: Isaiah 40–55 and 56–66 (called Third or Trito-Isaiah).

Second Isaiah (40–55)

We have seen in our discussion of the earlier prophets that they spoke to the situation in which they found themselves. Thus Jeremiah tried to persuade the people of Jerusalem that they were not safe from destruction even though they had the temple. The Babylonians represented the judgment of God and were a genuine threat to them if they did not repent. Second Isaiah spoke to those who suffered the consequences of the judgment—the destruction of Jerusalem and the exile of the people to Babylon. He was speaking to people who needed to be convinced that God was able to rescue them from exile and return them to their own land.

The Deuteronomic History and the exilic material in Jeremiah and Ezekiel gave an explanation of the people's predicament and presented the exile as an opportunity for repentance and for God to refashion the relationship on the basis of the promises and grace seen in Israel's history (Jer 31:31–34, Ezek 36:24–28). Second Isaiah built on these messages as he told the people of God's nature, of themselves as God's people, and of God's purpose for them. His message is delivered in vivid imagery and inspiring language (Isaiah 40:18–33).

Basic to the message of Second Isaiah is the understanding of God as the one who is in control, not only of Israel, but also of the whole of creation. The exiles feared that the destruction of Jerusalem and their consequent removal into exile demonstrated a weak God who was unable to rescue them when attacked by a foreign nation. Yahweh did not have the power to preserve the nation from defeat. If God was unable to do that, how could the Lord bring about their return? In answer, the prophet pointed to God as creator, the only God, the one who brought Israel out of Egypt, and the One whose control of the nations would achieve their return to the Promised Land.

Most references to creation are part of the argument to establish that God can bring to fruition any pronouncements made by the prophet. The promise that Jerusalem will be inhabited and the cities of Judah rebuilt (Isa 44:26, 28) begins with the declaration 'I am the Lord, who made all things, who stretched out the heavens alone, who spread out the earth—Who was with me?' (Isa 44:24). The promises that Cyrus would be God's instrument to bring about the return to Jerusalem concludes, 'I form light and create darkness, I made weal and create woe, I the Lord do all these things' (Isa 45:7). The foundation for the use of this argument is established at the beginning of the prophet's work. In a long and inspiring passage the prophet declares that God is the creator of all. No one helped God. No one advised God. God did it and now sits in control of all creation. Israel knew all this. As the prophet says, 'Have you not known? Have you not heard? The Lord is the everlasting God, the Creator of the ends of the earth. He does not faint or grow weary, his understanding is unsearchable' (Isa 40:28).

Such a strong claim leads to an equally strong statement against other gods. The claims made for God left no room for others, but the exiles in Babylon were surrounded by people who believed that they prospered because of their gods. The prophet's statements are a counter to the temptation for the people who are considering switching allegiance to the Babylonian gods. He pours scorn on the idols made by workmen and skilled craftsmen (Isa 40:18–19, 46:5–7), and on those who worshipped them (Isa 42:17, 44:9–20, 45:16–17). God cannot be likened to these idols, nor can anyone make a likeness of the Lord (Isa 40:18). God is the only God. If others make claims for their gods, let them prove these claims (Isa 44:7, See also Isa 44:21–4,

43:8–9, 45:21). God assures the people that they are the evidence to show to the nations that Yahweh is the only God (Isa 44:8 and 44:6).

The establishment of God's supremacy over the gods of other nations means that Israel may place its confidence in God to bring about salvation. It is also the basis upon which the prophet introduces Cyrus into his message. God, who is supreme over other gods, is also supreme over the nations. The earlier prophets made the same claim when they said that Assyria and Babylon were the instruments by which God would punish his people. Now this prophet says that God will stir up Cyrus of Persia to be the instrument of salvation and return (Isa 41:2,25). The prophet leaves no doubt that God is responsible for the Cyrus's rise to power. The God of creation and Lord of history has designated Cyrus as God's shepherd and the one to fulfil God's purpose for Israel (Isa 44:24–8). God has anointed Cyrus to subdue nations and to receive treasures for the sake of God's people (Isa 45:1–7), set the exiles free and rebuild Jerusalem (Isa 45:13).

The great historical reference points for Second Isaiah are the exodus from Egypt and the wilderness wandering. The importance of these two events is because the prophet and his people are in a similar situation to the Hebrews whom God released from slavery in Egypt. Second Isaiah proclaimed the release from Babylon as a second exodus. Many of the passages that refer to the return of the exiles recall the deliverance from Egypt. The summons to depart from Babylonia (Isa 52:11–12), recalls the departure from Egypt. Isaiah 43:16–17 recalls this event by reference to the Red Sea crossing. In Isaiah 51:9–11 the Red Sea crossing is equated with the struggle against the powers of chaos. However, this second exodus will have time for adequate preparation unlike the first exodus in which the people were forced to leave in haste.

The proclamations that announce the return through a transformed wilderness again recall the wandering in the wilderness before the exiles settled in the Promised Land. The experiences of the wilderness by the returning Babylonian exiles will be of joy and gladness, as all things rejoice in going forth. The people will be provided for (Isa 49:9–10) and led by God (Isa 42:16–17).

The relationship between Israel and God continued during the exile. The prophet proclaimed that Israel, the chosen of God, still belonged to and was in relationship with God, and would not be cast off by God (Isa 41:8–9, 43:10, 20, 44:1–2, 45:4, 49:7). Israel can depend on God who will strengthen, help, and uphold the nation with a victorious right hand (Isa 41:10, 44:2). The closeness of the relationship is shown when the prophet describes it as a marriage in which God is the husband (Isa 54:5). Israel's suffering will be removed and she will be restored like forsaken wife who has been called by her husband (Isa 54:5–8). What God was about to do in Cyrus was for Israel, whom God formed 'from the womb', and was about to restore to their own land (Isa 44:24–28).

God chose Israel to be God's servant. This term expresses both the relationship to God and the purpose of Israel. The term 'servant' occurs frequently in Second Isaiah. A group of poems often called the 'Servant Songs' (Isa 42:1, 49:1–6, 50:4–9, 52:13–53:12) may be isolated from the text as independent units because of their differences from their context, and their literary style. It is probable that they were once independent poems and that they refer to an individual who cannot now be identified. Moreover, it is probable that the prophet responsible for the major part of Second Isaiah wrote them

Where the term servant appears in passages other than the Servant Song it refers to Israel. A careful reading of the songs in their present context shows that the author of Second Isaiah intends us to understand that the songs now refer to Israel. In this way the author expresses the important truth for Israel that it had been called to reveal God to the nations (Isa 49:6, compare with Genesis 12:2–3). Furthermore, the songs put the suffering experience by Israel in a new light. God is turning this suffering to the divine purpose by which Israel suffers not only for itself, but also for others that they might turn back to God (53:4–6, 10–11).

In this prophet's use of the traditions of creation, the Exodus, and the wilderness wandering, he not only drew on them to show how God acted for people of Israel in the past, but also pictured what was to come. The release and return will be a new creation (Isa 43:1, 15, 44:2–3) and a new exodus (43:14–21, 51:9–11, 52:11–12).

The proclamation of a message of hope limits direct reference to earlier traditions by Second Isaiah. He does however refer to earlier prophecies of doom (Isa 43:22–28) and endorses these as the correct word for an apostate people. He thus points to the fulfilment of God's word through the prophets and includes in his message of salvation a warning, which is still necessary for his people. Furthermore, he re-enforces the point made by the earlier prophets that hope for Israel was through judgment.

An important pointer to Second Isaiah's knowledge of prophetic traditions is seen in his use of the phrase 'the Holy One of Israel' (Isa 41:14, 16, 20), which originated with Isaiah of Jerusalem. The earlier prophet's use of the term expressed God's judgment on the people who had turned away from God ('they have despised the Holy One of Israel . . .' Isa 1:4). Second Isaiah uses it to express God's continued activity towards the chosen people, now in the form of salvation oracle. God is called 'your Redeemer, the Holy One of Israel' (Isa 41:14, 43:14).

Third Isaiah (Isaiah 56–66)

A further collection of material is seen in Isaiah 56 to 66. The material in this section comes from the period after the exile. It has been gathered round a nucleus of material—Isaiah 60 to 62—which proclaims salvation, and has marked connections with material in Isaiah 40 to 55. These connections suggest that the author was a disciple of Second Isaiah, and that he applied his master's message to the problems faced by the returning exiles. The remainder of chapters, 56 to 66, have probably had a long history of literary growth with the final form in the time to Ezra and Nehemiah.

The people who returned to Jerusalem were still looking for the renewal proclaimed by Second Isaiah. The purpose of Isaiah 56 to 66 was to raise the confidence of the people so that they would continue to trust in God for their salvation. God would reverse the fortunes of the people of Israel. The Lord would not be angry forever, but would comfort and heal (Isa 57:16–18) and the conditions of the people would be transformed, for 'the Lord will arise upon you . . .' (Isa 60:2, see vv 1–3). Economic hardship would be removed (Isa 60:7, 62:8–9), political life would become stable (Isa 60:18), their ruined cities would be rebuilt (Isa 61:4), and their shame would be removed (Isa 61:7). The nations would see the New Jerusalem and be drawn to it (Isa 60:3). They would bring their treasures to Jerusalem (Isa 60:9), and acknowledge the mighty acts of God (Isa 62:2). The role of the nations is thus reversed. They were the instruments of God to bring judgment on God's people. Judgment is past and the new age is dawning in which the nations will serve Jerusalem and God's people (Isa 60:1–18).

Worship and sacrifice are important in the new era. Those who indulge in alien and impure cultic activities are condemned (Isa 57:3–13, 65:2–15). Provision for worship in the house of God will be made by the nations who come to Jerusalem. They will bring sheep and rams for the sacrifices and timber for the beautification of the sanctuary (Isa 60:7, 13).

The Sabbath is to be observed by all God's people. Such observance will be a test of those who belong to the community of God's people, particularly those who would otherwise be excluded such as foreigners and eunuchs. Those who observe the Sabbath will receive the blessing of God as the outcasts are gathered in (Isa 56:1–8, 58:13–14). There is a change of emphasis in the role of the Sabbath. Previously it had been an observance by those within the community. Now it becomes the means by which people enter the community. Membership will be no longer be decided by birth, but by resolution to accept the God of Israel as the only, true God.

In addition, it will be observed, and be acceptable to God if accompanied by care for the oppressed and needy (Isa 58:6–9). Worship and right actions are to be seen together in the New Jerusalem—a message, which was present in the pre-exilic prophets.

The material in this section is in the tradition of Isaiah 40 to 55. In addition, to the already noted extension of the earlier salvation material, it takes up expressions from it. For example, Isaiah 60:4a quotes Isaiah 49:18a as it describes nations bringing their gifts to God. Isaiah 61:1–3 is similar to Isaiah 42:1–4 and Isaiah 49:1–6, and has close connections to these two Servant Song passages. Good tidings are still to be proclaimed to God's people as they continue to look toward to salvation. Finally, Isaiah 62:10-11, which directs the people of Jerusalem to go out of the city to prepare the way for the returning exiles, is similar to Isaiah 52:11 which bids the exiles depart from Babylon to Jerusalem. There are also references to Isaiah 40:3 in 60:10 and 40:9–11 in Isaiah 60:11. (Note in particular Isa 62:11b and Isa 40:10b, which correspond exactly).

'The Holy One of Israel', seen to be important in the other parts of Isaiah, also appears in this collection. The nations will honour 'The Holy One of Israel' when they come to Jerusalem (Isa 60:9,14).

The purpose of Isaiah 40–66 is, first, to proclaim God's salvation to the people in exile in Babylon. This does not deny the judgment proclaimed by the earlier prophets, but builds on that understanding as they recognise that salvation for God's people can only come through judgment. Second, to portray God, as the one who is able and willing to bring release for the exiles from Babylon and return them to Zion.

Third, to show that Israel still had a purpose in the work of God for the world. Fourth, to show that this word of salvation and purpose persisted even though conditions for the returned exiles were different from what they expected. As the book concludes, there is a sense in which the longed-for glory of Jerusalem and its people is seen in the indefinite future. Isaiah 40 to 66 is thus a book of hope to all who look for God's salvation in the world.

Other minor prophets

Obadiah

Bible reading: Obadiah

Obadiah is the shortest book in the Old Testament. It consists of only 21 verses. Verses 1–18 denounce Edom for its exploitation of Israel's weakness after the fall of Jerusalem in 587 BCE, and verses 19–21 look to the restoration of Israel. The book has parallels with Jeremiah 49:7–16, particularly verses 1–4 with Jeremiah 49:14–16, and verses 5–6 with Jeremiah 49:9–10.

Obadiah takes up the tradition of the Day of the Lord. It will be a day of judgment for all nations (Obad v 15). The judgment and punishment of Edom is an example of what will come to all. However, the Day of the Lord is not the end of the world. It is a moment of crisis that will be followed by God's action in making things right again. Obadiah vv.17-20 describes the conditions to come on Mount Zion. The exiles will be restored and possess the land and God will have dominion over it (Obad v 21)

The book is probably part of a larger work of prophecy or of worship material, which dates from the exilic or early post-exilic period. Its purpose is to emphasise that God is the ruler of all, that God wants justice among the nations, and that Israel had a special place among the nations. That purpose would be fulfilled in Israel's restoration to the Promised Land.

Haggai and Zechariah

Bible reading: Haggai 1, Zechariah 2–°6, 9, 14

The prophetic works of Haggai and Zechariah 1–8 come from the early

Post-exilic period (520–518 BCE), and relate to the rebuilding of the temple after the return of the exiles from Babylon.

Although a start was made on rebuilding the temple soon after the exiles returned in 538 BCE (Ezra 3:10–13), the work does not appear to have progressed beyond the foundation stage by 520 BCE. The major reason for this was the poverty of the people who found their lives taken up with eking out an existence in Judah. Haggai reinterpreted the people's situation. He said that it was not a matter of poverty that prevented them rebuilding, but the lack of the temple was the cause of the present situation (Hag 1:1–11). If they rebuilt the temple, judgment would turn to blessing Hag 2:9).

The rebuilding was soon begun in response to Haggai's preaching. He encouraged the people by pointing to the glory that will bring to the temple when God shakes the nations and their treasure is brought to it. When this happens its glory will exceed that of the former temple (Hag 2:1–9).

Reference to the shaking of the nations appears to refer to events in the Persian Empire at the time. In 522 BCE, Cambyses the king of Persia, committed suicide and was succeeded by Darius. Rebellions broke out throughout the empire. Darius dealt with these and brought the empire under control in a relatively short time, but the upheaval appears to have suggested to Haggai that the old order was about to end and the new order centred on Jerusalem about to begin. So that this could happen, Jerusalem had to have a temple for the Lord God.

The message of the book of Haggai is that the most important thing for any community is its relationship to God. It was therefore a challenge to the people of the prophet's time that they acknowledge this and express it in rebuilding the temple. To people of later times it was a challenge to maintain the temple and to trust in God for the fulfilment of God's purpose for the people.

Haggai's prophetic activity lasted only a few months. It was left to Zechariah to maintain the enthusiasm of the people for rebuilding the temple. He did this by first warning the people that they should heed the words of the earlier prophets, as history showed their words of warning had been fulfilled (Zech 1:1–6). Then he proclaimed the coming age of salvation by means of a series of visions (Zech 1:7–6:15), and finally delivered oracles, which called for response to God by correct living (Zech 7:1–8:3).

Zechariah's call to heed the prophetic word is supported by recalling sayings from earlier prophets. The cry of lament found in the Psalms (for example, Ps 6:3) introduces a recollection of Jeremiah's predicted seventy years exile for Judah (Zech 1:12,compare with Jer 25:11, 29:10). The return 'of God to Jerusalem . . . and my house . . .'

(Zech 1:10) recalls Ezekiel's vision of the departure of the glory of God from the temple (Ezek 10:18–19) and its return in (Ezek 43:1–3). The gathering of the nations by God in Jerusalem to ensure that the city becomes a pilgrimage centre had been proclaimed by Isaiah and Micah (Zech 2:11, 8:20–22, compare with Isa 2:2–4, Mic 4:1–3).

There are also allusions to the Psalms as Zechariah recalls the traditions of Zion and the temple. He saw Jerusalem as the city that God had chosen so that God would be in the midst of the people. God will again choose Jerusalem as the religious centre of the nation (Zech 1:17, compare with Pss 46, 47).

Zechariah presents good news for the salvation of his people. He is sure of God's power will save them as an act of grace. All the old hopes for the temple and the city, which were recalled in the worship traditions, will be fulfilled. God will dwell with them in Jerusalem and the city will become a centre of pilgrimage for the nations.

This was not only an important message at the time of the rebuilding of the temple; it was an important element in sustaining the people's hope in the years that followed. In bringing together the hope associated with the rebuilding and the right way of life before God (Zech 8), Zechariah pointed the people to the reality of their ongoing life with God.

The note of hope which is clearly sounded in Zechariah 1–8 is reinforced in the latter half the book (Zech 9–14). The main feature of these chapters is that hope is no longer associated with the rebuilding of the temple. That has been accomplished. Nor is there any other explicit historical reference point. In a real sense these chapters point the message of the whole book to the future. They do this by presenting hope in terms of the last things when God will bring everything to fulfilment in himself (Zech 9:1–17, 10:3, 11:3), and by pointing to God's direct intervention in the history of Israel in order to renew the people in a great and final catastrophe (Zech 12:1–13:6). This second emphasis was developed in the apocalyptic literature of Israel, especially in the book of Daniel.

The overall emphasis of Zechariah is now one of hope for God's people. God will sustain them and bring about their salvation. The importance of the book, and particularly Zechariah 9–14, is seen in references to it in the New Testament passion narratives (Matt 21:5 and Zech 9:9; Matt 24:29 and Zech 12:10–14; Matt 26:15 and Zech 11:12; Matt 27:9 and Zech 11:12–13; Mark 14:27 and Zech 13:7).

Malachi

Bible reading: Malachi 2,4

The book of Malachi comes from the period after the rebuilding of the temple and probably about the time of Ezra and Nehemiah. It shows us the conditions among the people after the exile when religious observance was seen more as an extra than an essential thing for the people. Malachi attacks this, the laxity of the priests in the service of the temple (Mal 1:6–2:9), and the indifference of the people to the upkeep of the temple and its personnel (Mal 3:8).

The material is presented in a question and answer form. In the questions we hear the disillusionment of the people over the non-fulfilment of the promises from the past (Mal 2:17, 3:13–15). To these the prophet gives answers, which show pastoral concern for the faithful, and assures them that God will come and in that coming the hopes of the earlier prophets will be fulfilled (Mal 3:1–5, 3:16–4:3).

The prophet looks for indications of the people's concern for God and willingness to turn to God. For example, the offering of proper sacrifices and payment of tithes (Mal 3:10), respect for marriage laws (Mal 2:14), and rejection of divorce on the grounds of the suffering that would be imposed on a divorced woman (Mal 2:13–16). The people are assured of God's love for them, but they are reminded that the God who chose them could also reject them if they were unfaithful (Mal 1:2–5).

The purpose of the book is to rekindle and maintain the faith of the people, and to assure them that God's promises still hold for them. Furthermore, it reminds them of their responsibility as heirs to these promises.

Joel

Bible reading: Joel 1–2

Joel belongs to the same general period as Malachi. The book consists of two parts. The first is an extended proclamation concerning the Day of the Lord. The prophet believed the day was near and called the people to pray to God for mercy and help in their time of distress (Joel 1:2–2:17). The second part gives God's response to the prayer. God will have mercy on the people and grant new life to all who call on Yahweh (Joel 2:18–3:21). This will come through material blessings:

the fruits of the earth (Joel 2:18–27); spiritual blessings: the spirit poured out (Joel 2:28–29); signs and portents (2:30–31); and deliverance for all who call on God's name (Joel 2:32). Joel 3 returns to the Day of the Lord theme. The day will be a time of judgment for the nations, which will ensure that Jerusalem and Judah will survive.

A notable feature in Joel is the use of material from earlier prophets. For example, compare the phrase, 'the Day of the Lord'—Joel 1:15 with Isaiah 13:6, Joel 2:2 with Zephaniah 1:15, Joel 2:3, with Isaiah 2:4 and Ezekiel 36:35. Another theme picked up from earlier prophets is that of, 'judgment of the nations'—compare Joel 2:10 with Isaiah 2:4 and Micah 4:3 (note that Joel reverses the earlier saying). A final phrase, 'God roaring from Zion and Jerusalem', compare Joel 3:16 with Amos 1:2 and Isaiah 13:13.

The book proclaims God's judgment on those who reject the relationship and teachings, but blessing is poured out on those who are faithful.

Jonah
Bible reading: Jonah 1–4
Jonah appears to belong to the same period as Joel and Malachi. It may be described as a liturgical drama, presented as a story about a prophet, but it is more a statement about God. Jonah is referred to in 2 Kings 14:25 as one who prophesied the re-establishment of the borders of Israel under Jeroboam. The book takes the presumed nationalism of the prophet, stresses its narrowness, and satirises it. In spite of his nationalism, Jonah enables foreigners to meet God, the sailors (Jon 1:14–16), the people of Nineveh (Jon 3:6–10), and in the end, God's care for all people is established.

The book is clearly directed against the temptation that the community should see itself as the only one, which will be blessed by God. This temptation was strong because the earlier prophecies, which told of the destruction of foreign nations, had not been fulfilled, and Israel still suffered at their hands. It was necessary to remind the people that God's care extended to foreign peoples, especially those who acknowledged Yahweh as Lord

A brief review of the prophetic material

In our consideration of the prophetic books we have seen that they are made up of collections of material, which come from widely differing periods of Israel's life. We have seen that the earlier writings have taken and developed the traditions of Israel in order that the people would know what God had to say to them in their own day. These writings in turn have become part of the prophetic tradition and have been re-presented and actualised for new situations when they arose. In this process Jeremiah developed traditions from Hosea, and Ezekiel developed traditions from Hosea and Jeremiah. Within the books themselves we see the development and adaptation of the tradition of the prophet. In Jeremiah it is seen in the prose material and in Ezekiel in the development of judgment oracles into statements of hope for the exiles

In addition, we have seen that the prophetic books contain material that speaks of judgment and hope, with some of the hope material coining from a much later time in their history. In the case of Isaiah, the material in the book clearly applies to at least three periods of Israel's history—pre-exilic, exilic and post-exilic, but it is all put together in the one book. Further, in the book of the Twelve Minor prophets (Daniel to Malachi) we have material from many authors who came from widely separated periods in Israel's history.

This raises the point that in the tradition we have received there are only four books of prophets—Isaiah, Jeremiah, Ezekiel, and the Twelve. It is very unlikely that this is an accidental arrangement. Rather, it is a theological arrangement aimed at presenting those who read the books with the word of God. We have then to ask what the books have to say as the word of God in their canonical setting. The point is raised more clearly for Christians by the fact that although much of the prophetic material is concerned with judgment and punishment, New Testament writers understood it in terms of hope, and in particular, the coming of the Christian Messiah.

In both Jeremiah and Ezekiel the hope is based on God's actions for God's people. Both of these books are initially related to the exile of Israel. They make plain the reason for the catastrophe—Israel's disobedience. The reality of that is in no way diminished or obscured. It is an inevitable part of the relationship between God and Israel that disobedience led to judgment and punishment. These prophetic books are thus a warning to all people that their failure to respond to God with faithfulness will have dire consequences.

The further great emphasis of these two books is that God's faithfulness means that those who repent and turn back will be forgiven and brought into a restored and renewed relationship. That is the very basis of the hope Jeremiah and Ezekiel offer. But how real is such hope if the cycle of disobedience, judgment and punishment is simply repeated over and over again? Here these books take us a further step forward in hope. They tell of God providing those who are restored to God with a new heart and a covenant in which the motivation and strength to obey are provided by God's self (Jer 31:31–34, Ezek 36:26–8). Although these promises arose in an historical situation, they are not tied to that situation. They are present for God's people to appropriate in any and every age.

In spite of the apparent different historical reference points in Isaiah 1 to 39 and 40 to 66, the situation is the same in the book of Isaiah. Broadly, the first thirty-nine chapters deal with the theme of disobedience, judgment and punishment within Israel's relationship with God. It was God's desire to preserve the nation, but if they would not accept God's way and trust God then judgment must come. Even God's choice of Zion, and a covenant with the house of David could not avert this. But it would not be the end. Zion would again know the blessing of God (Isa 35). However, the section ends with the hint that there was a time of exile to come before that blessing (Isa 39:5–8).

Isaiah 40 to 66 accepts that the exile was inevitable because of Israel's disobedience to God. It strengthens that message from the earlier chapters as it accepts that the suffering of the exile was deserved. But it moves on from there to proclaim hope for those who suffer and gives an explanation for that suffering—it was to accomplish salvation for Israel. In addition, Isaiah 40 to 66 proclaims restoration, pointing to a renewed Jerusalem, which will be part of God's triumph for the chosen people, Israel. This will not be frustrated even though the people will pass through difficult times.

Above all the book of Isaiah proclaims the faithfulness of God and the need for people to trust and be faithful at all times. Again the message has historical links in its origins, but it is presented in such a way that its warnings and promises go beyond those historical situations into the future of God's people.

The book of the Twelve serves the same purpose. The individual books are not arranged in chronological order, but in an order, which develops the message of warning and promise. The way the books are set out is that 'warning' is the major theme of the books from Hosea to Micah. This is brought to a close by Nahum, which celebrates the end of Assyria and represents part of a transition to hope as God's triumph over the nation's enemies is proclaimed. It also serves as a conclusion to the chapter of Israel's history of involvement with Assyria.

The second part of the transition is Habakkuk, which reminds the people that God is active on their behalf and will continue to be so. Zephaniah completes the transition with its message of hope for the faithful and the promise that God is with Jerusalem.

The remaining books relate to the reconstruction after the exile and, in particular, the need to be faithful to God and to trust in that relationship. This is expressed in terms of the temple, but also in terms of confidence in God's purposes, which will be achieved as God fulfils everything spoken of by the messengers, that is, the prophets. The people can have full confidence and a definite hope in God. God is faithful and will not forsake them. It is significant that the 'book' ends with Malachi's message of faithfulness to God and the reminder that God chose the people, but God could also reject those who were unfaithful in the relationship. The message of hope is to the faithful of every age. So the two aspects are kept in tension. Hope is real. God's people are assured of the Lord's presence and action on their behalf. However, there is an underlying requirement of faithfulness for those who hear the word of hope.

Questions

1. How was Ezekiel's message different from that of Jeremiah? How did the situation make a difference to his message?
2. Deutero-Isaiah has more to say about God as creator than any other prophet. Discuss why this should be so?

8
Singing Songs to God

*§Poetry of the psalms * Types of psalms * The collection of the psalms * Psalms and Israel's traditions * The psalms today*

Bible readings: Psalms 8; 22; 23; 51; 103; 139; 150

This book of the Old Testament is sometimes referred to as 'the hymnbook of the Second Temple of Israel'. Such a description gives some clue to the contents and purpose of the book. It is a collection of material for use in worship—hymns and poems, which express the various elements that make up an act of worship for the people of God.

The Hebrew name for the book is The Book of Praises. Our name for it, Psalms, comes from the Greek, and means, songs. These names also give an indication of the contents of the book, which varies from praise and thanksgiving to confession and supplication.

To say that it is the 'hymnbook of the second temple' is to suggest that the collection was used in worship at some time in the post-exilic period. That is, these hymns and poems were collected for that particular purpose. We may then date the collection in the period after the exile, and after the dedication of the rebuilt temple in 515 BCE. That is not to say that the hymns and poems were composed in that period. Many of them belong to the period from David to the exile. In the collecting process those psalms that helped the people to celebrate their experience of God were included. Some psalms that came from the pre-exilic period of the kings of Israel and Judah were adapted so that they were suitable in the new situation; for example, the psalms that deal with the king (see below). These psalms maintained continuity with the past while helping the people of Israel to live in the present and face the challenge of the future. They speak of the faithfulness of God, and promise care for those who were faithful, and so emphasized the continuing basis of Israel's relationship with God.

The poetry of the psalms

It has been said already that the psalms are in the form of poetry. The indication of this in most of our translations is the way the material is presented. It is not written in full lines across the page as in the narrative material, but each verse is made up of a number of short lines. It is important that we remember this whenever we are dealing with material in the Old Testament. The poetry of the Old Testament, as with any other poetry, must be treated in a way that is true to that literary form. Only then will the richness of what the author has to say to us come through the poetry and not be hindered by our reluctance to enter into the picture and the experience that the poet's words suggest.

A simple example is Psalm 23. The poet draws on the way an eastern shepherd cared for his sheep. He does not mean that God is a shepherd, but in his attempt to describe God's care of his people the picture of that total care by the shepherd for his sheep comes to mind. The picture that this simple and beautiful poem presents is more effective in helping us to understand God's care and love than a long description of love. Indeed, it is only by the use of poetry that the great mysteries of God may be conveyed to the minds of people. (For further examples read Ps 22:1–14; 102:3–7 128:3–4; 139).

The two main characteristics of Hebrew poetry are rhythm, and a particular way of conveying the sense of the poem (sometimes called parallelism). The rhythm in Hebrew poetry is obtained through stress on the words in each line that gives a beat to the line. Unfortunately this is lost when the poetry is translated into English.

The sense aspect is usually retained in translation. In its most easily recognised form, what is said in the first line is repeated in different words the second line. For example:

> Why do the nations conspire,
> and the peoples plot in vain? (Ps 2:1)
> Let us burst their bonds asunder,
> and cast their cords from us. (Ps 2:3)
> O Lord, who may abide in your tent?
> Who shall dwell on your holy hill? (Ps 15:1)

In another form the thought of the first line is developed in the second line:

I cry aloud to the Lord,
and he answers me from his holy hill. (Ps 3:4)
To you, 0 Lord, I cried,
and to the Lord I made supplication. . . (Ps 30:8)
The Lord has established his throne in the heavens,
and his kingdom rules over all (Ps 103:19)

The third form has the second line giving the opposite sense to the first line:

for the Lord watches over the way of the righteous,
but the way of the wicked will perish (Ps 1:6).
0 let the evil of the wicked come to an end,
but establish the righteous . . . (Ps 7:9).

Awareness of these forms in the structure of the psalms helps us to appreciate the poetry, and to understand what the psalmist has to say to us.

Types of psalms

In our present day hymn books and books of worship we have various types of hymns and worship material. This is also true of the book of Psalms. Most psalms fit into one or other of the parts of corporate worship. Some have an individual emphasis, but it is probable that they too were used in public worship.

There are four main types of Psalms:
1. Hymns
2. Psalms for the nation
3. Psalms of thanksgiving
4. Individual prayers for times of need.

Within each type there are other distinctions and the types overlap, but we may accept this as a broad classification.

Hymns
These are generally songs or poems of praise to God, which enabled the people to celebrate who God was and what God had done for

them. For example; Psalm 113 is a hymn of praise to the Lord. The Lord's name is to be blessed forever (verses 2–3); the Lord is over all the nations (verse 4); and the Lord is incomparable in care for the poor and needy (verses 5-9). Psalm 146 also praises God, who is the creator and is faithful to the people in their need.

Other major themes are:

(a) God the lord of Israel's history. Psalm 78 is a good example of this as it recalls the history of Israel in which God continued to bless Israel in spite of its disobedience. Psalm 105 praises God for blessing the patriarchs and delivering Israel from Egypt.

(b) God is king. The nations are to know this for God comes to judge world.

> Say among the nations, 'The Lord is king!
> The world is firmly established, it shall never be moved.
> He will judge the peoples with equity' (Ps 96:10).
>
> He will judge the world with righteousness,
> And the peoples with his truth (Ps 96:13).

(c) Hymns for those who are on a pilgrimage to worship at Jerusalem.

These psalms recall the faithful care of God (121), the assurance that Jerusalem gave to God's people (84; 122), and the need to rely on God, and God alone (127).

Psalms for the nation

These psalms enabled the nation to respond to God because of God's action on behalf of Israel. Some of them are prayers for deliverance in time of trouble. These psalms lament that God has rejected the people and cast them off, making them a laughing stock among their neighbours, who taunt them (44:14). God is asked to remember the people and to take action to deliver them (44:24–26). Psalm 137 recalls the time of their exile in Babylon and laments the people's separation from God (verses 1–6). It then looks forward to the destruction of Babylon and the rejoicing that will follow it (verses 8-9).

There are prayers for blessing on the people and for their restoration. For example:

> May God be gracious to us and bless us
> and make his face to shine upon us. . . (Ps 67:1)
>
> Turn, 0 Lord! How long?
> Have compassion on your servants!
> Let the favour of the Lord our God be upon us,
> and prosper for us the work of our hands,
> O prosper for us the work of our hands! (Ps 90:13,17).

Psalms concerning the king have an important place in the book. Royal psalms such as Psalm 2 celebrate God's establishment of the king in Jerusalem. God will give the nations to Israel's king so their conspiracies and plots will come to nothing. The king's dependence on God for his glory and his victory over his enemies is remembered in Psalm 21. Psalm 45 is addressed to the king on his wedding day. It looks forward to a happy marriage that would help to establish the king's reign and assure the nation's future. The king is reminded of his responsibility to support the cause of truth and defend justice (verse 4). He is also reminded of his special relationship with God as the one anointed to lead God's chosen people (verses 6–7).

Other psalms offer prayers for the king who must rely on God if he is to be a worthy leader of God's people (61).

3 Psalms of thanksgiving

Many of the psalms classified as hymns are also psalms of thanksgiving, but there are some that give thanks for specific things God has done. At times of national deliverance the people were reminded that it was only by God's intervention on their behalf that they were spared (124). There are also psalms of thanksgiving for personal deliverance from fears and troubles (34), for restoration from the distress of being estranged from God (30), and for forgiveness (32).

God's continuing love and care is the subject of thanksgiving in Psalm 92. Steadfast love and faithfulness are seen in God's great works in the eventual downfall of the wicked and God's enemies (verses 59), and in the way that

> The righteous flourish like the palm tree,
> and grow like a cedar in Lebanon (verse 12).

Individual prayers in the time of need

There are many of these psalms and they cover a wide variety of subjects. The main characteristic of them all is that they place the individual before God to acknowledge utter dependence on God. A few examples will have to suffice here, but lists of these psalms may be found in the introductions to commentaries on the Psalms such as, *The Cambridge Commentary* JW Rogerson and JW McKay (Cambridge University Press, Cambridge, 1977) and the New Interpreter's Bible, volume 4 (Abingdon Press, Nashville, 1996) 641–681).

Prayers for forgiveness have had extensive use in the church. Psalm 51 is the best known with its acknowledgement of sin (vv 3–5), plea for cleansing (vv 6–12), and commitment to teach others the ways of God (v 13). The depth and beauty of expression in this psalm has won for it a continuing place in the worship traditions of the church.

Closely related to prayers for forgiveness are those that express a longing for the nearness of God. Psalm 25 combines these two themes in a beautiful expression of devotion to God. It expresses trust in God to protect those who wait on God (vv 1–3), a prayer to know God's ways (vv 4–5), reminders of God's willingness to forgive (vv 6–10), a request for forgiveness (vv 13–18) and a prayer to be sustained, protected and guided by God (vv 16-21).

Of the psalms that express trust in God, Psalm 23 is the best known. (See above). Psalm 16 is another good example. It opens with a request for preservation and a statement of faith:

> I say to the Lord, 'You are my Lord;
> I have no good apart from you' (verse 2).

After discussing the help of other gods, the psalmist proclaims the assurance that comes from God who gives security and joy (vv 3–8).

Many of these psalms have won a place in the private devotions of people through the centuries, as well as in the liturgies of the church. Beauty of expression, the deep personal knowledge of God experienced by the authors and the ability to express how people feel before God, cause many to turn to the Psalms in time of need.

The individual psalms were not limited to use in private devotions, any more than they are today. In some cases they may have been adapted for public worship, but even in their 'individual' form they have an important place in public worship as the 'I' and 'me' take on the double meaning of the individual alone, and the worshipping group as a whole. When we use Psalm 51 as a prayer of confession and forgiveness, we identify ourselves as individuals before God and as a community that seeks forgiveness and renewal.

These few examples of the variety in the book of Psalms show what a great resource it was, and is, for the worshipping community of God. It provides material for worship related to the many aspects of the life of God's people.

The collection of the Psalms

There are indications that our present book of Psalms is the gathering together of earlier collections. The headings at the beginning of many psalms appear to indicate this. Seventy-three psalms are headed, 'to David'. Tradition has ascribed all of these to Davidic authorship, but that is unlikely. Much more probable is that these psalms were from a Davidic collection and that, some of them may have been written by David. The psalms from David would then have formed the nucleus of a collection that was in the tradition of David, who was noted as a musician and singer. (It was this skill that first brought him to the court of Saul [1 Sam 16:17–23]). The 'David' psalms are distributed throughout our present book. Other collections have been associated with the names of Korah (eg Pss 42 to 4.9) and Asaph (eg Ps 73 to 83). Again, this may indicate the source of these psalms.

Another collection is to be seen in Psalms 42 to 83. In these the word God (Hebrew, Elohim) appears to have been substituted for that which is usually translated Lord (Hebrew, Yahweh). This can be seen when we compare Psalms 14 and 53, which are versions of the same psalm. The change of name was probably made when the collection was formed.

The doxologies placed at the end of Psalms 41, 72, 89 and 106 may also indicate earlier collections. They suggest that these psalms mark the end of originally separate collections that have now been brought together. The doxologies are not the work of the authors of the psalms to which they are attached. They appear to have been added after the collection was complete. Psalm 150 is an extended doxology that brings the book as a whole to a close. The doxologies appear to serve the purpose of marking divisions in the completed book. These divisions may be the result of an author's attempt to make a parallel with the five books of the Pentateuch.

The Psalms and Israel's traditions

All of the major traditions of Israel are found in the psalms. This should not surprise us. As the material for Israel's worship, the psalms necessarily present the traditions about God and God's relationship with Israel so the people could respond to God with adequate worship.

Creation

The tradition of God as creator occurs frequently in the book of Psalms. The major point the authors emphasise is that God has made everything and is supreme over all creation. Thus in Psalm 8 the writer considers the status of humans and contrasts them with the glory of the heavens that God made.

> When I look at your heavens, the work of your fingers,
> the moon and the stars that you have established;
> what are human beings that you are mindful of them,
> mortals that you care for them? (vv 3–4).

God also made humankind, and human glory is in being a little less than God, and having authority in God's creation.

> Yet you have made them a little lower than God,
> and crowned them with glory and honour.
> You have given them dominion over the works of your hands;
> You have put all things under their feet (vv 5–6).

In Psalm 19 the glory of the heavens and the placing and ordering of the sun tells of the glory of God (vv 1–6). This revelation of God in creation is set beside God's revelation through the law (vv 7–10), and the worshipper is led to obedience through contemplation of them both (vv 11–13).

A more extended account of creation is given in Psalm 104. It attributes all of creation to God (v 24). Everything God made is dependent on God (vv 27–30). The psalm ends with the psalmist glorifying God and asking that his meditation may be pleasing to God.

> I will sing to the Lord as long as long as I live;
> I will sing praise to my God while I have being.
> May my meditation be pleasing to him,
> for I rejoice in the Lord (vv 33–34).

Understanding God as creator established the greatness of God, assured the people of God's ability to fulfill the word given to the people, and confirmed God as the provider for the people. The psalms enable people to respond to the creator with praise and humility, and to seek continued blessing.

Exodous, wilderness and settlement traditions

The great saving acts of God remembered in these traditions are recalled in a number of psalms. The emphasis is on the graciousness of God who acted for the people in these great events. The aim of this presentation was to have the people make a suitable response of thanksgiving and obedience to God.

Psalm 106 opens with thanks for God's enduring love and mighty deeds (vv 1–2), recalls that those who do justice are blessed (v 3) and calls on God to remember the worshipper(s) when the people are delivered (vv 4–5). Verses 6–39 recall the traditions of the Exodus, wilderness and conquest of the land, and the sins of the people associated with each event. Alongside this God's continuing grace and care for the sinful people is recalled. For example,

> they did not remember the abundance of your steadfast love,
> but rebelled against the Most High at the Red Sea.
> Yet he saved them for his name's sake,
> So that he might make known his mighty power (vv 7b–8)

The recital reaches its climax in verses 36–39 when idolatrous and faithless practices of the people in the Promised Land are recalled and God's anger was aroused so that the people were given over to punishment by the nations (vv 40–43). But even here God's grace to the people continued and 'for their sake he remembered his covenant. He caused them to be pitied by all who held them captive' (verses 45b–46).

The psalm ends with a cry to God to save the people so that they may give thanks and praise to God (vv 47–48).

Here we see the traditions used to remind the people of God's action in creating the people Israel, leading them and caring for them with faithfulness and love. It also shows that the people's persistent disobedience led to punishment, but that God would forgive them when they cried to God because they were God's people, the people with whom God made the covenant (v 47). With this spoken understanding of God and their need for forgiveness and renewal, the people called on God to save them.

This is a psalm which would be most appropriate in the worship of the people who were in exile as they remembered the history of their relationship with God and saw that their only hope of release and return to Judah lay with God. So they asked, 'Save us, 0 Lord our God, and gather us from among the nations . . .' (verse 47). After the exile it served as a source of encouragement and hope for a people who struggled against great odds to re-establish themselves in their land.

Psalm 78 is similar to Psalm 106 in its recall of the traditions and the people's faithlessness, but it concludes with a statement affirming God's choice of Zion and 'his servant David' (vv 68–72). This psalm must have been composed after the fall of the northern kingdom of Israel (see v 67). It develops the same point as Psalm 106—punishment for God's people was inevitable because of their faithlessness. This was an important theme of the exilic period. The confident assertion of the choice of Zion and David pointed to hope for the exiles being in the faithfulness of God who would fulfill the promise that one of David's line would always be on the throne of Israel (2 Sam 7).

Psalm 105 develops the theme differently. It celebrates what God did for the people by recalling the traditions of the promise to

Abraham, Isaac and Jacob, to give them and their descendants the land of Canaan (vv 7–11). It recalls Joseph and the time the people spent in Egypt (vv 16–25), the Exodus and the plagues God sent to convince Pharaoh that the people should be released (vv 26–38), and God's provision and protection of the people as Moses led them through the wilderness (vv 39–41). All of these actions by God were founded on the promise to Abraham.

> 'For he remembered his holy promise, and Abraham his servant' (42).

When the people said this psalm they celebrated what God had done for them in the past, but they were also assured of the reliability of God's promise. The promise was made when the people were few in number (v12), and it may have appeared to be ended when they were slaves in Egypt, but by God's action in bringing Israel out of Egypt and through the wilderness, that promise was fulfilled. The response required from the people was that they should keep God's statutes and observe the laws (v 45).

This psalm could have been said at any time in Israel's history. It emphasises the essentials of the relationship between God and Israel—God's acts for the people and their need to respond to God with obedience, thanksgiving and praise.

In these three psalms we see the creative use made by the psalmists of the traditions of their people. In this way the people of Israel were constantly reminded of all that God had done for them, to celebrate their relationship with God, and respond with worship and praise.

The King

There are seventeen psalms which draw on or develop Israel's understanding of the king and his relationship to God and Israel. These psalms originated in the period of the monarchy and were used in celebration of the king's role in Israel. The king was not only a political figure in Israel, he also was a religious figure. He had to represent God to the people and represent the people to God.

These royal psalms celebrate various aspects of the king's function in Israel at the time of his coronation or some other important event. Psalm 2 is a good example of this. It establishes the relationship between God and king—the king is God's anointed and when the nations act against Israel, they are acting against the Lord and the

Lord's anointed (vv 1–3). God, enthroned in heaven, laughs at the nations' actions, for God *has 'set my king on Zion, my holy hill'* (verse 6; see verses 4-6), and declared him to be 'my son' (verse 7). The psalm concludes with a call to the kings of the earth to serve the Lord with fear (v 11). Other enthronement psalms conclude with a promise of victory over the king's enemies (eg Psalm 21:8–12; 72:8–11).

Psalm 72 is in the form of a prayer that would be appropriate for an enthronement or other royal occasion. It asks that the king may judge with righteousness, have a long life, have victory over his enemies, defend the weak and needy, and have an abundance of wealth and fame. In a real sense it also sets out the way the king should reign, making clear to him those things that God requires of him, and reminding him that he is dependent on God that he might have justice and righteousness in his reign.

As we have seen above, Psalm 45 celebrates the king's wedding. It also emphasises the closeness between God and the king when it refers to 'your divine throne' (verse 6). Alternative translations are 'Your throne is a throne of God' or 'Thy throne, 0 God.' The psalm looks to the king to be a successful warrior in the cause of truth and right. On all such royal occasions the king's function as the anointed of God, who was responsible for right order and justice, was celebrated, and a time of right rule anticipated.

One characteristic that must also be noted is that God is always the one who provides what the king needs to fulfill his role. In this way the king's position as ruler under God is emphasised. It makes clear the king's responsibility to lead the people in the way of God, to acknowledge God, and to promote the ways of justice and truth.

The Royal Psalms also give us a good example of how material could be re-interpreted to serve a later time. These psalms were originally used in the time when Israel had a king. After the exile, when the collection of psalms was made, there was no king but the psalms were preserved and reinterpreted as references to the coming messiah. The promise of victory and the role of the king as preserver of justice, truth and peace were seen to apply to the Messiah. These psalms thus came to have a present application of hope for a people who struggled to live as God's people while under the rule of foreign powers. They also pointed to the future when God's reign would be known in all the earth.

The Psalms for today

The Royal Psalms show us one reason why the psalms are used so much in the worship of the church. From the beginning the church understood these psalms as statements about Jesus Christ. The hope for the messiah was seen in them as they proclaimed the coming king as the God-sent leader. The church saw that Jesus was the leader who fulfilled that hope. Not only is he the fulfilment, but we could not think of him as Messiah without these psalms and the way they were interpreted by the people before Christ. Like so much of the Old Testament, the psalms find their fulfillment in him.

Another, and perhaps more important reason for our use of the psalms, both in public and private devotions, is the way they present to us a timeless expression of a living faith, which is close to the New Testament, and the needs of us all. They are sublimely beautiful, and yet they speak of the ordinary and everyday striving of all people who would live with God. They express needs and hopes that are common to the human race in all ages. The outward details may vary, but the God of the psalmists is the God of Jesus Christ who offers himself to his people in love and concern, and bids them come to him and live.

Questions

1. How did the Psalms come into being?
2. For what purposes were they read?
3. Give a picture of God from the Psalms.
4. What do the psalmists understand by salvation?

9
Books for Special Occasions

---

§ Discussion of Ruth, Esther, Lamentations, Song of Songs

Ruth

Bible reading: Ruth 1–4

This book presents us with a short story in which the main characters are Naomi, an Israelite woman, Ruth, Naomi's Moabite daughter-in-law and Boaz, a kinsman of Naomi's late husband. The story is told with such simplicity and beauty that it has become one of the best-loved parts of the Old Testament. In particular, the way in which Ruth's faithfulness to Naomi and her gracious character are portrayed makes it very attractive.

The book tells of an Israelite, Elimelech, his wife Naomi, and their two sons, who journeyed to Moab in a time of famine and settled there. The two sons married Moabite women, but a short time later all three men died. Naomi heard the famine had passed and decided to return to Israel and make her home in Bethlehem. In spite of Naomi's insistence that the daughters-in-law remain with their own people, Ruth pledged her loyalty to Naomi and declared she would follow her wherever she went in the unforgettable words, 'where you go I will go, and where you lodge I will lodge; your people shall be my people, and your God my God; where you die I will die, and there I will be buried' (Ruth 1:16–17).

The main part of the book (Ruth 2–4) is taken up with an account of how Ruth became the wife of Boaz, the kinsman of Elimelech. Naomi played a significant part in this, and at the end of the story, when Ruth and Boaz had a son, it was Naomi who gained recognition from her neighbours for, by her efforts, she had ensured that the dead man's name (Elimelech) was kept alive in Israel (Ruth 4:14–16). A further point to the story is given in that the child was the father of Jesse, the father of David, Israel's greatest king (Ruth 4:17).

The book makes a number of points, which are important in Old Testament religion. The institution of the levirate marriage, in which a man assumed responsibility for his dead brother's wife and raised children by her in the name of the brother is used by Ruth. The law for this is in Deuteronomy 25:5–10, with another example found in Genesis 38, Judah and Tamar. However, this law cannot strictly apply in Ruth because Boaz is not a brother of Elimelech, rather a distant relative. Ruth used it to suggest to Boaz that he did have responsibility to her and, in acting on that, Boaz showed more justice than Judah, who refused to support Tamar.

In addition, we find in Ruth that great value is placed on 'faithfulness' in human relations. The book tells a very human story in which Ruth's loyalty to Naomi is a high point. Her faithfulness transcended the fear and difficulties of being a foreign woman in Israel without the support of husband or direct family. Indeed, the fact that she is named as the 'Moabitess' several times demonstrates that she comes from a hated tribe of people. The story is told also that we might see how God is in control through all of life's events. It displays God's guidance for those who seek goodness and who are faithful in their relationships with each other.

A third point comes as a counter to the emphasis on exclusiveness, which is found at some points in the Old Testament. For example, in Deuteronomy the people are commanded to have nothing to do with neighbouring races when they take possession of the Promised Land. In particular, marriage with foreigners is forbidden (Deut 7:1–5). A major aspect of the Ezra and Nehemiah reforms was their overt proclamation to remove foreign influences from Judah. They re-emphasised the command against marriage to foreigners, and Ezra went so far as to insist that those married to foreign women should divorce them (Ezra 10:10–12, Neh 13:23–31). In the story of Ruth we see a foreign woman accepted in Israel who became the ancestress of the great king David. In this way the book presents a wider outlook than the narrow nationalistic view expressed elsewhere.

Esther

Bible reading: Esther 1–2

The book of Esther is also a short story, but with a different theme from that of Ruth. It tells of a beautiful Jewish girl who became queen of the Persians and Medes and was able to use her position to thwart a plan to kill all the Jews in Persia. Esther was guided by her uncle

Mordecai who had incurred the hatred of the king's adviser, Haman. As an expression of his hatred Haman arranged a day when all Jews would be killed. Mordecai persuaded Esther to use her influence with the king so that Haman's plan could not only be thwarted, but also turned against him. As a result, Haman was hanged and the Jews were given permission to strike their enemies, who were wiped out. The day on which this great victory for the Jews occurred was established as the feast of Purim. The Jews celebrated this feast in the post-exilic period.

Discerning the purpose of the book has been a problem for Christians through the centuries. It appears to have two purposes, both of which help us to see the reason for its inclusion in the Old Testament. First, it gives the basis and background for the popular Jewish festival of Purim. The name of the feast comes from the word for casting lots (*pur*), the means by which Haman sought guidance in his plan to remove all the Jews (Esther 3:7, 9:24–8).

Second, the book celebrates the triumph of the Jews over adversity, an important point when we consider the history of the people. As such the celebration would encourage generations of Jews who suffered adversity in the period after the exile to stand firm and remain confident that they would overcome their own enemies.

The book is not religious, as we usually understand the word. It does not mention God and God's hand in the affairs appears to be indirect at best. However, it does emphasise the point that when we read of God's people in the Old Testament we are reading about a nation that existed in the ancient world and had to struggle to maintain that existence. It was through these people that God chose to reveal self to the world.

Lamentations

Bible reading: Lamentations 1–4

The book of Lamentations consists of five chapters, each of which is a poem with a special alphabetic form. The first four poems are in what is known as an acrostic form. That is, each verse or part begins with a letter of the Hebrew alphabet in alphabetic order. The fifth poem is not in the acrostic form, but it does have twenty-two verses, which corresponds to the number of letters in the alphabet. The use of this form may have been an aid to memory, or it may have had some particular significance in worship. Its occurrence in the Psalms (for example, Psalm 119) suggests this possibility, and the contents of the poems in Lamentations are appropriate for use in celebrating the faith of post-exilic Israel.

The historical background to the book is the last years of the kingdom of Judah, especially from the death of Josiah in 609 BCE to the destruction of Jerusalem and the temple, and the exile of many of the people to Babylon (Lam 2). The book represents the reactions of the people to these events and reflection on the significance of such disasters for Israel's understanding of its relationship with God. The book is a selection of material, which enabled Israel to see the events as part of the relationship between God and the nation.

The great problem faced by Israel after the fall of Jerusalem was to understand how this calamity fitted into their understanding of God as a God of love, power and salvation, and the God who had chosen Israel and given it the covenant. Were the old beliefs and hopes still to be held or did these events mean that Israel's belief about God and their relationship was wrong? People questioned whether God had any further plans for Israel, and if God had, how should they react to the one who had brought such punishment upon them.

Such questions have a note of despair about them and the poems reflect this. They do not avoid the horror of the siege, slaughter and eventual destruction of the city and its temple, all of which appeared to deny the purpose of God. But the author sets alongside this a firm faith in the God of Israel. His reaction was not to question whether God was still the God of Israel, but rather how the events should be interpreted as part of God's actions for Israel, and from them, how God's will for the people may discerned.

The basic point made in the book is that the exile was the result of Israel's sin (Lam 1:8–12). The people had sinned and rebelled against their God, therefore God brought the Babylonians against them to punish this disobedient people (Lam 1:14–15). In this the author shows that the prophets' words of judgment and doom were fulfilled. Now, what they had foretold had happened. Jerusalem's fate may appear extreme, but it was deserved.

What then was Israel to do? Acknowledge their sinfulness and accept that their punishment was just? The poet did this as he considered the calamity. However, that was not the end. And here the poet displayed his great faith and insight into the faithfulness of God.

He knew the future was bleak, but he saw a future for his people if they would wait on God and trust God to save them in God's own time.

The poet saw that Israel's one hope was in God who had shown by faithfulness to the people in times past that God was to be trusted in the present situation and in the future. It was this message that enabled Israel to live through the exile, reconstruct its life as the people of God and return to its homeland when Cyrus ended the exile in 538 BCE

Song of Solomon

Bible reading: Song of Solomon 1–8

Song of Solomon sometimes referred to as the Song of Songs, is a collection of love songs. It contains nothing that is specifically religious. The songs are set against the background of springtime in Palestine and celebrate the love of a man for a woman. Some of the songs appear to have been written for use at weddings. It is most probable that the songs were first used in the celebrations of the people and were intended to express their unaffected joy in the physical aspects of human relationships.

Why such a book of songs is in the Old Testament has been a puzzle for people over many centuries. Some have suggested that it is to be read as an allegory. That is, the bridegroom is God and the bride the congregation of Israel. The songs suggest that God cares for the people in the same way and woos them in order to seek a response. Christian commentators have adapted this in suggesting that the bridegroom is Christ and the church is his bride.

Others have suggested that the songs arose in the worship of the Canaanites and were adapted by Israel to assist it to celebrate the way God provides the fertility and fruitfulness of the earth. However, Israel does not appear to have had a festival where such a celebration took place.

Others again suggest the songs represent a drama, which celebrates married love. The weakness of this interpretation is that it requires a story to be imposed on the songs rather than finding a story developing in the collection.

The book is best seen as a collection of songs that celebrate the mysteries of human love and belongs in the context of the marriage festival. As such, within the context of the Old Testament, it affirms the wholesomeness of this love and sets it within the faith understanding of the people of God.

Questions

1. How does the book of Ruth counter the tendency of the Jews to be an exclusive race?
2. What understanding of God comes to us from the book of Lamentations?
3. Overcoming adversity. Discuss in relation to the books Ruth, Esther and Lamentations

10
Words to Make One Wise

---

*§ Origins of Israel's wisdom literature * Folk wisdom * Court wisdom* Discussion of Proverbs, Ecclesiastes, Job * Facing issues*

The wisdom literature of the Old Testament is often neglected by students of the Bible, yet these writings represent an important body of tradition and teaching, which could rank alongside the message of the law and the prophets (Jeremiah 18:18). Such a valuation may appear to be too generous when we see that there are only three books that may be classified as wisdom literature in the Old Testament—Proverbs, Ecclesiastes and Job. A greater appreciation of the importance and influence of the wisdom teachers is gained when we see that wisdom material appears in other books of the Old Testament. For example: in the stories of Joseph (Gen 37 to 47) and Solomon (1 Kgs 3 to 11), both of whom were 'wise men'; and in Psalms 1, 37, 49, 73, 112. References to proverbs and riddles (both wisdom forms) appear in the Deuteronomic History and in the prophets (Jud 14:14, Isa 10:15, Jer 31:29, Ezek 16:44; 17:2).

Further wisdom material is found in the apocryphal books of Ecclesiasticus and the Wisdom of Solomon. These books show the continued importance of wisdom and give an indication of the way the literature changed to meet the needs of the people. The importance of wisdom teaching generally is to be seen in its occurrence in the literature of ancient Egypt and Mesopotamia. In both areas literature similar to Old Testament wisdom material is found.

Origins of Israel's wisdom literature

Two main streams have come together to form Israel's wisdom literature—folk wisdom and court wisdom.

Folk wisdom

This type of wise saying is to be found in most cultures at an early stage of their development and continues to live on as the society develops. It arose and was preserved in family and tribal groups and usually is in the form of a short saying that sums up an attitude to aspects of life, or gives guidance in one's approach to living. In later periods the original reason for the saying may be lost, but the essential meaning is still retained. For example, we may still hear, 'look before you leap', 'the early bird catches the worm', 'a stitch in time saves nine', and 'you can't change horses in mid-stream', without being too much concerned about horses, birds or stitches as such.

Many examples of these sayings are found in the Old Testament in the form of apt sayings or words of guidance. For example, 'The fathers have eaten sour grapes, and the children's teeth are set on edge' (Jer 31:29; Ezek 18:2); 'can the Ethiopian change his skin, or the leopard his spots?' (Jer 13:23); 'Out of the wicked comes forth wickedness (1 Sam 24:13). Many similar sayings are found in the book of Proverbs.

Sometimes this popular wisdom was used to recall the past and so give warning; for example, when a girl was threatened with rape she said, 'such a thing is not done in Israel, do not do this wanton folly' (2 Sam 13:12); or as a source of guidance, for example 'They were wont to say in old time, "Let them enquire at Abel . . ."' (2 Sam 20:18).

The many references to wisdom of this type, particularly in the prophetic books, shows that it retained its influence among the people throughout the Old Testament period. The prophets used it both as a point of contact with the people and as a reminder of these general guides for life.

Court wisdom

The second stream of wisdom arose in a more sophisticated area of Israel's life. When the monarchy was introduced to Israel it brought with it the need to develop an organisation that could deal with the political requirements of a kingdom, both internal and external. This resulted in an administrative group gathered round the king to ensure that his policies were carried out in all the territories he controlled. The people who made up the group were necessarily well educated so they could carry out their tasks. A main qualification was to be able to write so they could conduct the king's correspondence and keep the necessary records. They were probably responsible for the larger collections of the traditions of Israel as we find in J and E in the

Pentateuch, and the court histories that form major sources in the Deuteronomic History.

A second qualification was to be able to advise the king on the policies he should adopt with his own people and in his relations with foreign powers. This required them to know other languages and to understand the cultures of their neighbours. They acquired a great deal of knowledge and wisdom, so much so that they became professional wise men whose influence was felt, not only in the court, but in the whole nation. They reflected on life, and the wise sayings that came from this reflection became available to others.

The sayings of the wise were made known through their teaching and, in particular, through the teaching of those who had been trained to become part of this special group to carry on this work. Some of the wisdom material we have in the Old Testament was produced for this teaching function. A considerable part of the book of Proverbs appears to have originated in this way. It is set in a teacher-pupil (or father-son) context and gives instruction that would be required by those who were to be scribes and advisers of the king.

The king himself may have been well skilled in the functions of the court wise men. It is not unreasonable to assume that the king's sons would be educated at least as well as those who were to become royal advisers. Certainly the tradition that locates Solomon in the line of the wise men is well established, so much so that he has become the patron of wisdom in the Old Testament, and is said to have produced many wise sayings and songs. His fame as a wise man extended beyond the borders of Israel to the neighbouring nations (See 1 Kgs 4:29–34).

Extensive schools of wise men existed in Egypt and the kingdoms of the Mesopotamian area from as early as 2000 BCE, as writings from these areas show. Israel was influenced by these schools in two ways; first, by accepting them as a model, especially in the structure of the wisdom school within the royal court to advise the king. The schools of Egypt and Mesopotamia had this important function. Second, by using some of the material from these schools as the basis for Israel's wisdom literature. For example, Proverbs 22:17 to 24:22 is very similar to the 'Instructions of Amen-em-hotep', and the story of Job has close parallels in both Egyptian and Mesopotamian literature. However, we should not think that Israel's wisdom writers merely borrowed material from others. It is also likely that there existed material that was common to the wisdom schools but was used by the schools in their own particular way.

The teaching of these schools aimed at equipping students to live a long, happy and useful life. This is not to be a self-centred life, but rather one which recognized responsibility to others and to the divine order that was over all. Indeed, happiness and success could only come to the one who was obedient to the divine order. To go against it would surely lead to disaster. Israel's wisdom writings follow the same broad lines, but they also reflect Israel's belief about God and God's requirements of the people.

The Proverbs

Bible readings: Proverbs 1–2, 8–9, 15–16, 30–31

There is much in this book that fits in with our understanding of wise or proverbial sayings. That is, sayings of one or two short sentences that convey to us some of the accumulated wisdom related to everyday living that is handed down from one generation to the next. In Proverbs the form is generally of two or three lines giving parallel statements about a topic. For example:

> A soft answer turns away wrath,
> but a harsh word stirs up anger (15:1).
> A false witness will not go unpunished,
> and a liar will not escape (19:5).

There is also much that is clearly not of this type, but intended to form part of the teaching material for those who would hold positions of responsibility in relation to the king and the court. It is not intended to be a guide to the people of the community as a whole. For example:

> Righteous lips are the delight of a king,
> and he loves him who speaks what is right (16:13).

The presence of these two types of sayings suggests that the book is a collection of materials intended for use in a school or for private study. This is confirmed by the arrangement of the book. It has a series of teaching discussions on wisdom in chapters 1 to 9; proverbs attributed to Solomon in chapters 10–22 and 25–29; sayings of the wise in 22:17 to 24:34; and sayings of Agur son of Jakeh, 30:1–33 and Lemuel, King of Massa, 31:1–9. The headings to each of the sections show that the book was made up from a number of sources.

The book is ascribed to Solomon (1:1) but its structure shows that it was not written by him. The headings in chapters 10 and 25 may indicate that Solomon was responsible for the sayings that follow, but the phrase 'Proverbs of Solomon' may only mean that these collections have a nucleus that goes back to Solomon's time. The book as it now stands is from the post-exilic period, but some of the proverbs it contains come from the earlier periods of Israel's history. The book then is a post-exilic presentation of the accumulated wisdom of Israel. Its purpose is to preserve that material and to make it available to the people of the post-exilic period as they faced the challenges presented in being part of the Persian empire, and later, the Greek empire.

The general emphasis in Proverbs is on practical everyday living. It has nothing to say about religious duties as such, nor about worship and cultic festivals, which have a major place in the other Old Testament material. The book gives practical advice in the form of 'do's and don'ts' on such things as the choice of friends (13:20; 22:24), and in particular women friends. Marriage is a good thing (18:22), but its happiness depends on the choice of a suitable partner (31:10–31). There is a lot of space given to warnings against a wicked woman, the harlot and the adulteress (chapter 5 and large parts of chapters 6 and 7). The last chapter however, describes the ideal wife, who is not only faithful, but a shrewd business woman to the advantage of her husband (31:10–31).

The young man is also warned against laziness (20:4–13) and drunkenness (23:19–21), both of which inevitably lead to poverty. The author sees no virtue in poverty. It is a sign of lack of wisdom and success. It is to be avoided by acting on the teachings of the wise. However, if there must be a choice between wealth and wisdom, the choice must always be for wisdom. To be a poor wise man is much to be preferred to being a rich fool.

The way to wisdom is through discipline. This is necessary for the young who must have discipline to develop character and to acquire learning. Physical punishment is an important part of this discipline. It is a service to children and a sign of love for them (13:24; 22:15).

An important sign of wisdom is the care with which people speak. A wise person recognises the power of words and so uses them with care, avoiding gossip and statements that may hurt others. Indeed, words make a positive contribution to securing the position of the wise as they are used to persuade and to correct (11:12–13; 18:21; 25:15).

The emphasis in Proverbs is on good practical advice. But it is grounded on the understanding that God is in control of the world and it is God's way that is the basis of the moral teachings that are given. Although the book does not give direct religious teaching it does presume a view of religion that is positive and leads to a responsible life. The aim of the teacher is that the pupils will live the life of the wise and acknowledge that they are accountable to God (3:1–12).

Ecclesiastes

Bible readings: Ecclesiastes 1, 3, 8

This book is different from all other books in the Old Testament—it casts doubts on the view that Israel was the chosen people of God and that God's will had been made known to Israel. The author is not an atheist, far from it. Rather, for him, the existence of God is the reason for pessimism. God exists but cannot be known, and what God requires of humanity is a mystery. The best that we can do is to observe what is happening about us, seek understanding through our experience, and accept what cannot be changed. All human effort to change our lot is doomed to failure. The same fate comes to human and beast, which cancels out all human values.

This is an expression of resignation expressed in a mood of disillusionment. It is in stark contrast to the main themes of the Old Testament, which stress faith, hope and obedience. The author based his attitude to life on a need for caution and moderation with the hope that he may thus be able to enjoy being alive. This enjoyment is the only satisfaction that is available to humans.

It is not surprising, in the face of such pessimism, that the writer finds little value in religious practices (5:1–7). Nor is wisdom an answer to his problems. He is set on the search for wisdom, but the search is frustrating—'a striving after wind . . .' (1:14. See 1:12–18). Although wisdom is superior to folly, it is cancelled out by the common fate of all people (2:12–17). Pleasure brings no lasting satisfaction (2:1–11), nor does wealth (5:10–6:9). Wealth, honour, and long life are worthless without contentment and the happiness that God permits (6:1–9).

We may well wonder how such a book became part of the Old Testament. The answer is that, like the other books, people read it and found that it helped them in their relationship with God. For some who clung to their belief in spite of all that was happening which seemed to deny God, it was encouraging to read the reflections of one who could find no support in the orthodox presentations of religion and life, yet still believed in God and tried to find enjoyment in life.

Another reason for the book's acceptance may be that its presence among the sacred writings allowed people to have honest doubts. The book represents the experience of us all. We have our doubts and times of pessimism, which are expressed best and examined within the witness of the community of faith and its traditions. By its very existence Ecclesiastes forces us to look afresh at the affirmations that come to us through the tradition of God's revelation and guidance.

Some additions have been made to the book to remind readers that they must approach the book with an awareness of its wider context. They are reminded that people will face the judgment of God (11:19), and that they should fear and obey God. 'Fear God, and keep his commandments, for this is the whole duty of everyone. For God will bring every deed into judgment, including every secret thing, whether good or evil.' (12:13–14). The questioning and pessimism have not been removed, but they have had the position of orthodox religion put beside them to point the reader to the wider context of Israel's traditions. Readers are thus encouraged to allow the traditions represented by Ecclesiastes and those from the Law and the Prophets to interact as they read and reflect upon them. In this way their understanding of God and the way of God is enriched.

Job

Bible readings: Job 1–2, 4–7, 20–21, 38–42

The book of Job tells of the struggles of a man who tries to understand the mysteries of life. In Job this centres on the question of why the innocent suffer. Job's innocence is clearly established. He had all those things that in his day indicated he was a righteous man. He was rich, had a family and friends, and was in favour with God who pointed to him as an example of a righteous man (1:8). Suddenly he lost all of these things and became a poor and lonely man. His health was gone and his body stank. The question, 'Why should this happen to Job?' is the major point of discussion between Job and the friends who came to comfort him.

In all the discussions Job maintains that he should not be made to endure such suffering. He has done nothing to deserve it, so, by ordinary justice it should not have come to him. He demands to put his case to God. The friends try to counter this and put forward various arguments to explain Job's situation. Eliphaz suggests that Job is wrong in thinking himself innocent. It is not possible for anyone to be completely innocent of sin; therefore suffering is never undeserved. Bildad proposes that Job may be suffering for the sins of others, particularly some member of his family. Zophar charges Job with being a hypocrite. It is quite clear to him that the magnitude of the suffering of Job shows that he has sinned greatly, and he should acknowledge it. All of these arguments make a direct connection between sin and suffering. The fourth friend, Elihu, suggests that suffering may come so that we may learn from it. Job's present suffering will be of benefit to him if he will react to it in the right way.

Job rejects all of these arguments and continues to demand to present his case to God. Finally, God does confront him, but does not enter into the debate with him. Rather, God points Job to the great mysteries of the world about him, particularly in creation. Job sees that suffering is one of these mysteries. So even here there is no answer to the question of suffering. Rather there is comfort for Job in the presence of God. God has come to him so that he now knows that his suffering has not cut him off from God. His cry to meet with God has been answered and in that experience his trust and certainty of God are increased (42:5). He can believe, even though he is suffering.

The book of Job presents a skeptical view of the ready answers which orthodox religion gives to the problem of suffering. By doing this it highlights the difficulty of believing in God in a world in which so much seems to contradict God's power and presence. It also points beyond argument about God to the experience of God as the basis of belief. This experience does not promise answers to the great questions of life, but it does make us aware of them within the context of God's presence with us as we seek the answers and engage in the struggles of life. When Job was confronted by God he became more aware that he was human, small and frail, but he was not condemned nor rejected. So he could express his faith in God. He could believe.

Facing issues

Wisdom literature is different from other material in the Old Testament with its worldly and questioning approach to human problems. As mentioned earlier this was an important contribution to the people's life and so gained acceptance alongside the other material that deals with law and obedience, promise and grace. But wisdom teaching was not a static thing. There are signs of development in the books we have in the Old Testament. There is also evidence of development and application to new situations in the apocryphal books. In both Ecclesiasticus and The Wisdom of Solomon there is a much greater interest in religious questions, particularly those that faced the people in the last 200 years before Christ. God's revelation to the people and their required response was an important issue for the writers of this material. The relationship between wisdom and righteousness, and life after death, are also important. These were among the things raised for the Jews by their contact with the philosophies of the Greeks. In grappling with these issues the later wisdom writers drew on and applied the traditions of those who had gone before them. Tradition, creatively used, was a continuing aid to the people as they faced new situations.

Questions

1. What is wisdom literature? What purposes did it have in the life of Israel?
2. Does wisdom teaching have a place in the proclamation of the gospel today?
3. What does the book of Job tell us about suffering?
4. How far is the wisdom writer's view of life a genuinely religious one?

11
Hidden Strength in Time of Trouble

*§ General themes of apocalyptic * A literature examination of major themes * Differences between apocalyptic and prophetic writing *Discussion of Daniel*

Apocalyptic material

Bible reading: Daniel 1–12

The word 'apocalyptic' conjures up a variety of images in people's minds: the end-time, a cataclysmic event, bizarre images, secret numbers with hidden meanings, God's intervention, judgment and the salvation of a few chosen people. However, if we are going to study it seriously in relation to the biblical text, consideration must be given to the period in which it arose and some understanding of the type of literature used.

Although there is a wide variety of apocalyptic literature available from the period 200 BCE–100 CE, the major study book for our purposes is the book of Daniel. There are small segments of apocalyptic type literature in Zechariah 9–14, Isaiah 24–27, Ezekiel 38–39, and parts of Joel 3. This particular form of writing took place in the period known as the intertestamental period (200 BCE–100 CE), and was produced by Jews living in Babylon and Egypt as well as in Palestine.

The apocalyptic writings were included in the early Greek translations of Christian bible until the Protestants removed them in the reign of James 1 (1658). The early Latin versions omitted the Apocrypha, but it became reinstated in the Roman Catholic Bible at the Council of Trent. However, it is only in recent years that the Apocrypha has been included in translations of Protestant bibles. We now have what the early Christian communities used as the basis for their preaching and teaching. Some examples of this literature include, 1 Esdras, Wisdom of Solomon, Susanna, 1 and 2 Maccabees). It is also found in the Dead Sea scrolls, the ancient documents found at

Qumran in 1955, some of which we already have in the Bible (for example, Isa 24–27), and others which were quite new to scholars.

The root meaning of the word apocalyptic is 'to reveal' or 'to uncover' and refers to the revelation of God's word or truth. It is a type of writing, which is quite distinctive in style and message. It was a literary style that appeared when there was a major crisis in the nation and the words of the prophets had been silent for about two hundred years. The first example of this literature was written during the reign of King Antiochus Epiphanes the Fourth (175–163 BCE) of the Seleucid Empire who was ruler over Judah at this time. In the latter part of his reign he was very cruel and oppressive when the Jews refused to accept Greek culture and practice because it was in direct opposition to the Law of Moses. It was a time of terror and brutal persecution, and in this period books like Daniel were written. The only Christian book accepted as part of the canon in a similar style is the book of Revelation. This also emerged from a time of terrible persecution, which, in the case of Christians, was that promulgated by Domitian (81–96 CE). Much of the imagery and language was borrowed directly from the book of Daniel.

To understand these writings it is necessary to appreciate the type of literature used and to realise it is not the literal prose of our time. It was written to give hope and encouragement to a people who were suffering because of their faith. God seemed distant because it was impossible to believe that the terrible situation in the present world was part of God's plan. The imagery is bizarre and often incomprehensible, with vivid descriptions of judgment on those nations who were the oppressors of God's people. One example is in Daniel 7 in which animals represent nations or persons: Babylon is represented by a lion, Media by a bear, Persia by a leopard, and the Messiah by a white bull in 1 Enoch, and by a great ram in Judas Maccabaeus.

There was a considerable number of ideas or themes current in apocalyptic literature, but they are not all represented in every piece of writing that is available. The idea of resurrection is present in some writings and not in others. Different understandings of the Messiah, of how and when that person will come—are all expressed in different ways, and the method of judgment is not the same throughout. The general theme of apocalyptic material will be presented and then the book of Daniel examined in more detail.

Apocalyptic themes

When there was a time of persecution, God seemed to be far away and inactive within the affairs of the world. God was still in control, but people perceived it was only as a transcendent being and not present in the events of history. To enable God's messages to reach the people, intermediaries and messengers were necessary; therefore angels play an important role in apocalyptic writing and visions were a means by which God's ways were revealed to a chosen few. There was a heightened belief that God's power extended to all the ends of the earth. It was present in the beginning of time and would be there at the end of time. God's reign encompassed both heaven and earth.

A feature that is practically constant in all the writings is the hope for the 'end-time'—that moment when God would intervene and bring about judgment in order that the faithful would be saved and the unfaithful punished. This upheaval, often couched in cataclysmic terms, would bring to an end the present period of history and usher in a new age or reign of God. The writings sometimes included a Messiah, either earthly or transcendent, who would figure in this final judgment and overthrow all the evil power of the world. Sometimes it was God who broke in first and then the Messiah reigned, while in other descriptions this order was reversed: sometimes there would be a resurrection of the dead who had been faithful and sometimes a resurrection of both faithful and unfaithful to face the judgment of God. Apocalyptic writings vary in their use of the elements spoken of above except for the constant one of knowing that God would intervene in some way.

The end-time in apocalyptic literature was clearly depicted as being at the end of a specific period in history. History was divided into segments determined by God and revealed to some of the great names of the past. God had spoken in the past and was still acting his history. So the sign of the time discerned by the writer would reveal the close of the present age and usher in a new golden age of peace and justice for the faithful. There was a dualism of thought in which the present time of evil and persecution represented the time of darkness before the age of light dawned. There was the concept of a fight between the power of darkness and the power of light. It was evident that the writer assumed that God's power would prevail and win over the evil power of the world. God's triumphant victory would save the righteous. There would be a remnant and hope for the faithful few.

The writings were anonymous but presented as written by some great person of the past, for example, the Assumption of Moses and the Psalms of Solomon. The new writer would present his revelation as given originally to one of the great heroes of the past. In attributing the literature to this famous person it gave an authority and respect to the current literature. The exception to this is the book of Daniel for whom we cannot find an easily identifiable hero.

The writings tended to be exclusive, understood by only a select few who could interpret the language and the secret messages conveyed in the highly symbolic imagery, cryptic words and numbers. This led to a general suspicion about this type of writing and is one of the reasons for the small amount of apocalyptic literature in the Old Testament.

The message contained within apocalyptic literature was addressing a crisis and issuing a call to the people to he faithful to God within the midst of persecution and oppression. It was a message of assurance that God could and would act in history and that the righteous who were loyal and faithful, would find peace and hope in God's purposes. It came into full maturity at the time of the Maccabees, but it has its roots in three possible areas as discussed in the following paragraphs.

In the prophetic writings there are traces of apocalyptic type ideas; for example, Ezekiel 38, 39; Isaiah 24–7; Zechariah 9, 12–14. The message of God came via the use of visions and not just by direct speech as it had to many of the prophets (Jeremiah, Amos). In prophetic literature God acts continuously in history and not just at the end of a specific period in time. There is a tendency in some of the writings toward the use of highly imaginative symbolism to describe events. In addition, present in prophetic literature was the idea of a Day of Judgment, or the Lord's Day. This was given different emphases by particular prophets, but in apocalyptic literature it came to mean judgment on the unfaithful and salvation for the faithful at the end of history.

It could be that apocalyptic writings have their root in the wisdom writings of the past. The wise interpreted life as it was experienced and reflected on it to enable people to live fully and properly in the present age. They could interpret signs, following the example of Joseph who interpreted the signs for Pharaoh. Because of this ability to read the signs of the times, some scholars have suggested they were the authors of apocalyptic literature.

Another possible source for this literature is the writings and practices of the Babylonian and Persian peoples, especially those related to the disciplines of astrology, numerology, demonology, angelology and Zoroastrianism. It is likely that apocalyptic writers were influenced by many of these practices.

The writings could have come from the Hasidim, the Pious Ones, who originally were the scribes and teachers of the Torah and became the Pharisees of the New Testament era. These people would have been influenced and aware of both their prophetic and wisdom background and in contact with officials of the courts of Persia. Influenced by their past traditions and by the surrounding culture, the Hasidim created a completely new type and form of writing, which was God's message to a generation in the midst of strife and fear.

While we recognise the similarities, it must be quite clear that apocalyptic literature is unique in its final form and it is not good enough to see it only as a development of either prophetic or wisdom traditions of the past. The major differences between prophetic and apocalyptic literature are:

1. Apocalyptic material was always written and never preached as prophecy had been.

2. God is revealed to the writers by visions and angels. God did not speak directly to them as he did to the prophets.

3. Judgment would be at a specific end-time in history and not the continuous judgment proclaimed by the prophets.

4. Apocalyptic literature was secretive compared with the open proclamation addressed to all people by the prophets.

The overriding similarity was the belief that God was in control and had the power to bring in the kingdom. Both types of writing contained hope for those who remained faithful, although in the case of apocalyptic literature it was an otherworldly hope rather than hope to be fulfilled in this world.

This literature must be viewed as a particular medium through which the word of God was proclaimed. To interpret literally the language of either Daniel or Revelation only succeeds in distorting the message. We have to go back into the mind of the author, and try to comprehend the images and symbols for that time and place.

Daniel

Bible reading: Daniel 1–12

This book was written about 165 BCE in the time of Judas Maccabaeus. It reflects a situation in which the Seleucids had control of Judah and king Antiochus Epiphanes the Fourth was trying to stamp out Judaism and encourage Greek ways. Many of the high officials of Judah were willing to comply with this move to Greek cultural practice such as the use of Greek names. For example, a high priest of the time was known as Jason instead of the Hebrew, Joshua. Further influences involved the use of the Greek language, dress and fervent interest and participation in all athletic activities. The king became very angry with those pious Jews who were against these changes, especially those relating to worship and sacrifice to other gods associated with the games. The king even had his own image printed on coinage of the time, indicating he was divine.

In response to the Jews who remained faithful to the Torah and Hebrew custom, the king forbade circumcision of young babies and violently killed them and their mothers if this procedure was found to be exercised. Scriptures were seized and destroyed and a decree was issued in 167 BCE forbidding Jews to live by their ancestral law. The final indignity was the desecration of the temple when the king introduced the god Zeus into the temple and swine's flesh was offered up as sacrifice. This abomination triggered off uprisings that eventually led to the downfall of the Seleucid kings and the restoration of the temple in 163 BCE.

During this time writers gathered a number of older stories from the exile, as they seemed to apply to some of the questions that were being asked in the period 167–64 BCE. Language and symbolism were taken from the Persian culture and used by the writers to help express a message of hope.

As previously mentioned, the prophetic literature was used as a source by the author, who created out of this material a completely new and unique form for his time. The book is divided into two parts—Daniel 1–6, 7–11, within which there are differences in language. Daniel 1–2:4a are in Hebrew, 2:4b–7: 28 are in Aramaic, 8–11 are in Hebrew. There is no satisfactory answer to the question, 'Why was the book written in two languages?' However, it may be that the stories in Aramaic were issued anonymously and separately to encourage those suffering under persecution. The author then took these and added in classic Hebrew an introduction and the description of the four later visions.

Daniel 1–6 portrays Daniel and his three companions whose persistent loyalty to the one God never wavers despite their time of training, trials and persecution. Their faithfulness and courage resulted in the acclamation of King Nebuchadnezzar, who finally acknowledged God as Lord. Each chapter in the book has a prologue, a trial of the faithful and an epilogue. The stories have not come from the same era but were gathered here to proclaim God's word in a new and different situation. Daniel 7–11 is written in the first person singular, and contains accounts of four visions depicting different historical situations and an announcement of the 'end-time'.

There are similarities to the role and person of Joseph at the court of the Egyptian Pharaoh. Joseph was part of the saving history of the Jews: he interpreted the signs depicted in the Pharaoh's dreams and made wise decisions about life with the resultant rise to fame in a foreign court. Daniel had many parallel experiences, and it is these similarities that suggest to scholars that the wisdom traditions are one of the roots of the apocalyptic writings.

The author is very vague about certain aspects of the Babylonian period and there are inaccuracies, which support the probability that it was written in a period much later than the exile. Furthermore, there were no persecutions during the exile. The Jewish exiles lived in peaceful co-existence with their Babylonian neighbours.

It is suggested that the Hasidim, the group that developed from the scribes and teachers of the synagogue, were the authors of the book of Daniel. They were the people who defended the traditions and knew the past writings. They were also familiar with wisdom writing, the law and the prophets and were intent on keeping the faith alive in a time of persecution.

The message of Daniel

The stories of Daniel were used for the purpose of proclaiming God's word anew in a crisis situation. We use the same method today when we read the teachings of Jesus and hear God's word speaking to us in our own time. The stories in Daniel speak to questions, which were troubling the Jews, for example, 'can a Jew accept and use a foreign name as the high priest was doing?' Daniel and his three companions were given Babylonian names and in the story there was no problem with acceptance and using them in their situation. Jews living in 165 BCE could identify with Daniel and use Hellenistic versions of their own Hebrew names. When it came to the question of eating foreign food, which was forbidden in the Torah, there was an alternative suggestion given. They could eat vegetarian food (Daniel 1:12–15). The lesson to the Jews in the period 165 BCE was not to break their law, but seek alternative ways, on some issues.

However, there was no way around the situation in which the king tried to prevent Daniel praying to Yahweh (Dan 6). The foreign king punished Daniel, but God protected him from injury in the lion's den. Furthermore, in Daniel 3 it was clear that there could be no compromise on the issue of worshipping golden images. Daniel and his friends were thrown into the fiery furnace and again God protected them. On some issues it was possible to seek a compromise, but in regard to the matter of worship, there was no compromise acceptable to God. People were expected to remain true to God, even if they were not always saved (Dan 3:18): there was no compromises—the Jews were expected to remain faithful.

The dream of Nebuchadnezzar was interpreted to mean that he and his kingdom would suffer punishment, but a stump would remain and be restored (Daniel 4). This is an unusual element in Old Testament scripture when a Gentile remnant would be saved under God's judgment. The contrast between Daniel 4 and 5 shows in the latter, a king who would not be saved and who could suffer complete destruction because he was so corrupt. The latter king will never acknowledge the power and glory of God as King Nebuchadnezzar does in the previous chapter. These two chapters are deliberately set side by side to portray what should be the right attitude of a king.

The second part of the book (Dan 7–11) is connected to the first by a description of the dream in chapter 7. The four visions are vivid and almost incomprehensible in the imagery used. The beasts represent nations, and, in Daniel 8:3–8, the two horns of the ram represent the successive kings of Media and Persia. The he-goat from the west is speaking of Greece and its king, Alexander the Great. For the first time in the Old Testament an angel is given a name, Gabriel (Dan 8:16) and he interprets the vision for Daniel. The promise at the end of this interpretation proclaims that the power of Antiochus will be broken without any human agency (Dan 8:25).

The fourth vision occurs in chapter 10, with the last three chapters reading as a unity. They culminate in the writer's expectation of what the divinely appointed end would be like (Dan 12:1–4). A great prince, Michael, will arise and will be in charge of the faithful people of Israel. There will be a general awakening of the dead (Dan 12:2) and some will be judged good and some bad. The words are to be shut up and sealed until the time is right for their release.

This book spoke to a particular time in history and for a particular reason. The message was to encourage the faithful in the face of terrible persecution. There will be hope for both the living and dead if they remain true to the one God. Yahweh can be trusted to overcome evil and with the conviction that God will not desert faithful people. The Jews can identify with Daniel as he is portrayed in the stories, finding through them and the visions, the hope to remain steadfast in light of their dark times.

This book can speak to our time when it is understood from its own historical viewpoint and message. It can be foolishly misused as a key to future events and fixing definite dates for God's purposes. The faith and witness of the book to call the faithful to remain true to God, the Father of our Lord Jesus Christ is still an important message of our church today. It can inspire us because it reflects the faith of people who remained true to God through an horrific period of Israel's history.

Questions

1. What ideas of permanent value can be found in apocalyptic writings?
2. What was Daniel's message and in what situation did it occur?
3. Show the similarities and differences between prophetic and apocalyptic writings.

Epilogue

As Christians of the twenty-first century we have the Bible as a of faith and belief. In it the Old and New Testaments are bound together to make the sacred writings of the church. Within these writings each part affects the other parts. The Old Testament tells us much about God and God's dealings with people. It ends with the relationship between God and the people in a bad state of repair because the people were not able to offer God perfect obedience. However, it ends with hope as it points to further action by God in which the problem of obedience will be overcome when God writes the law on the hearts of the people (Jer 31:31–4), and when God puts a new spirit within them and gives them a new heart (Ezek 36:26). The New Testament testifies that in Jesus Christ God has done this thing for all people. The promises are fulfilled.

However, the value of the Old Testament for the Christian is not limited to its preparation for Jesus and the New Testament. There is great benefit to be gained from studying what the different writers had to say, for they tell of the faith and spiritual progress of a people who were aware of a special relationship with God. These writings highlight the challenge that faces all who would live the life of faith as they question the values of the day and call people to live by a faith that commits the whole of life to God in hope and trust. It is the Bible that brings us knowledge of God, the Father, the Son, and the Holy Spirit. Our study of it equips us to live our lives with God in the present age recognising that the Spirit is always challenging us to new ideas and possibilities.

Glossary

Anathoth	A village just north of Jerusalem.
Apocrypha	Books of the Old Testament period that were not accepted as part of the Canon of sacred writings of the Jews. They were included in the Greek and Latin translations of the Old Testament and appear in some English versions.
Apostasy	Forsaking one religious faith for another.
Aramaic	A language which began with a people in the area of the Euphrates river gradually spread over the area of the Euphrates and Tigris rivers and down to the Mediterranean coast to Palestine, including Israel.
Ark	A box containing the stone tablets on which were written the Ten Commandments. It had special significance for the people of Israel as a sign of God's presence with them. Also, the name given to the vessel built by Noah to house human and other species in the time of the great flood (Gen 6–9).
Covenant	The agreement or bind that was the basis of the relationship between God and Israel. It is summarised in the words, 'I will be your God, they shall be my people' (Jer 31:33).
Cult	The way in which people organise their worship. For example, the worship offered in the temple in Jerusalem with its sacrifices, prayers and psalms.

Cyrus	Founder and ruler of the Persian empire (550 to 330 BCE). He defeated Babylon and allowed the exiles to return to Judah in 538 BCE.
Decalogue	The Ten Commandments.
Deuteronomic	Term applied to writings that show the influence of the thought and theology of the book of Deuteronomy.
Deutero-Isaiah	Isaiah chapters 40 to 55.
Diaspora	The scattering of the people of Judah (Jews), which began with the fall of Jerusalem in 586 BCE. Some were taken into exile in Babylon and others fled into neighbouring countries. By the time of Christ there were Jews in most of the major centers round the Mediterranean Sea.
Elohim	One of the names used for God in the Old Testament. (Translated as 'God' in most English versions.)
Elohist	The title given to one of the compilers of the early traditions found in the Pentateuch. The term comes from the compiler's use of the name Elohim for God.
Exegesis	The study of a biblical passage to determine its meaning.
Exodus	The departure of the Israelites from Egypt. The book of Exodus relates to this event.
Hasidim	A group of Jews ('loyal ones') who were active during the period when the Greeks controlled Judah. They strongly opposed Greek policies that threatened Jewish religious practices.

Holiness Code	A code of laws found in Leviticus 17 to 26. Its name comes from the requirement that the people should be holy because the Lord God is holy (Lev 19:2).
Immanuel	The name of the child whose birth Isaiah said would be a sign that God would save the people (Judah) from their enemies, Syria and Israel (Isa 7:14). The name means 'God with us', Isaiah's promise and the name were later applied to the birth of Jesus in Matthew 1:23.
Intertestamental	Refers to the period of history between the end of the Old Testament record and the beginning of the New Testament. It also refers to the Jewish writings that came from that period (200 BCE–100 CE).
Israel	The name of the twelve tribes of people who settled in Palestine after the exodus from Egypt. The name goes back to Jacob, whose name was changed to Israel after he 'wrestled with God' (See Gen 32:24–32). The name was retained by the ten northern tribes after the division of the kingdom in 922 BCE.
Judah	One of the twelve tribes that settled in Canaan (Palestine). After the division of the kingdom at the end of Solomon's reign, the southern portion took the name of the dominant tribe, Judah.
Liturgy	The form of public worship.
Liturgical	Relating to the form of public worship.
Levites	Members of the tribe of Levi. The tribe became priests for the people of Israel, so the term often refers to the priests.
Mosaic	Of things or ideas relating to Moses.

Nazarite	A person who took a vow to dedicate their life to God. Numbers 6 lists the requirements of the 'Nazarite vow'.
Oracle	In Old Testament use, a message from God spoken by a prophet.
Palestine	Area of land between the Mediterranean Sea to the West and the Jordan River, Sea of Galilee and Dead Sea to the East.
Patriarchs	Ancestors of the people of Israel–Abraham, Isaac and Jacob.
Pentateuch	The first five books of the Old Testament–Genesis, Exodus, Leviticus, Numbers and Deuteronomy.
Pharaoh	Ruler (king) of Egypt.
Priestly	Like a priest or influenced by a priest or priests. In the Old Testament, 'priestly material' is that which shows the influence of the priests of Israel.
Primeval	The earliest period of the earth's history.
Prophet	An inspired person who speaks the word of God.
Proverb	A short, wise saying that becomes popular because it helps people to remember important truths. (Proverbs are common in most cultures.)
Psalm	Sacred song or hymn.
Psalmist	One who writes a psalm.
Pseudepigrapha	Writings that were presented under a false name. For example, books supposed to have been written by important persons from Israel's past.

Revelation	Knowledge made known to a person by God or an agent of God.
Sabbath	The seventh day of the week appointed as a day of rest and religious observance in Israel.
Samaritan	A person from the province of Samaria during the Persian, Greek and Roman empires. Samaritans claimed to be God's people by descent from people of the northern kingdom (destroyed in 721 BCE), but this claim was rejected by the Jews. Bitterness between Samaritans and Jews continued into New Testament times—*'For Jews have no dealings with Samaritans'* (John 4:9).
Seer	One who interpreted 'signs', such as unusual events and dreams, to find the will of God. Seers were also consulted by people who wanted God's guidance.
Semites	The group of nations said to be descended from Shem (Gen10:21). It includes the Israelites, Arameans, Arabs and Assyrians. There are similarities between the languages of the peoples.
Sojourner	A temporary resident.
Stele	An inscribed stone slab set up to mark an important event.
Syncretistic	Used of a religion that has a mixture of elements of two or more different religions. It is not true to any of the original religions.
Terebinth	A small tree common in the Mediterranean area.
Theology	The study of the knowledge of God.

Tithe	A tax of one tenth paid by Jews to the temple.
Torah	Guidance or instruction that comes from God. It became the name for the first five books of the Old Testament, which contain instruction in the form of 'law'.
Tradition	Stories, beliefs and customs preserved and handed on for generation to generation.
Transcendent	Existing apart from the material world and, therefore, not subject to the limitations of the world.
Tribe	A group of families which claimed descent from a common ancestor. The tribe took its name from the ancestor, for example, the tribe of Judah, which claimed descent from Judah, the son of Jacob.
Vassal	One holding land or office under the rule or favour of an overlord or master.
Wisdom	The ability to decide between good and evil and to carry the decision through into appropriate action.
Yahweh	The name of the God of Israel as revealed to Moses (Ex 3:15).
Yahwist	Title given to one of the compilers of the early traditions found in the Pentateuch. The term comes from the compiler's use of Yahweh as the name of God.
Zion	The hill of Jerusalem on which the temple was built.
Zoroastrianism	A religion that began in Persia in the seventh century BCE. The name comes from its founder, Zoroaster.

Further Reading

Anderson, BW, *The Living World of the Old Testament*, fourth edition (Harlow Essex: Longmans, 1988).

Bright, John, *A History of Israel*, third edition (London: SCM Press, 1981).

Brueggemann, Walter, *An Introduction to the Old Testament: The Canon and Christian Imagination* (Louisville: John Knox Press, 2003).

Clements, RE, *The World of Ancient Israel* (Cambridge: Cambridge University Press, 1991).

Collins, John J, *Introduction to the Hebrew Bible* (Minneapolis: Fortress Press, 2004).

Gillingham, Susan E, *One Bible: Many Voices: Different Approaches to Biblical Studies* (London: SPCK, 1998).

Holdsworth, J, *The Old Testament,* SCM Study Guide (London: SCM Press, 2005).

Kaiser, O. *Introduction to the Old Testament* (Oxford: Blackwell, 1975).

Laffey, Alice, *An Introduction to the History of Israel and Judah* (Valley Forge: Trinity Press International, 1993).

New Interpreter's Bible, volume one (Articles on the Bible and the Old Testament) (Nashville: Abingdon, 1994).